A WORLD MADE NEW

A WORLD MADE NEW

Eleanor Roosevelt

and the Universal Declaration

of Human Rights

MARY ANN GLENDON

RANDOM HOUSE

NEW YORK

All rights reserved under International and Pan-American Copyright Conventions.
Published in the United States by Random House, Inc., New York, and simultaneously
in Canada by Random House of Canada Limited, Toronto.

RANDOM HOUSE and colophon are registered trademarks of Random House, Inc.

Library of Congress Cataloging-in-Publication Data
Glendon, Mary Ann.
A world made new : Eleanor Roosevelt and the Universal Declaration of Human Rights
/ Mary Ann Glendon.
p.   cm.
Includes index.
ISBN 0-679-46310-0 (alk. paper)
1. United Nations. General Assembly. Universal Declaration of Human
Rights—History.   2. Roosevelt, Eleanor, 1884–1962.   I. Title.
K3238.31948 .G58 2001   323—dc21   00-062555

Random House website address: www.atrandom.com
Printed in the United States of America on acid-free paper
24689753
First Edition

Book design by J. K. Lambert

TITLE-PAGE PHOTO:
*Eleanor Roosevelt with E. Gross and P. C. Jessup
at the UN conference in Paris, September 22, 1948
(courtesy Franklin D. Roosevelt Library)*

For Claire and Giulia Giangravé

Our Father, who has set a restlessness in our hearts and made us all seekers after that which we can never fully find, forbid us to be satisfied with what we make of life. Draw us from base content and set our eyes on far-off goals. Keep us at tasks too hard for us that we may be driven to Thee for strength. Deliver us from fretfulness and self-pitying; make us sure of the good we cannot see and of the hidden good in the world. Open our eyes to simple beauty all around us and our hearts to the loveliness men hide from us because we do not try to understand them. Save us from ourselves and show us a vision of a world made new.

Eleanor Roosevelt's nightly prayer, from *Mother R.*,

by Elliott Roosevelt and James Brough

ACKNOWLEDGMENTS

Heartfelt thanks are due to my agents Lynn Chu and Glen Hartley for their enthusiasm when this project was in its earliest stages; to Joy de Menil, the editor of my dreams; and to Dean Robert Clark for his unfailing support and encouragement.

Among those who provided me with assistance along the way, I am especially grateful to Habib Malik for access to his father's private diaries and papers; to historians John Hobbins and A. W. Brian Simpson, for collegial generosity that included commenting on the manuscript and sharing their own research; and to Gregory Carr of the Carr Center for Human Rights Policy at Harvard University's Kennedy School of Government, who made it possible for me to obtain material from the Soviet archives.

The manuscript benefited greatly as well from the comments, at various stages, of: Paolo G. Carozza, Douglas Cassel, Anthony D'Amato, Avery Dulles, Giorgio Filibeck, Jack Goldsmith, Thomas Kohler, Donald P. Kommers, Daniel S. Lev, Edward Lev, Diarmuid Martin, Paul McNellis, Michael Novak, Samantha Power, Henry Steiner, and the students in my human rights course at Harvard Law School.

It was my good fortune to have research assistance from an extraordinary group of young men and women: Thomas Cotton, Mary Eileen Glendon, Harry Kemp, Nikita Lomagin, David Mascari, Susan Norton, Michael O'Shea, Reeghan Raffals, Barak Richman, and Lynne Robbins.

I also received valuable help from William Alford, director of the Harvard Law School East Asian Legal Studies Program; Ismini Anastassiou de Shali and Maria Sara Rodriguez Pinto of Santiago, Chile; Margaret H. McAleer of the Library of Congress; Victoria Schultz of the United Nations Video Section; Shirin Sinnar of the Columbia Law School Class of 2003, and Sumner Twiss of Brown University.

Finally, I am deeply appreciative of the generous support for this project provided by the John M. Olin Foundation and the John Templeton Foundation.

CONTENTS

PREFACE

When the Athenian navy was poised to invade tiny Melos in 416 B.C., the terrified islanders sent emissaries to try to reason with the masters of the sea. The Athenians' scornful rebuff has echoed down the centuries: "You know as well as we do that right, as the world goes, is only in question between equals in power, while the strong do what they can and the weak suffer what they must."[1]

History has provided plenty of support for that brutal dictum, from the enslavement and massacre of the Melians down to the present day. Yet centuries later, in the wake of atrocities beyond Greek imagining, the mightiest nations on earth bowed to the demands of smaller countries for recognition of a common standard by which the rights and wrongs of every nation's behavior could be measured. The moral terrain of international relations was forever altered late one night in Paris, on December 10, 1948, when the General Assembly of the United Nations adopted the Universal Declaration of Human Rights without a single dissenting vote.

Early in 1947, with the horrors of two world wars fresh in their memories, a remarkable group of men and women gathered, at the behest of the newly formed United Nations, under the chairmanship of Eleanor Roosevelt, to draft the first "international bill of rights." So far as the Great Powers of the day were concerned, the main purpose of the United Nations was to establish and maintain collective security in the years after the war. The human rights project was peripheral, launched as a concession to small countries and in response to the demands of numerous religious and humanitarian associations that the Allies live up to their war rhetoric by providing assurances that the community of nations would never again countenance such massive violations of human dignity. Britain, China, France, the United States, and the Soviet Union did not expect these assurances to interfere with their national sovereignty.

In the years that followed, to the astonishment of many, human rights would become a political factor that not even the most hard-shelled realist could ignore. The Universal Declaration would become an instrument, as well as the most prominent symbol, of changes that would amplify the voices of the weak in the corridors of power.[2] It challenged the long-standing view that a sovereign state's treatment of its own citizens was that nation's business and no one else's. It gave expression to diffuse, deep-seated longings and lent wings to movements that would soon bring down colonial empires. Its thirty concise articles inspired or influenced scores of postwar and postcolonial constitutions and treaties, including the new constitutions of Germany, Japan, and Italy. It became the polestar of an army of international human rights activists, who pressure governments to live up to their pledges and train the searchlight of publicity on abuses that would have remained hidden in former times. Confirming the worst fears held in 1948 by the Soviet Union and South Africa, the Declaration provided a rallying point for the freedom movements that spurred the collapse of totalitarian regimes in Eastern Europe and the demise of apartheid. It is the parent document, the primary inspiration, for most rights instruments in the world today.[3]

Together with the Nuremberg Principles of international criminal law developed by the Allies in 1946 for the trials of German and Japanese war criminals and the 1948 Genocide Convention, the Universal Declaration of Human Rights became a pillar of a new international system under which a nation's treatment of its own citizens was no longer immune from outside scrutiny. The Nuremberg Principles, by sanctioning prosecutions for domestic atrocities committed in wartime, represented a determination to punish the most violent sorts of assaults on human dignity. The Genocide Convention obligated its signers to prevent and punish acts of genocide, whether committed in times of war or in peace.[4] The Universal Declaration was more ambitious. Proclaiming that "disregard and contempt for human rights have resulted in barbarous acts which have outraged the conscience of mankind," it aimed at *prevention* rather than punishment.[5]

Today, the Declaration is the single most important reference point for cross-national discussions of how to order our future together on our increasingly conflict-ridden and interdependent planet. But time and forgetfulness are taking their toll. Even within the international human rights movement, the Declaration has come to be treated more like a monument to be venerated from a distance than a living document to be reappropriated by each generation. Rarely, in fact, has a text been so widely praised yet so little read or understood.

The Declaration marked a new chapter in a history that began with the great charters of humanity's first rights moment in the seventeenth and eighteenth centuries. The British Bill of Rights of 1689, the U.S. Declaration of Independence of 1776, and the French Declaration of the Rights of Man and Citizen of 1789 were born out of struggles to overthrow autocratic rule and to establish governments based on the consent of the governed. They proclaimed that all men were born free and equal and that the purpose of government was to protect man's natural liberties. They gave rise to the modern language of rights.

From the outset, that language branched into two dialects. One, influenced by continental European thinkers, especially Rousseau, had more room for equality and "fraternity" and tempered rights with duties and limits. It cast the state in a positive light as guarantor of rights and protector of the needy. Charters in this tradition—the French constitutions of the 1790s, the Prussian General Code of 1794, and the Norwegian Constitution of 1815—combined political and civil rights with public obligations to provide relief for the poor. In the late nineteenth and early twentieth centuries, as continental European Socialist and Christian Democratic parties reacted to the harsh effects of industrialization, these paternalistic principles evolved into social and economic rights.

The Anglo-American dialect of rights language emphasized individual liberty and initiative more than equality or social solidarity and was infused with a greater mistrust of government. The differences between the two traditions were mainly of degree and emphasis, but their spirit penetrated every corner of their respective societies.

When Latin American countries achieved independence in the nineteenth century, these two strains began to converge. Most of the new nations retained their continental European–style legal systems but adopted constitutions modeled on that of the United States, supplementing them with protections for workers and the poor. The Soviet Union's constitutions took a different path, subordinating the individual to the state, exalting equality over freedom, and emphasizing social and economic rights over political and civil liberty.

In 1948 the framers of the Universal Declaration achieved a distinctive synthesis of previous thinking about rights and duties. After canvassing sources from North and South, East and West, they believed they had found a core of principles so basic that no nation would wish openly to disavow them. They wove those principles into a unified document that quickly displaced all antecedents as the principal model for the rights instruments in force in the world today.

When read as it was meant to be, namely as a whole, the Declaration's vision of liberty is inseparable from its call to social responsibility (inspired in part by Franklin Roosevelt's famous "four freedoms"—freedom of speech and belief, freedom from fear and from want). Its organic unity was, however, one of the first casualties of the cold war. The United States and the Soviet Union could not resist treating the Declaration as an arsenal of political weapons: each yanked its favorite provisions out of context and ignored the rest. What began as expediency hardened into habit, until the sense of an integrated body of principles was lost. Today the Declaration is almost universally regarded as a kind of menu of rights from which one can pick and choose according to taste.

The fact that nations and interest groups increasingly seek to cast their agendas or justify their actions in terms of human rights is one measure of the success of the human rights idea. Nearly every international dispute today sooner or later implicates human rights; nearly every exercise of military force claims some humanitarian justification. Yet the more the Declaration is pulled apart and politicized, the higher the risk that protection of human rights will become a pretext for imposing the will of the strong by armed intervention or economic pressure.

One of the most common and unfortunate misunderstandings today involves the notion that the Declaration was meant to impose a single model of right conduct rather than to provide a common standard that can be brought to life in different cultures in a legitimate variety of ways. This confusion has fostered suspicion of the Universal Declaration in many quarters, and lends credibility to the charge of Western cultural imperialism so often leveled against the entire human rights movement.

Eleanor Roosevelt understood these dangers. She was fond of saying that documents expressing ideals "carry no weight unless the people know them, unless the people understand them, unless the people demand that they be lived."[6] This book aims to take seriously Mrs. Roosevelt's injunction to "know" the Universal Declaration—not for the sake of "originalism," but because, in a world marked by homogenizing global forces on the one hand and rising ethnic assertiveness on the other, the need is greater than ever for clear standards that can serve as a basis for discussions across ideological and cultural divides. Until something better comes along, it is, as Mrs. Roosevelt once remarked of the UN itself, "a bridge upon which we can meet and talk."[7]

⚊

This book is the story of how the idea of an international human rights standard became a reality, of the obstacles it overcame, and of current threats to the Declaration's brave attempt to improve the odds of reason and conscience against power and interest. The story of the Declaration is, to a large extent, the story of a journey undertaken by an extraordinary group of men and women who rose to the challenge of a unique historical moment. The brief interlude between the end of World War II and the definitive collapse of the Soviet-American alliance lasted just barely long enough to permit major international institutions such as the UN and the World Bank to be established and for the framers of the Universal Declaration to complete their task. The members of the first Human Rights Commission were well aware that they were engaged in a race against time: around them, relations between Russia and the West were deteriorating, the Berlin blockade raised the specter of another world war, the Palestine question divided world opinion, and conflict broke out in Greece, Korea, and China. Shortly after the Declaration's adoption, the window of opportunity closed, to remain shut for forty years.

The growing hostility between the United States and the USSR was only one of many daunting obstacles confronted by the Declaration's drafters. They had to surmount linguistic, cultural, and political differences and overcome personal animosities as they strove to articulate a clear set of principles with worldwide applicability. Their final product, they all acknowledged, was imperfect, yet they succeeded well enough to give the lie to claims that peoples with drastically opposed worldviews cannot agree upon a few common standards of decency.

For everyone who is tempted to despair of the possibility of crossing today's ideological divides, there is still much to learn from Eleanor Roosevelt's firm but irenic manner of dealing with her Soviet antagonists; and from the serious but respectful philosophical rivalry between Lebanon's Charles Malik and China's Peng-chun Chang. There is much to ponder in the working relationship between Malik, a chief spokesman for the Arab League, and René Cassin, an ardent supporter of a Jewish homeland, who lost twenty-nine relatives in concentration camps. When one considers that two world wars and mass slaughters of innocents had given the framers every reason to despair about the human condition, it is hard to remain unmoved by their determination to help make the postwar world a better and safer place.

With the exception of Eleanor Roosevelt, most of the members of the committee that shaped the Declaration are now little remembered outside their home countries. Yet they included some of the most able and colorful public figures of their time: Carlos Romulo, the Filipino journalist who won a Pulitzer Prize for his articles predicting the end of colonialism; John P. Humphrey, the dedicated Canadian director of the UN's Human Rights Division, who prepared the preliminary draft of the Declaration; Hansa Mehta of India, who made sure the Declaration spoke with power and clarity about equal rights for women well before they were recognized in most legal systems; Alexei Pavlov, brilliant nephew of the conditioned-reflex scientist, who had to go the extra verst to dispel suspicions that he was still bourgeois; and Chile's Hernán Santa Cruz, an impassioned man of the Left who helped assure that social and economic rights would have pride of place in the Declaration along with traditional political and civil liberties.

Among the Declaration's framers, four in particular played crucial roles: Peng-chun Chang, the Chinese philosopher, diplomat, and playwright who was adept at translating across cultural divides; Nobel Peace Prize laureate René Cassin, the legal genius of the Free French, who transformed what might have been a mere list or "bill" of rights into a geodesic dome of interlocking principles; Charles Malik, existentialist philosopher turned master diplomat, a student of Alfred North Whitehead and Martin Heidegger, who steered the Declaration to adoption by the UN General Assembly in the tense cold war atmosphere of 1948; and Eleanor Roosevelt, whose prestige and personal qualities enabled her to influence key decisions of the country that had emerged from the war as the most powerful nation in the world. Chang, Cassin, Malik, and Roosevelt were the right people at the right time. But for the unique gifts of each of these four, the Declaration might never have seen the light of day.

In this book I have tried to bring the Declaration's history to life in the voices of the participants themselves as recorded in diaries, letters, memoirs, interviews, and records of meetings, as well as other contemporary accounts. Much of this material is previously unpublished and sheds new light on the politics and origins of the Declaration: the extensive diaries and papers of Charles Malik to which I was given exclusive access; documents from the archives of the Soviet Politburo that began to be declassified in the fall of 1999; a biography of Peng-chun Chang prepared by his children; and (from the Malik collection) verbatim transcripts of Human Rights Commission meetings. The material presented here also fills a gap in the biographies of Eleanor Roosevelt by providing a more comprehensive account of her role in what history, as well as she, judged to be her greatest achievement.

The story of the parent document of the modern human rights movement is the story of a group of men and women who learned to cooperate effectively despite political differences, cultural barriers, and personal rivalries. It is an account of their attempt to bring forth from the ashes of unspeakable wrongs a new era in the history of rights. It is an unfinished story, whose course will be influenced, for better or worse, by actions and decisions being taken today.

The tale begins in the spring of 1945, when a war-weary world began to prepare for peace, and dream of freedom.

A WORLD MADE NEW

*Churchill, Roosevelt, and Stalin—the Big Three leaders—flanked
by their military advisers at Yalta, February 1945.*

CHAPTER I

THE LONGING
FOR FREEDOM

Politics, it has been said, is "the arena where conscience and power meet, and will be meeting until the end of time."[1] Conscience so often fares poorly in such encounters that we celebrate the occasions when Power gives her more than a tip of the hat. In April 1945, as delegates from fifty lands gathered in San Francisco for the United Nations founding conference, Power was much on display. Battleships leaving the Pacific harbor with men and matériel were a grim reminder that the war with Japan was still raging. The tides of war in Europe, however, had turned in favor of the Allies, and the "Big Three" (Britain, the Soviet Union, and the United States) had begun jockeying for the positions they would hold in the new world order. As part of their planning for the postwar era, the Allies invited to the San Francisco conclave all states that had declared war on Germany and Japan by March 1, 1945.

The Allied leaders had agreed in principle on the need for an international organization to prevent future aggression, assure the stability of frontiers, and provide a means for resolving disputes among nations, but the most vigorous supporter of the idea was Franklin Roosevelt. The American president was mindful that the failure of the first such organization, the League of Nations, was due in no small measure to President Woodrow Wilson's inability to convince the Senate to ratify the treaty establishing it. A driving force behind the League's formation after World

War I, Wilson had been bitterly disappointed. To prevent a repetition of that debacle, Roosevelt had begun speaking to the American people about his hopes for a new world organization during the war. "Nations will learn to work together," he insisted, "only by actually working together."[2] In a radio address on Christmas Eve 1943, he emphasized that the main purpose of such an organization would be to keep the peace. The United States had no interest, he said, in Allied domination over other nations: "The doctrine that the strong shall dominate the weak is the doctrine of our enemies—and we reject it."[3]

Now, with the confidence born of approaching victory, Roosevelt believed the time had come to make up for the mistakes of the last peace. Shortly after his inauguration in January 1945, he told Congress of his hopes to replace the old international system of "exclusive alliances and spheres of influence" with a "universal organization in which all peace-loving nations will finally have a chance to join."[4]

Eleanor Roosevelt had long shared those hopes. When her husband asked her to accompany him to the opening session of the UN founding conference in April, and on a trip to England and the continent in May, she was delighted—not least because his enthusiasm allayed her growing anxiety about his health. Labor Secretary Frances Perkins had objected that a trip to the war zone would be too dangerous, but the president replied that he expected the war to be over by then. He had long looked forward, he told Perkins, to a victory tour with the First Lady at his side: "Eleanor's visit [to England] in wartime was a great success. I mean a success for her and for me so that we understood more about their problems. . . . I told Eleanor to order her clothes and get some fine things so that she will make a really handsome appearance."[5]

With spring flowers in bloom and war's end at last in sight, an exuberant president began to prepare for the San Francisco conference.

The features of the future UN that were of most interest to the Great Powers had been settled already at two much more exclusive meetings. In the summer and fall of 1944, representatives of Britain, China, the United States, and the USSR had met at Dumbarton Oaks to do preparatory work on what would become the UN Charter. One month earlier, at Bretton Woods in New Hampshire, the Allies had established the main institutions of the postwar economic order—the International Monetary Fund and the International Bank for Reconstruction and Development (the World Bank).

Determined to avoid Wilson's main error, Roosevelt actively courted Republican support for the United Nations. When the time came to choose representatives for San Francisco, he made a point to include prominent GOP leaders: former Minnesota Governor Harold Stassen, future Secretary of State John Foster Dulles, and Senator Arthur Vandenberg, the ranking minority member of the Senate Foreign Relations Committee.

The Soviets went along with the project, but without much enthusiasm. Their chief concern for the immediate postwar period was to protect the frontiers of the motherland from renewed aggression. On the eve of the Normandy invasion, according to former Yugoslav Communist Party official Milovan Djilas, Stalin told Djilas: "Perhaps you think that just because we are the allies of the English we have forgotten who they are and who Churchill is. They find nothing sweeter than to trick their allies. . . . Churchill is the kind who, if you don't watch him, will slip a kopeck out of your pocket. . . . Roosevelt is not like that. He dips in his hand only for bigger coins."[6]

George F. Kennan, a shrewd observer then serving in the U.S. embassy in Moscow, sized up Russia's position this way: "Insofar as Stalin attached importance to the concept of a future international organization, he did so in the expectation that the organization would serve as the instrument for maintenance of a US-UK-Soviet hegemony in international affairs."[7] That arrangement could be satisfactory to the Soviets only if Britain and America accepted the sphere of influence the USSR was establishing in Central and Eastern Europe in the summer of 1944.

Churchill and the British Foreign Office were skeptical of the Soviet Union's value as a partner in promoting future peace and wary of Stalin's expansionist aims. Anthony Eden, Churchill's foreign minister, viewed Soviet policy as "amoral" and the American attitude as "exaggeratedly moral, at least where non-American interests are concerned."[8] Regarding the UN, Churchill's expectations were modest. "Jaw Jaw is better than War War," he conceded, but he was more interested in postwar cooperation among the Western European nations than in a worldwide organization. "I must admit," he told foreign affairs adviser Sir Alexander Cadogan, "that my thoughts rest primarily in Europe. . . . It would be a measureless disaster if Russian barbarianism overlaid the culture and independence of the ancient States of Europe. Hard as it is to say, I trust the European family may act unitedly as one under the Council of Europe."[9]

Churchill and the Foreign Office, determined to resist any erosion of British imperial power, were not about to become champions of human rights. The issue of the future of colonial dependencies was, in fact, a major source of friction between Britain and the United States. Roosevelt favored the evolution of the British colonies into independent states and free trading partners, while the United Kingdom envisaged that they would become self-governing dominions in a special relationship, including trade relations, with one another and the mother country.[10] The British suspected, not without reason, that the United States' anticolonial policy was driven in part by its own economic and military aims.

When representatives of the Big Three met at Dumbarton Oaks, they were united by the desire to win the war, but each had different goals and concerns for the peace.[11] In the draft proposals for the UN Charter that issued from this meeting, human rights were mentioned only once, briefly, at the suggestion of the United States. Britain and the Soviet Union rejected the American delegation's proposal that promotion of human rights be listed among the UN's main purposes but agreed to its inclusion among the provisions dealing with economic and social questions.[12] Edward R. Stettinius, Jr., head of the American delegation, noted in his diary that Roosevelt "seemed gratified by these developments and felt the inclusion of the human rights sentence was extremely vital. He seems rather surprised that the Soviets had yielded on this point."[13]

The most divisive issue at Dumbarton Oaks was the structure and powers of the Security Council, the future UN's executive organ. Stettinius argued, with Eden's backing, that a state should not be allowed to exercise its veto power in a dispute to which it was a party. Stettinius had been put in charge of the U.S. Dumbarton Oaks team at the last minute, after the wartime secretary of state, Cordell Hull, fell seriously ill. He was a wunderkind of the business world who had resigned his chairmanship of the board of U.S. Steel at age forty to join Roosevelt's brain trust. But he was no match for the USSR's foreign minister, Vyacheslav Molotov, known as "Old Stone Ass" for his staying power in negotiations. Molotov would not budge from his position that there should be no exceptions to the veto power. Unable to resolve the issue, the diplomats left it to be settled in person by Stalin, Churchill, and Roosevelt, who were soon to meet in Yalta to make concrete arrangements for the shape of the peace.

Eleanor Roosevelt was worried about the strain that the Yalta meeting would place on the president. "After the inauguration," she wrote in her memoirs, "it was clearer every day that Franklin was far from well."[14] But he seemed so energized when he spoke of his plans that she suppressed her concerns: "Franklin had high hopes that at this conference he could make real progress in strengthening the personal relationship between himself and Marshal Stalin. He talked a good deal about the importance of this [relationship] in the days of peace to come, since he realized that the problems which would arise then would be more difficult even than those of the war period."

In February 1945 the Big Three leaders and their advisers gathered at Yalta, a resort on the Black Sea. Once the site of an ancient Greek colony, Yalta was dotted with handsome villas that had belonged to the Russian nobility. Stalin was an expansive host. Churchill welcomed the "genial" Crimean climate, with its "warm and brilliant sunshine."[15] But the American president, though striking a jaunty pose in photographs from the conference, looks gaunt, frail, and ill.

The most controversial items on the Yalta agenda involved the Soviet Union's plans for the security of its frontiers. Stalin's main concern, he announced, was to reach a firm agreement with the United States and Britain to protect his country from any resurgence of German military ambitions. To this end he insisted that the postwar governments of the countries along the Soviet Union's western border had to be friendly to Russian interests. He had already taken steps toward that goal: Bulgaria and Romania, Germany's allies, were under Soviet control, and the Red Army had occupied Warsaw just two weeks before the conference. In January the USSR had recognized a committee of Polish Communists and sympathizers as the legitimate provisional government of Poland, over the protests of Britain and the United States, who had previously recognized a rival group.[16]

Churchill, hoping to dilute the Soviet Union's power on the European continent, proposed that France should have an active role in policing postwar Europe. He was ultimately successful in obtaining a seat for

France as the fifth permanent member (with Britain, China, the United States, and the USSR) of the United Nations Security Council. This seems not to have troubled Stalin, since the Soviet Union's position that there should be no exceptions to the veto power substantially prevailed.

Discussion on the status of Poland was protracted and acrimonious. Finally the three leaders reached an agreement, calling for the Communist-dominated provisional government to be "reorganized on a broader democratic basis with the inclusion of democratic leaders from Poland itself and from Poles abroad."[17] To Stalin, "democratic" meant anything that was not fascist. To Roosevelt, it meant free elections. "I want this election in Poland to be the first one beyond question," he told Stalin. "It should be like Caesar's wife . . . they say she was pure." Stalin's bantering reply was ominous: "They said that about her, but in fact she had her faults."[18]

The agreement on Poland was vague and toothless, but in view of Soviet military dominance in Eastern Europe, there was little more that Roosevelt and Churchill could gain by means of negotiation. "It was not a question of what Great Britain and the United States would permit Russia to do in Poland," Stettinius later wrote, "but what the two countries could persuade the Soviet Union to accept."[19]

To Eleanor Roosevelt, FDR seemed far from discouraged upon his return. Yalta was important to him, she wrote, but only as a step: "He knew there had to be more negotiation, other meetings. He hoped for an era of peace and understanding, but he knew well that peace was not won in a day—that days upon days and years upon years lay before us in which we must keep the peace by constant effort."[20]

Signs that the president's health was failing fast could no longer be ignored. On March 1, for the first time, he remained seated while addressing Congress. The famous voice was less distinct than on previous occasions. On April 12, a week before the opening of the San Francisco conference, news came from Warm Springs, Georgia, that Franklin Delano Roosevelt had succumbed to a cerebral hemorrhage. The president who had led America through the war would not be there to shape the peace.

⚊

The loss of its most powerful supporter was a severe blow to the future United Nations. Though Stalin did not view the new peace and security organization as enough of a threat to his plans to stand in its way, his disdain for the vision of an inclusive "universal organization" had surfaced at Yalta. Many small nations, he remarked to dinner companions, had the absurd belief that the Great Powers had fought the war in order to liberate them.[21] Churchill, as prime minister of a country with a vast if crumbling colonial empire, was in no position to disagree. When Stettinius (who had been promoted to secretary of state in November 1944) broached the subject of establishing UN trusteeships in non-self-governing territories (a euphemism for colonies), Churchill became agitated, swearing that "not one scrap of British territory" would ever be included in such arrangements if he could prevent it.[22]

Though FDR had been the only Allied leader to push for a human rights reference in the Dumbarton Oaks proposals, the truth is that the promotion of fundamental rights and freedoms was far from central to the thinking of any of the Big Three as they debated the shape and purpose of the United Nations. This was not surprising: it was not self-evident that the proposed international organization ought to be concerned with such matters. For one thing, international lawyers regarded a state's treatment of its own citizens, with rare exceptions, as that nation's own business.

That began to change, however, in the waning days of the war, as appalling details of the Nazi reign of terror were coming to light and the Allies faced the question of how to deal with major war criminals. Both Roosevelt and Stalin had pushed for some kind of public international trial. Churchill, however, was strongly opposed, maintaining that the chief leaders should be summarily executed once they were properly identified.[23] He reluctantly capitulated only after the deaths of Mussolini, Hitler, and Goebbels in April and May 1945 had removed the most notorious offenders.

In August 1945, six months after Yalta, the Allies issued a charter setting forth the guidelines that came to be known as the Nuremberg Principles. Largely crafted in Washington, these principles stated that to wage a war of aggression was a crime against international society and that to persecute, oppress, or do violence to individuals or minorities on political, racial, or religious grounds in connection with such a war, or to exterminate, enslave, or deport civilian populations, was a crime against humanity.

But the Nuremberg Principles left the issue of *peacetime* violations of human dignity untouched. So had the founders of the League of Nations after the First World War. The League's Covenant had contained no mention of human rights, and the same might well have been true of the UN Charter. On the eve of the San Francisco conference of 1945, one thing was clear: The Great Powers were not going to take the initiative in making human rights a centerpiece of their postwar arrangements. It was not in their interest to do so.

This had not gone unnoticed in the world at large, where the winds of change were gathering force. Men and women throughout the broken world were yearning not only for peace, but for a better and freer existence. By destroying lives, leveling cities, and displacing peoples, the two world wars had unsettled fixed, familiar patterns of living. Amid the ruins, something new was stirring. When the fighting that had drawn soldiers to battlegrounds in Europe, North Africa, and the Pacific Islands came to a close, victory bells had awakened pent-up longings in the hearts of women and men in every corner of the earth. Soldiers and civilians alike had become aware that the way things had been was not necessarily the way they had to be. In Southeast Asia and North Africa, anger was building against Britain, France, the Netherlands, and other powers loath to relinquish their overseas empires. Over 250 million people were still living under colonial rule, and millions more belonged to disadvantaged minorities in the United States, Latin America, and the Soviet Union. A new chapter in the history of human rights was about to unfold.

When delegates began to arrive in San Francisco from fifty far-flung lands in April 1945, they included a number of individuals who hoped that the new organization would concern itself with much more than collective security.[24] Many had been inspired by Allied descriptions of the war as a fight for freedom and democracy. They had read or listened eagerly to Franklin Roosevelt's 1941 "four freedoms" speech, which linked future peace and security to respect for freedom of speech and expression, freedom to worship God in one's own way, freedom from want, and freedom from fear.[25] Those sentiments were echoed in the Atlantic Charter, the press statement issued by Roosevelt and Churchill after their shipboard meeting prior to the U.S. entry into the war. At the beginning of 1942, the Allies, calling themselves the "united nations," issued a joint declaration that began by stating that victory was essential in order "to defend life, liberty, independence and religious freedom and to preserve human rights and justice in their own lands as well as in other lands." These efforts to articulate the meaning of the struggle had sounded chords that would reverberate long after the war ended.

☞

Among the delegates most determined to hold the Allies to their wartime rhetoric was Carlos Romulo of the Philippines. One of the more flamboyant characters in the UN's early history, Romulo had won a Pulitzer Prize in 1941 for a series of newspaper articles forecasting that the days of colonialism in East Asia were numbered. When Japan invaded the Philippine Commonwealth, he joined the U.S. Army, serving as an aide to General Douglas MacArthur at Bataan and Corregidor, where he earned a Silver Star and a Purple Heart with two oak leaf clusters. Some say it was Romulo who came up with MacArthur's famous words, "I shall return."[26] His political opponents often made disparaging remarks about his height, which he put at five feet four and they at five two. But cocky Romulo made up in ego for what he lacked in stature. In a *Reader's Digest* article titled "I'm Glad I'm a Little Guy," he compared himself to Francis of Assisi, Beethoven, Keats, and Napoleon, all "shorties" who, he said, had been spurred to strive for higher achievements.[27]

In the summer of 1944, as a member of the Philippine government-in-exile, Colonel (soon to be General) Romulo had attended the Bretton Woods economic conference. Romulo came away from that meeting indignant that the major powers "had already set themselves up to be the ones to decide what the economic pattern of the postwar world should be."[28] He told reporters that the economic arrangements made by the Allies would one day have to be reexamined in the light of the needs and ideals of developing nations. The Dumbarton Oaks conference, a month after Bretton Woods, did nothing to ease his concerns: it was closed to all except China, Great Britain, the Soviet Union, and the United States. (Most of the decisions made by Roosevelt, Churchill, and Stalin at Yalta were kept secret until the end of the war, and the full text of the Yalta agreements was not disclosed until 1947.)

In San Francisco, Romulo sensed that the movers and shakers were not listening to what he and other delegates from lesser powers had to say. Even the Russians, who talked a good game of liberation from oppression, behaved "towards all of us representatives of smaller countries as though we scarcely existed. They acted as if they owned the world, strutting around like conquerors in their ill-cut suits with bell-bottom trousers."[29] Great Britain's Cadogan was better dressed and more polished, but his letters to his wife reveal that Romulo's suspicions were far from fanciful. As the Big Four approached agreement on the powers of the Security Council, Cadogan wrote that he expected a final decision in a day or two, but "we shall have all the little fellows yapping at our heels, and it won't be easy. Of course one could crack the whip at them and say that if they don't like our proposals there just damned well won't be any World Organization. But I don't know that that would pay, and it would have to be put tactfully."[30]

Romulo, who believed that the single most important issue in the postwar era would be colonialism, was not one to suffer in silence. Nor was the "third world soldier" (as he called himself) given to observing diplomatic niceties. When the question of the future status of "non-self-governing territories" came up, he became a thorn in the side of representatives from countries with large colonial possessions. Belgium, Britain, France, and the Netherlands attempted to finesse the issue of independence through a pledge to work for a gradual transition to "self-government," but Romulo insisted that this did not get to the heart of the matter.

"Self-government," Romulo claimed, was not the same as independence. Some colonies were already largely self-governing internally, but their inhabitants were aiming for nationhood, with full equality in the family of nations. "Mr. Chairman," he said, "the peoples of the world are on the move. They have been given a new courage by the hope of freedom for which we fought in this war. Those of us who have come from the murk and mire of the battlefields know that we fought for freedom, not for one country, but for all peoples and for all the world."[31] By his own account, Romulo became "a nuisance, a gadfly, a pest. I prowled corridors, buttonholed delegates, cornered unwilling victims in hotel lobbies and men's rooms."

His persistent efforts, supported by the Soviets, yielded significant, if not fully satisfying, results. The objective of promoting the "self-determination of peoples" was included among the purposes of the UN in the Charter's Preamble. Romulo was disappointed, however, that the Charter provisions dealing with non-self-governing territories obligated the states responsible for those territories only to "develop self-government" with no mention of independence. He took some consolation from the fact that the purposes of the UN trusteeship system included the promotion of their "development towards self-government or independence." The trusteeship system was created to administer the overseas possessions stripped from the Axis powers and to replace the mandate system set up by the League of Nations after the First World War to administer former German and Turkish territories.

The following year, 1946, when the Philippines gained independence from the United States, Romulo elaborated on the position he had taken in San Francisco: "We of the Philippines know the aspirations and yearnings of the dependent people of the Far East because we are part of their world. We know how they hunger for freedom. We know, too, the fears and resentments they have long harbored in their hearts. We know that to these people self-government is a meaningless word, while independence stands for all their hopes and dreams. Although we had no authority to speak *for* these millions in the Far East who were not represented at the Conference, we could speak *of* them and plead their cause."[32]

Romulo and several other delegates also pressed in San Francisco for a position on racial discrimination—much to the discomfort of the United States and some colonial powers. Reminding the assembly that many different races had fought together in the war, he and representatives from Brazil, Egypt, India, Panama, Uruguay, Mexico, the Dominican Republic, Cuba, and Venezuela agitated in favor of various antidiscrimination proposals.[33] Their combined efforts, supported by China, France, and the Soviet Union, produced the Charter's radical challenge to the social status quo throughout the world: an emphatic statement that human rights belong to everyone "without distinction as to race, sex, language, or religion."

Another spokesman for small nations at San Francisco was Australian Foreign Minister Herbert V. Evatt, who spearheaded a widely supported attempt to limit the requirement of unanimity among Britain, China, France, the United States, and the USSR, the five permanent members of the Security Council (that is, the veto power of each of them). As it happened, the frequent use of the veto power would soon dash hopes for the UN's future as a cooperative peacekeeping body. The movement to curb it was, of course, doomed, but its energy so alarmed the United States that President Truman telephoned the Australian prime minister to request that Evatt be reined in. The insurgence was quelled only when the Big Three made it clear that the issue was non-negotiable. U.S. delegate Thomas

Connally, chairman of the Senate Foreign Relations Committee, dramatized the point by ripping a piece of paper to shreds as he warned that any
change in the veto arrangements would be equivalent to tearing up the
Charter.[34]

But Evatt scored an important victory in another area. Insisting that the
key issues of the peacetime era would be economic, his Australian delegation argued that a permanent system of security could be effective only
if it had a foundation in economic and social justice. Evatt especially
stressed full employment. Referring to the role of the Great Depression in
the rise of militaristic, totalitarian regimes in Germany, Japan, and Italy,
he wrote: "The great threat to human freedom which we have been combating for five years arose out of and was made possible by an environment dominated by unemployment and lacking freedom from want."[35]
Widespread support for the Australian position led to strengthening the
Charter's provision for an Economic and Social Council (ECOSOC),
making it a "principal organ" of the UN, alongside the Security Council.

One of the youngest delegates to the San Francisco conference was getting the sense, as Romulo and Evatt had done, that "the big 3 or 4 or 5 decide among themselves, and we cannot make much difference."[36] Charles
Malik, thirty-nine, from the recently independent Lebanese Republic,
sympathized with Romulo's general outlook but was appalled by his
bombastic manner. Malik was a philosophy professor who had been recruited into diplomatic service only months before. "Many people talk
rhetorically in order to produce an impression, e.g., this awful man General Romulo," he noted in his diary. "The mere thought that I might be
doing that is enough to paralyze my powers of speech."

Malik used his own turn at the podium to criticize the conference
agenda as too limited in scope. "We are dealing," he complained, with
"mere framework and form."[37] He traced that problem to the Dumbarton
Oaks proposals, which he described as disappointingly superficial—
envisaging "political, military, judicial, economic, and social measures for
the maintenance of international peace and security," while failing to address the underlying causes of aggression and conflict. Certain outwardly
peaceful and secure situations, Malik pointed out, "do not spring from genuine justice. . . . There is a peace that only cloaks terrible inner conflicts;
and there is a security that is utterly insecure."

Sharing Romulo, Evatt, and Malik's desire to enlarge the aims of the new organization were the delegates from the Latin American states, the largest single bloc at the conference. Among them at that time were several that were struggling to establish constitutional democracies, and Mexico, which had adopted a socialist constitution in 1917.[38] Their focus was on the rights that they had recognized in their own twentieth-century constitutions and were then internationalizing in a draft document that would become the 1948 American Declaration of Rights and Duties.

That document was a tribute to the century-old Pan-American vision of Simón Bolívar. After leading independence wars in Venezuela, Colombia, Panama, Ecuador, Peru, and Bolivia, Bolívar had convened representatives of these new republics in 1826 to discuss a united South America. Early in the twentieth century the continent's pioneering internationalists formed an inter-American conference that met at regular intervals. In 1945, just before the San Francisco conference, representatives of twenty-one Latin American countries gathered in Mexico City and resolved to seek inclusion of a transnational declaration of rights in the UN Charter. In San Francisco, Panama submitted a draft proposal for such a bill and joined delegates from Cuba, Chile, and Mexico in pressing hard for movement on that front.

Also intent on promoting a broad spectrum of rights were representatives from more than forty nongovernmental organizations (mostly U.S. based) who had been invited as consultants and observers.[39] These NGOs, as they are now called, included Catholic, Jewish, and Protestant groups, legal associations, and labor and peace organizations. In the nineteenth century the habit of mobilizing for the redress of injustice and the relief of suffering worldwide had become part of the culture of many developed countries. Now, in the century of mass slaughters, the heirs of various movements for the abolition of slavery, workers' rights, universal suffrage, and other reformist causes joined forces in the struggle for human rights.

The role played at San Francisco by the "smaller nations," as Romulo and others called them, has often been overlooked. (The term *smaller* referred to their clout, not necessarily to their size.) Though the proceedings were dominated, and to a certain extent stage-managed, by the Big Three, with China and France admitted by courtesy to the inner circle, the voting power and influence of the other forty-five countries was far from negligible.

While the delegations from Latin America were especially active, those from war-torn Europe took few initiatives. Vera Dean, who attended the conference as an observer for the Foreign Policy Association, remarked that the Europeans appeared like "convalescents from a grave illness." The problem of Russia's future relations with its wartime allies, she added, dominated the San Francisco proceedings "as if it had been written in invisible ink throughout the otherwise scrupulously technical agenda."[40]

Conscience was thus present in numbers at the San Francisco meeting, but Power did not at first pay much attention. Even as the conference unfolded, the Soviet Union was tightening its control over Poland, reneging on its Yalta promise to admit democratic elements into the government, and sending its secret police to arrest Poland's non-Communist leaders.[41] The United States continued to support the reference to human rights in the UN's general statement of purposes, but it opposed proposals by Latin American delegates to include a bill of rights in the Charter and rejected their suggestion that the Charter should contain a commitment to set up special commissions for education, culture, and human rights.[42] Such commissions, the U.S. delegation said, could be established as and when needed by the future Economic and Social Council, as had been proposed at Dumbarton Oaks.

In May 1945, with the conference well under way, a number of developments at last helped to open a path for human rights advocates. After exchanging views inconclusively at Yalta on how to deal with war criminals (Churchill still wanted to shoot them), Churchill, Roosevelt, and Stalin had left the matter to be discussed by their foreign secretaries in San Francisco.[43] When Britain finally dropped its opposition to formal trials on May 3, the way was clear to begin establishing a tribunal. That evening Sir Alexander Cadogan wrote his wife, "The question of the major war criminals seems to be settling itself, as they seem to be getting bumped off satisfactorily in one way or another."[44] Anticipating the British decision, Harry Truman, who became president upon Roosevelt's death, had announced on May 2 that Supreme Court Justice Robert H. Jackson would represent the United States "in preparing and prosecuting charges of atrocities and war crimes against such of the leaders of the European Axis powers . . . as the United States may agree with any of the united nations to bring to trial before an international military tribunal."[45] Jackson took a leave of absence from the bench to help develop the Nuremberg Principles and to act as the chief U.S. prosecutor at the trials held in 1945 and 1946.

That same week, representatives of several American NGOs secured a meeting with Edward Stettinius. The busy secretary of state accorded them all of twenty-five minutes, telling them at the outset that there was little hope of securing more recognition for human rights than had been granted at Dumbarton Oaks.[46] The group's spokesman, Frederick Nolde of the Joint Committee for Religious Liberty, led off with a high-minded exhortation, urging the United States, in keeping with its best traditions, to show leadership on the issue. He was followed by Judge Joseph Proskauer of the American Jewish Committee, who made a more political case, emphasizing the intensity and diversity of interest in human rights among the voting public. Reinforcing Proskauer's point, labor leader Philip Murray rose to affirm the "wholehearted" support of the Congress of Industrial Organizations (CIO). Then Walter White of the National Association for the Advancement of Colored People spoke of "the importance of including colonies and other dependent peoples within the concept of human rights." The last speaker, Clark Eichelberger of the American Association for the United Nations, had a specific request. It was especially important, he said, for the United Nations to set up a *commission* on human rights.

Stettinius's diary for that period shows him embroiled in tense negotiations with the Soviets and beset with divisions among his advisers on how best to deal with these allies who were already becoming enemies. Whether the secretary was moved by any of the arguments he had heard, or whether he was just throwing the NGOs what he thought was a crumb, the United States made a single exception to its opposition to the naming of special commissions in the Charter: It would agree to a Human Rights Commission.[47]

This marked a crucial turning point. It is unlikely that human rights would have figured prominently in the UN Charter without the support of the U.S. State Department. The Soviet Union entered no objection, secure in the knowledge that the Charter would protect purely domestic affairs from UN intervention.[48]

Meanwhile delegates from Brazil, Canada, Chile, Cuba, the Dominican Republic, Egypt, France, Haiti, India, Mexico, New Zealand,

Panama, and Uruguay kept up the pressure for giving human rights an even higher profile in the Charter. Support for these initiatives grew when the euphoria of V-E Day, May 8, was followed by the shocking first photographs from the concentration camps.

By the time the UN Charter was completed on June 26, principles of human rights were woven into its text at several points.[49] They were given pride of place in the Preamble, which begins with a ringing announcement of the member nations' determination:

> to save succeeding generations from the scourge of war, which twice in our lifetime has brought untold sorrow to mankind, and
> to reaffirm our faith in fundamental human rights, in the dignity and worth of the human person, in the equal rights of men and women and of nations large and small, and
> to establish conditions under which justice and respect for the obligations arising under treaties and other sources of international law can be maintained, and
> to promote social progress and better standards of life in larger freedom . . .

The affirmation of equal rights in the Preamble, so far ahead of the realities of the time, was reinforced in Article 1 of the Charter, which recites the purposes of the United Nations. Prominent among the new organization's aims is respect for the "self-determination of peoples" and for "human rights and for fundamental freedoms for all without distinction as to race, sex, language or religion." Self-determination of *peoples* and human rights for all *individuals* would prove difficult to harmonize, but the Charter established that both aims were fundamental. Then, in Article 56, the nations solemnly pledged themselves to promote those rights and freedoms. Among the tasks assigned to the Economic and Social Council was that of establishing "commissions in economic and social fields for the promotion of human rights."[50]

Harry Truman gave his first major speech as president at the San Francisco Opera House on the occasion of the signing of the UN Charter on June 26. "Experience has shown how deeply the seeds of war are planted by economic rivalry and by social injustice," he said.[51] Economic and social cooperation are "part of the very heart of this compact." He was looking forward, he told the delegates, to the framing of an "International Bill of Rights."

Eleanor Roosevelt followed from a distance the proceedings she had hoped to attend with her husband. "One feels in the San Francisco conference," she wrote to her aunt Maude Gray, "that a strong hand is missing."[52] She was sad, she added, that FDR "could not see the end of his long work which he carried so magnificently." On the day the Charter was signed, she greeted the event with cautious optimism in her syndicated "My Day" column: "I don't believe that greed and selfishness have gone out of the human race. I am quite prepared to be considerably disappointed many times in the course of cooperation, . . . but I want to try for a peaceful world. The ratification of the Charter as soon as possible, in compliance with President Truman's wishes, will, I think, make easier every step we take in the future."

The following month, her late husband's wise bipartisan strategy paid off: the U.S. Senate approved the UN Charter by an overwhelming majority, 89–2.

⚓

The idea of universal human rights thus found a place in the UN Charter, but it was a glimmering thread in a web of power and interest. What might come of it was far from clear. The Charter did not say what those rights might be, and no one knew whether any rights really could be said to be universal, in the sense of being acceptable to all nations and peoples, including those not yet represented in the United Nations.

The Great Powers had gone along with the human rights language, but they made sure that the Charter protected their national sovereignty: "Nothing contained in the present Charter shall authorize the United Nations to intervene in matters which are essentially within the domestic jurisdiction of any State, or shall require the Members to submit such matters to settlement under the present Charter; but this principle shall not prejudice the application of enforcement measures under Chapter VII."[53] Chapter VII's exception to that principle, limited to situations where the Security Council determines that international peace and security are threatened, could be controlled by any of the Big Five through their veto power.

Smaller nations, however, had more reason to be concerned. On the one hand, the addition of human rights references to the Charter might encourage stronger states to intervene in their affairs under pretext of championing the rights of their citizens, as Hitler had done in Czechoslovakia. On the other hand, many tyrants including Hitler had hidden behind the bulwark of national sovereignty, seemingly protected in the Charter as well. How can human rights be secured while discouraging bad-faith military adventures or economic sanctions in their name? When is intervention in a country's internal affairs legitimate, and when not? What is intervention? The vague domestic-jurisdiction language of the Charter shed little light on these problems. They would remain tough nuts to crack.

How Conscience would fare in the tug-of-war between human rights and national interests in the new international organization was anyone's guess. Much would depend on the new Human Rights Commission. A key figure on that Commission would be scholarly Charles Malik, who left the San Francisco meeting feeling like an alien. He wrote in his diary: "Intrigue, lobbying, secret arrangements, blocs, etc. It's terrible. Power politics and bargaining nauseate me. There is so much unreality and play and sham that I can't swing myself into this atmosphere and act."[54]

Charles Malik had yet to meet Eleanor Roosevelt.

CHAPTER 2

MADAM CHAIRMAN

The Creation of
the Human Rights Commission

On New Year's Eve 1945, after the photographers that had surrounded such notables as Senators Thomas Connally and Arthur Vandenberg finally dispersed, a tall woman in a black coat boarded the *Queen Elizabeth* bound for Southampton. Eleanor Roosevelt, along with Connally, the Texas Democratic chairman of the Senate Foreign Relations Committee, and Vandenberg, the Michigan Republican who was the committee's ranking minority member, was headed for the first meeting of the UN General Assembly in London. Neither she nor anyone else suspected that, at age sixty-two, she was on a course that would lead to the most important achievement of her already distinguished public life.

When President Truman had asked her to be a member of the U.S. delegation to the UN, the widow of the wartime president was doubtful: "How could I be a delegate to help organize the United Nations when I have no background or experience in international meetings?"[1] Those reservations about her qualifications were shared by many members of the foreign policy establishment. The opposition to her nomination included not only prominent Republicans such as John Foster Dulles, who would later be Dwight Eisenhower's secretary of state, but distinguished Democrats, including Senator William Fulbright. The former regarded her as too liberal, the latter as too inexperienced. Fulbright was concerned that her presence on the delegation would signal a lack of seriousness about the UN.[2]

There was also the risk, from the perspective of these foreign-policy professionals, that the outspoken former First Lady would be a loose cannon in her new environment. As a political activist and popular journalist, she had developed a formidable reputation for her independence of mind and determination to champion progressive causes. During her White House years she had even used her newspaper column to criticize decisions of her husband's administration, such as a provision of his economic recovery program that resulted in the layoff of married women.[3] FDR accepted these public disagreements with equanimity, telling his wife on one occasion: "Lady, this is a free country. Say what you think. If you get me in Dutch, I'll manage to get myself out. Anyway, the whole world knows I can't control you."[4] Wags of the day said that FDR's prayer was "Dear God, please make Eleanor tired." No wonder the foreign-policy establishment was nervous.

The decision, however, was the president's. And Harry Truman was less concerned with possible risks than with keeping the prestige of the Roosevelt name associated with his administration. Besides, Truman was the last person in the world to be dissuaded by Mrs. Roosevelt's inexperience in foreign affairs. When he was thrust into the highest office in the land the preceding April, he had had to work hard to bring himself up to speed on foreign policy. In his biography, David McCullough relates that Truman, with a summit meeting at Potsdam looming in July, "had no experience in relations with Britain or Russia, no firsthand knowledge of Churchill or Stalin. He didn't know the right people. He didn't know [Ambassador to the Soviet Union] Harriman. He didn't know his own Secretary of State, more than to say hello."[5] Franklin Roosevelt, for all his political astuteness, had not bothered to prepare the vice president to take over in the event of his death.

Truman pressed Mrs. Roosevelt to accept the UN assignment. Later she wrote that she might not have agreed "if I had known at that time . . . that the nomination would have to be approved by the United States Senate, where certain senators would disapprove of me because of my attitude toward social problems and more especially youth problems. As it turned out, some senators did protest to the President against my nomination, but only one, Senator Theodore G. Bilbo of Mississippi, ac-

Eleanor Roosevelt and President Harry S. Truman
at his desk in the Oval Office.

tually voted against me."[6] The sticking point for Bilbo, apparently, was the former First Lady's devotion to the cause of racial equality.

What overcame Mrs. Roosevelt's hesitation was the belief, shared by family and friends, that the UN appointment might be the best solution to the problem with which she had been wrestling since the death of FDR in April: how to make a new life for herself.[7] In the months since leaving the White House, she had been pondering her future, dealing all the while with various family crises, personal and financial. From the time she had been a young woman, she had thrown herself into helping the most neglected members of society, her empathy aroused perhaps by her own experiences as a lonely, unloved child whose mother had regarded her as an ugly duckling. After years of involvement in Democratic Party politics at all levels, in which she had spoken out on behalf of her own favorite causes—women's rights, the end of racial discrimination, improvement of working and housing conditions—she was resolved to remain active in public life. But since the death of her husband she could not see her way forward clearly. The new international organization might, she thought, be a place where her talents and energies would be useful and where she could pursue her lifelong interest in humanitarian causes.

Truman's use of the atomic bomb to end the war with Japan in August 1945 had broadened the horizon of her concerns. That awesome decision, whose morality is still debated, did bring World War II to an immediate end, but Mrs. Roosevelt saw that it also put an end to isolationism. With that event, she had written in her column, "we came into a new world—a world in which we had to learn to live in friendship with our neighbors of every race and creed and color, or face the fact that we might be wiped off the face of the earth."[8]

Looking back a few months after her decision, she told the readers of her newspaper column:

> I [took this assignment] because it seemed I might be able to use the experiences of a lifetime and make them valuable to my nation and to the people of the world at this particular time. I knew, of course, how much my husband hoped that, out of the war, an organization for peace would really develop. It was not just to further my husband's hopes, however. . . . It was rather that I myself had always believed that women

might have a better chance to bring about the understanding necessary to prevent future wars if they could serve in sufficient numbers in these international bodies.[9]

As the date of departure approached, however, Eleanor Roosevelt's anxieties returned. She wrote in her "My Day" column: "I am told we will be 'briefed' (whatever this may mean) during the trip," adding that "I need it in the worst possible way."[10] To her daughter, Anna, she said, "Say prayers that I'm really useful on this job for I feel very inadequate."[11] Later she confided to Irene Sandifer, the wife of her State Department adviser:

[Y]ou can never know how terribly frightened I was when I got on that ship that night to go to London. I came to the ship alone and I was simply terrified. I felt that I was going to do a job that I knew nothing about, I knew I did not know anything about it. . . . And if I had known then how Senator Vandenberg and Mr. Dulles felt about me I do not believe I could ever have had the courage to go.[12]

When the time came, however, as so often before in her life, she did what had to be done. She donned her hat and coat, tossed her trademark fox furs over her shoulder, and boarded the ocean liner still painted gray from use as a troop ship. As soon as she was settled in her cabin, she wrote to Anna, "Just a line from the ship to tell you I am comfortable & tho' the responsibility seems great I'll just do my best and trust in God."[13] The next day she got up early and began studying stacks of State Department documents on the issues to be discussed in London. Her remedy for insecurity was the same as Harry Truman's: hard work and preparation.

"Last night was bad," she wrote on January 2, "fog horn most of the night, heavy roll and much colder."[14] It was but one of many bad nights Eleanor Roosevelt had passed since the shocks of the previous spring. Her grief over FDR's death had been compounded by the discovery that after urging her to remain at the family residence in Hyde Park, he had spent his last days in Warm Springs with Lucy Mercer Rutherfurd, whom he had promised never to see again after the long-ago affair that had nearly ended the Roosevelt marriage. In the days following FDR's death, Mrs. Roosevelt learned for the first time that her husband had begun seeing

Mrs. Rutherfurd at the White House while she was away—and that these visits had occurred with Anna's full complicity.[15]

While these wounds were still fresh, the ex–First Lady found herself faced with unaccustomed money problems, owing to the length of time it took to probate her husband's estate. Nor did bereavement produce a moratorium on the various marital and financial difficulties of her adult children, who still looked to Mother for advice and help.

Years of practice in dealing with disappointments large and small carried Mrs. Roosevelt through the immediate trauma. When President Truman asked if there was anything he could do for her, she was composed enough to respond, "No, thank you, Mr. President. But is there anything I can do for you, for you are the one who is in trouble now?"[16] Resorting to the strategy that had carried her through hard times before, she kept busy, attending to the tasks at hand, writing her newspaper column, and answering voluminous correspondence. She strove to join her personal suffering to the sorrows of millions who had been deprived by war of all they held most dear, including hopes and illusions. In "My Day" for April 17 she wrote, "When you have lived for a long time in close contact with the loss and grief which today pervades the world, any personal sorrow seems to be lost in the general sadness of humanity."[17] Eleanor Roosevelt did not hold with self-pity.

Later, in an introspective passage of *This I Remember,* she recalled that she had had "an almost impersonal feeling about everything that was happening" at the time of her husband's death:

> The only explanation I have is that during the years of the war I had schooled myself to believe that some or all of my sons might be killed and I had long faced the fact that Franklin might be killed or die at any time. . . . That does not entirely account for my feelings, however. Perhaps it was that much further back I had had to face certain difficulties until I decided to accept the fact that a man must be what he is, life must be lived as it is, circumstances force your children away from you, and you cannot live at all if you do not learn to adapt yourself to life as it happens to be.[18]

Love for her only daughter seems to have helped her overcome the pain of betrayal, judging from the affectionate letters she continued to write to her "darling Anna" and her ready responses to Anna's calls for financial and moral support. Regarding FDR, she was later to say, "All human be-ings have failings, all human beings have needs and temptations and stresses. Men and women who live together through long years get to know one another's failings; but they also come to know what is worthy of respect and admiration in those they live with and in themselves. If at the end one can say: 'This man used to the limit the powers that God granted him; he was worthy of the love and respect and sacrifices of many people, made in order that he might achieve what he deemed to be his task,' then that life has been lived well and there are no regrets."[19]

While the *Queen Elizabeth* plowed across the choppy North Atlantic, Mrs. Roosevelt threw herself into her new job. She participated actively in daily meetings with the other members of the U.S. delegation, faithfully doing her homework each evening. Her fellow delegates were all major players in foreign affairs. Besides Senators Connally and Vandenberg, there was former Secretary of State Edward Stettinius, who had served as the ailing Roosevelt's right-hand man at Yalta. After a brief stint in the cabinet at the end of the Roosevelt administration, Stettinius had been re-placed by Truman appointee James F. Byrnes and was now headed to London as the first U.S. ambassador to the United Nations. Secretary Byrnes, also a delegate, traveled separately by air. Among the five alter-nates was John Foster Dulles, then serving as foreign affairs adviser to Thomas E. Dewey, who had been the Republican presidential nominee in 1944 and would be again in 1948.

The stature of the members of the bipartisan U.S. delegation was evi-dence of the seriousness and breadth of the U.S. commitment to the UN at the time. Vandenberg, a hard-core isolationist before the war, had be-come a major voice of internationalism not only in the Senate, but also in the GOP. Secretary Byrnes had announced that the Truman administration intended to continue FDR's internationalist policies. He told Congress, "This can be relied on, because it is supported by Republicans as well as Democrats and will be adhered to regardless of which party is in power."[20]

The newcomer's willingness to work, and her quickness in grasping the gist of technical material, did not go unappreciated. Her young State Department aide, Durward Sandifer, wrote his wife from shipboard that Mrs. Roosevelt was making "a great impression on the advisers with her alertness and sincerity and her avid desire for information."[21] Before they landed, Senator Vandenberg asked her whether she would be willing to serve as the American representative on the UN's Third Committee on

Social, Humanitarian, and Cultural Affairs (one of seven main committees set up to deal with specific matters designated as 1) political and
civil, 2) economic and financial, 3) social, humanitarian, and cultural, 4)
trusteeship, 5) administrative and budgetary, 6) legal, and 7) special political). Mrs. Roosevelt suspected that the third committee was thought to be
a "safe" place where she could do little harm.[22] But she told Vandenberg
that she would serve wherever she was needed and requested as much information as possible on "Committee Three."[23]

The UN General Assembly held its opening session on January 10, 1946,
in Central Hall, Westminster, specially renovated for the occasion at the
request of King George VI.[24] The participants in the San Francisco conference had settled on London as the site for that first meeting, pending
the decision on a permanent home for the new organization. The mood of
the delegates was less hopeful than it should have been on such a historic
occasion, for relations between the Soviet Union and the West were becoming increasingly strained. Six months earlier, Truman, Churchill, and
Stalin had met at Potsdam to make plans for the political future of Eastern
Europe, the occupation of Germany, and the conclusion of the war with
Japan. Truman had gone to the summit with hopes of developing a work-
able relationship with Stalin, but the Russian leader had been implacable
where Eastern Europe was concerned. Like others in the West, Truman
began to fear that the Soviet Union's expansionist aims would not stop
there. It was the first and last time that Truman and Stalin would meet.

The day after the opening ceremonies, Mrs. Roosevelt, still anxious
about her role, wrote to Anna, "My contribution to this meeting, beyond
the fact that I am Pa's widow & by my presence seem to remind them all
of him is very insignificant."[25] Not least among her fears was that a poor
showing on her part might set back the cause of women's advancement.
After her return she confessed, "[D]uring the entire London session of the
Assembly I walked on eggs. I knew that as the only woman on the delegation I was not very welcome. Moreover, if I failed to be a useful member, it would not be considered merely that I as an individual had failed,
but that all women had failed, and there would be little chance for others
to serve in the near future."[26]

There were few women at the General Assembly in those days, and
those present were mostly alternate delegates or advisers. Trying "to think

of small ways in which I might be more helpful," Mrs. Roosevelt began inviting the sixteen other women to tea in her sitting room at Claridge's hotel.[27] She found that in such informal sessions a group of colleagues could often make "more progress in reaching an understanding on some question before the United Nations than we had been able to achieve in the formal work of our committees." That discovery would later stand her and the human rights project in good stead.

As the London meeting progressed, Mrs. Roosevelt began to worry less about her own role than about the impression that other countries were acquiring of the United States. Secretary of State Byrnes struck her as "afraid of his own delegation" and therefore "afraid to decide on what he thinks is right and stand on it."[28] As for Vandenberg and Dulles, "they are rude and arrogant and create suspicion." But Byrnes's nervous "over-cordiality" struck the wrong note, too. The proper course seemed plain to the woman who had nagged her husband for years to be less cautious and more proactive in advancing civil rights: "I think we must be fair and stand for what we believe is right. . . . We have had that leadership and we must recapture it."

She threw herself with her customary vigor into the work of the third committee, which was occupied with the problem of the million or more war refugees from Eastern Europe who were living in displaced persons camps. "A new type of political refugee is appearing," she wrote to her daughter, "people who have been against the present governments and if they stay at home or go home will probably be killed."[29] The representatives of Communist governments, however, were claiming that war refugees who did not want to return to their countries of origin were mostly "quislings or traitors."

The argument quickly became acrimonious, foreshadowing future debates in the Human Rights Commission where proposals for "freedom of movement" would provoke alarmed and strenuous opposition from representatives of the closed Eastern European regimes. "It was ironical perhaps," Mrs. Roosevelt later remarked, "that one of the subjects that created the greatest political heat of the London sessions came up in this 'unimportant' committee to which I had been assigned."[30]

The USSR sent its heaviest hitter, then Deputy Foreign Minister Andrei Vishinsky, to argue that the displaced persons must be sent back to their homelands, like it or not. Vishinsky, whose résumé included service as chief prosecutor in Stalin's infamous treason trials of the 1930s, was renowned for his keen mind and sharp tongue. Since no one on the American delegation besides Eleanor Roosevelt was very well informed on the refugee question, her colleagues, after much conferring among themselves, asked her to respond.[31] When she rose to speak, she conceded that war criminals deserved punishment but pointed out that many refugees did not wish to return to their homelands simply because they disagreed with the existing regimes. Such persons, she said, did not deserve to be called "quislings" and should not be required to return. Would the Soviet Union, she inquired, want to see political refugees forcibly repatriated to Franco's Spain? With an eye toward gathering votes from the numerous Latin American delegates, she worked in a reference to the Great Liberator, Simón Bolívar. Let the displaced persons be free to make their own decisions, she urged. The majority of the third committee agreed.

Those members of the American contingent who hadn't known it before realized that their self-deprecating colleague was no babe in the political woods. Even Vandenberg and Dulles began to understand that the former First Lady could be an important asset to the United States in international settings. At the close of the London session, they approached her and said, "We must tell you that we did all we could to keep you off the United States delegation. We begged the President not to nominate you."[32] But now, as Mrs. Roosevelt later recounted with satisfaction, her erstwhile critics conceded, "We found you good to work with. And we will be happy to do so again."

Shortly after her return to New York, Eleanor Roosevelt received an assignment that finally allowed her to resolve her indecision about future plans. The UN's newly formed Economic and Social Council asked her to serve on a small "nuclear" commission charged with making recommendations concerning the structure and functions of the permanent Commission on Human Rights envisioned in the UN Charter. The nine nuclear committee members were chosen as individuals rather than as representatives of governments. Coming on the heels of her London performance, Roosevelt's nomination must have been a tribute to her personally, as well as a move to bind the United States more closely to the project and to appropriate the world-famous Roosevelt name. With a growing sense of the importance of the UN work, and increased confidence in her own ability to make a contribution, she agreed.

By the time the nuclear committee convened at Hunter College in New York from April 29 to May 20, 1946, the division between the Soviet Union and the West had been openly acknowledged by Stalin and Churchill. In February the Soviet leader had declared in a Moscow speech that peaceful coexistence between communism and capitalism was impossible. George Kennan had sent what came to be known as his "long telegram" from the Moscow embassy, advising the U.S. State Department that Stalin meant what he said. Kennan further advised that the Soviet regime, while not likely to be moved by appeals to reason or humanity, would often back off when faced with strength.[33] Then, on March 5, Winston Churchill (now ex–prime minister since the Labour Party's victory in July) turned up the heat with his famous "Iron Curtain" speech, warning against the danger of Soviet hegemonic ambitions. Truman, still hoping to get along with the Soviets, but determined not to appease them, took no public stand for the time being.[34]

Meanwhile the planning for a UN Human Rights Commission slowly went forward. The nuclear committee's first act was to elect Mrs. Roosevelt its chair. The meeting in other respects was less auspicious: only six of the nine members were in attendance.[35] At one point, after French member René Cassin had spoken for fifteen or twenty minutes without pausing for translation, the interpreter broke down in tears and fled the room, leaving Mrs. Roosevelt, who fortunately was fluent in French, to summarize his remarks as best she could. Three days before the meeting ended, a new Soviet representative arrived, claiming that the USSR was not bound by any decisions in which his predecessor had joined because the first man had had no authority to vote.[36]

The committee's most important recommendation was that the first project of the permanent Human Rights Commission should be to write a bill of human rights. Mrs. Roosevelt recounted in *Foreign Affairs,* "Many of us thought that lack of standards for human rights the world over was one of the greatest causes of friction among the nations, and that recognition of human rights might become one of the cornerstones on which peace could eventually be based."[37] After three weeks of discussion the group managed to produce only one other major recommendation: that the members of the permanent Human Rights Commission should be named by the UN on the basis of their individual qualifications, rather than appointed by the member states.[38] This recommendation was summarily rejected by the Economic and Social Council, but the idea of an international bill of rights, long in the air, was now on its way to becoming a reality.

In June 1946 the Commission on Human Rights was established, along with a separate Commission on the Status of Women. The human rights commissioners would be representatives of eighteen member states, with five from what were still being called the Great Powers (the United States, the Soviet Union, the United Kingdom, France, and China). Thirteen seats would be rotated at staggered three-year intervals among the other nations. The first Commission was composed of delegates from Australia, Belgium, Byelorussia, Chile, China, Egypt, France, India, Iran, Lebanon (represented by Charles Malik), Panama, Philippines (represented by General Romulo), Ukraine, USSR, United Kingdom, United States, Uruguay, and Yugoslavia.[39] The decision made political sense. As John P. Humphrey, the Canadian international law expert who was named the first director of the Human Rights Division of the UN Secretariat, observed, "[T]here would be no point in preparing texts which would not be accepted by governments."[40]

The new body was given the task of preparing an international bill of rights and devising means for its implementation.[41] Humphrey and his staff were to assist with research and technical services. Drafts and proposals were already pouring into the UN Secretariat, and Humphrey began assembling documentation immediately upon his appointment in August 1946.

In January 1947 the Commission on Human Rights held its first session in the UN's temporary quarters in an old gyroscope factory at Lake Success, New York. John Humphrey recalled a mood of "optimistic excitement" on the opening day:

> All the visitors' seats in the Council chamber were occupied when the session opened. The importance which governments attached to the commission was manifested by the quality of their representatives, many of whom were also playing or would later play important roles in the General Assembly and the Security Council. Two of them, Charles Malik and Carlos Romulo, later became presidents of the General Assembly.[42]

Eleanor Roosevelt was unanimously elected chairman. That, according to Humphrey, had been expected. The preceding August, when he assumed his post in the Secretariat, he quickly gathered that "the most important person in the United Nations human rights program was already Eleanor Roosevelt."[43] Her enormous prestige, both as a reminder of the late president and in her own right as an effective champion of humanitarian causes, was "one of the chief assets of the Human Rights Commission in the early years."

Peng-chun (P. C.) Chang, head of the Chinese UN delegation, was chosen as vice chairman. Chang was a Chinese Renaissance man—a playwright, musician, educator, and seasoned diplomat, devoted to traditional Chinese music and literature but conversant with Islamic and Western culture as well. In January 1946 he had given an unusual speech at ECOSOC's historic opening meeting. Quoting from the Chinese thinker Mencius, Chang said that ECOSOC's highest aim should be "Subdue people with goodness."[44]

Lebanon's Charles Malik, enthusiastically nominated by Romulo, became rapporteur, or secretary, responsible not for keeping the minutes, but for summarizing and preparing official reports on the committee's work. This triumvirate, symbolically representing West, East, and, in the case of Malik, a crossroads of many cultures, constituted the leadership of the Human Rights Commission throughout the entire period of the preparation of the document that became the Universal Declaration of Human Rights.

Malik knew the Bible well enough to have been intrigued by the similarity between Mencius' maxim and Romans 12:21 ("Seek not to overcome evil with evil, but overcome evil with good"). Over time, Malik and Chang would discover other affinities and would learn to work effectively together. But a serious personal and philosophical rivalry between these two intellectual giants of the Commission was one of the factors that got the human rights project off to a rocky start.

Not everyone, moreover, shared the mood of "optimistic excitement" as the Commission began its work. The Soviet delegate, Valentin Tepliakov, sent a gloomy report to Moscow: "We weren't able to make the changes that we wanted to make, such as to bring the representative of the Soviet Union or Yugoslavia into the leadership of the Commission."[45] What made matters worse, he complained, was that "the Chinese representative as well as the Lebanese representative are partisans of the position of the representative of the United States." Though Chang and Malik were more independent than Tepliakov surmised, the Soviet Union would suffer throughout the drafting process from its inability to count on more than four certain votes for its positions (its own plus those of Byelorussia, the Ukraine, and Yugoslavia). The euphoria of the opening day quickly dissolved as the commissioners began to grapple with the formidable task ahead.

A ROCKY START

The First Meeting of
the Human Rights Commission

Sixteen member states (all but Byelorussia and the Ukraine) were represented at the first session of the Human Rights Commission, held at Lake Success, New York, from January 27 to February 10, 1947.[1] The abandoned factory that served as the UN's temporary headquarters from 1946 to 1950 had been used to manufacture spare parts for airplanes during the war. The setting was conducive to business. The plain old building offered few amenities, and its quiet Long Island surroundings provided few distractions.

Most of the delegates were strangers to one another. Eleanor Roosevelt and René Cassin, both in their sixties, were the oldest of the group; Charles Malik, at forty, was the youngest. The only women members were Roosevelt and Hansa Mehta, an Indian legislator. An activist in the movement that led to India's independence in August 1947, Mrs. Mehta had been a sharp, outspoken critic of Britain's colonial policies of detention without trial, censorship, and confiscation of property.[2]

Mrs. Roosevelt, who had just written in a popular magazine, "Men and women both are not yet enough accustomed to following a woman and looking to her for leadership," knew she had her work cut out for her in more ways than one.[3] Named "the woman most admired by other American women" in a January 1947 poll, she was acutely conscious of herself as a role model. On January 16 she reflected on growing older in her "My

Day" column. She was "a little sad," she informed her readers, because "[t]oday I received the notice of the cancellation of my driving license for reckless driving in connection with the accident I had last summer."[4] Her own lapse of attention, she admitted, had caused her to hit another car. Although no one was seriously injured, the incident had prompted her to wonder whether, at the age of sixty-two, "it is wise to curtail one's activities." One thing, she said, was certain: "If you give up any activity, it is much more difficult to start in again." On the brink of the most challenging assignment of her life, Eleanor Roosevelt was not inclined to curtail any of her activities. She reapplied for a driver's license and meanwhile arranged to be driven to Lake Success.

The entire two-week session was devoted to general discussion about how the Commission's work should be organized. From the outset, fault lines appeared, cutting in many directions and foreshadowing difficulties that would endure throughout and beyond the process of preparing the Universal Declaration. The different preoccupations of cold war antagonists were evident in one of the few concrete decisions to emerge from the meeting: to recommend that the Economic and Social Council create two subcommissions. The Sub-Commission on the Prevention of Discrimination and the Protection of Minorities was established at the suggestion of the Soviets; the Sub-Commission on Freedom of Information and the Press was created at the behest of Britain, France, and the United States. This was but the beginning of continual finger-pointing by American and Soviet UN representatives at the respective weaknesses of their countries. (Well before World War II, the Soviets used America's race problem to fuel their propaganda machine, publicizing the unequal treatment of blacks and presenting communism as the solution.)

Another major bone of contention concerned how and by whom an international bill of rights would be implemented. Petitions addressed to the new Commission were already pouring in from all over the world. Often inartful and handwritten, they came from individuals who claimed they were victims of rights violations and were unable to secure remedies or even hearings in their own countries. The UN had no apparatus for dealing with these complaints, and the new Commission could do no more than instruct the Secretariat to acknowledge receipt while they struggled with the questions that would occupy them for the next two years. Should the Commission recommend the establishment of international forums where such complaints could be heard? Or should it content itself with

Eleanor Roosevelt, to her class on human rights, "Now, children, all together: 'The rights of the individual are above the rights of the state.'"

producing a declaration of standards and goals toward which each nation should strive on its own?

Colonel William Roy Hodgson of Australia and Mrs. Mehta were adamant that an international bill of rights would be meaningless without some machinery for enforcement. Neither of these individuals would prove easy to ignore. Low-voiced Mrs. Mehta combined the assurance of a member of the Brahmin caste with a fierce dedication to women's rights and national self-determination. She and her husband had both been imprisoned by the British for civil disobedience. Noisy Colonel Hodgson, a champion of the interests of small nations, was one of Australia's leading experts in international relations. A U.S. State Department memo noted that he demonstrated "an extremely critical attitude towards most foreign countries" and a "peppery aggressive manner" that seemed to be aggravated by consumption of alcohol.[5] The memo conceded, however, that the Australian's "blustering and provocative approach is said often to hide a very thorough knowledge of the question under consideration." Hodgson put forward a proposal for an entirely new sort of legal institution—an International Court of Human Rights that could hear complaints from individuals that their rights had been infringed by their own governments.[6]

The United States, for its part, took the position that the Commission should concentrate first on framing a declaration of principles "as a standard to be observed by members."[7] The world was impatient for movement on human rights, Mrs. Roosevelt said, and since the problem of implementation was bound to be time-consuming, it should be taken up after the bill of rights was completed. Her political intuitions were sound. The first international tribunal where individual complaints could be heard would not appear until the European Court of Human Rights opened its doors in 1959 to persons in states that had accepted its jurisdiction. It was not until 1976, when the Covenant on Political and Civil Rights went into effect, that men and women were given the opportunity to present complaints to a UN body against nations that had agreed to this procedure. Fortunately the Human Rights Commission did not wait.

The lengthiest and most heated discussions at Lake Success involved political philosophy. The meeting began calmly enough with general agreement on P. C. Chang's suggestion that there should be a preamble setting forth the premises upon which the bill was based.[8] "A standard should be established," he said, "with a view to elevating the concept of man's dignity." René Cassin added a theme upon which he was to insist throughout the drafting process: the affirmation of one common human nature and the fundamental unity of the human race.[9]

The politically inexperienced Charles Malik jumped in with such vigor as to precipitate the Commission's first big argument. His voice comes across in the transcript as more than a little pompous as he lectures his elders. When we speak of human rights, he said, "we are raising the fundamental question, what is man?" When we disagree about human rights, he went on, we are really disagreeing about the nature of the person. "Is man merely a social being? Is he merely an animal? Is he merely an economic being?"[10]

Malik's intervention drew a sharp response from the most voluble of the Communist delegates, Yugoslavia's Vladislav Ribnikar, who asserted that human liberty consists in "perfect harmony between the individual and the community" and that the common interest, as embodied in the state, takes priority over individual claims.[11] In 1943, Ribnikar, the scion of the family that once owned the Belgrade newspaper *Politika,* struck his friend C. L. Sulzberger of *The New York Times* as being "as far left as an editor of a moderately liberal newspaper in the United States."[12] Shortly thereafter, however, Ribnikar joined the partisan resistance and cast his lot with Marshal Tito. The State Department's background sheet on him noted, "In private, Ribnikar is said to profess a friendliness toward Great Britain and the United States, but publicly he has followed the government line in extolling the Soviet Union on all occasions."

Whatever his private views may have been, Ribnikar had mastered the Marxist jargon of the day. "The psychology of individualism," he opined, "has been used by the ruling class in most countries to preserve its own privileges; a modern declaration of rights should not only consider the rights favored by the ruling classes."[13] In nations where "the social principle comes first," he explained, the state "has one purpose, to create conditions necessary for the fulfillment of the interest of each individual."

Malik leaped in again. "The deepest danger of the age," he said, is posed by a collectivism that demands "the extinction of the human person as such in his own individuality and ultimate inviolability."[14] He proposed four principles to guide the work of the Commission. First, the human person is more important than any national or cultural group to which he may belong. Second, a person's mind and conscience are his most sacred and inviolable possessions. Third, any pressure from the state, church, or any other group aimed at coercing consent is unacceptable. Fourth, since groups, as well as individuals, may be right or wrong, the individual's freedom of conscience must be supreme.[15]

After the midday break on February 4, the minor official the Soviet Union had sent to the meeting, Valentin Tepliakov, called Malik's four principles completely unsuitable as a basis for the bill of rights.[16] "I do not understand," he said, professing puzzlement at Malik's reference to "pressure" exerted on individuals. "What does he mean?" The rights of the individual, he insisted, must be seen in relation to the individual's obligations to the community, which is "the main body which provides for his existence, and the enjoyment of the human rights which belong to him." On one point he was absolutely unambiguous: "We cannot divide the individual from society."

This debate annoyed more pragmatic members of the group, like Hansa Mehta, who wanted to get on with the work at hand. After Tepliakov spoke, Mrs. Mehta intervened impatiently. "We are here to affirm faith in fundamental human rights," she said. "Whether the human person comes first or the society, I do not think we should discuss that problem now." The Commission "should not enter into this maze of ideology."[17]

The next morning Mrs. Roosevelt at last weighed in. Taking care not to further polarize the issue, she observed, "It seems to me that in much that is before us, the rights of the individual are extremely important. It is not exactly that you set the individual apart from his society, but you recognize that within any society the individual must have rights that are guarded."[18] The Commission might not have to decide with absolute certainty whether government exists for the good of the individual or the group, but "I think we do have to make sure, in writing a bill of rights, that we safeguard the fundamental freedoms of the individual."

The United Kingdom's Charles Dukes, a staunch trade unionist and Labour Party man, did not comment directly on Mrs. Roosevelt's view but joined in the attack on Malik, blasting him for failing to realize that "we must pay the price for the advantages that result from our calling upon the State to safeguard our liberties, both in the sense of personal freedoms and also in the direction of a minimum degree of economic security."[19] The price, he explained, was that of "limiting [one's] own freedom [so as to] receive the benefits of any group organization, whether it be religious, ethical, economic, State, whatever it may be." It was hard to imagine any freedoms, political or economic, he said, without "somebody in the form of the State" making provision for them.

René Cassin straddled the fence. While he shared the view that "the human being is above all a social creature whose life and development and whose progress have been made possible only because he could lean on his neighbors," he agreed with Malik on the overriding importance of an individual's freedom of conscience.[20] "This right," he said, is what "gives man his value and dignity."

Malik responded to his interlocutors like the philosophy professor he had until recently been. He rebuked Mrs. Mehta for thinking that the Commission could avoid "ideological" disputes. "Whatever you may say, Madam, must have ideological presuppositions," he observed, "and no matter how much you may fight shy of them, they are there, and you either hide them or you are brave enough to bring them out in the open and see them and criticize them."[21] Later, when he had become more adept at the delicate dance of diplomacy, Malik would have responded less tartly, keeping India's vote in mind.

Turning to the statements of Tepliakov and Dukes, he dismissed as "artificial" any sharp antithesis between the individual and society. Human beings are both individual and social, he said. He would be pleased to explain to the Soviet delegate what he meant by condemning "pressure" exerted on individuals: The human person, though bound by social responsibilities, nevertheless has "the right to say *no* to any social pressure, and to legal protection of that right so that the person who dares to say *no* will not be physically eliminated." Malik agreed with the English representative that one must pay the price of the benefits one receives from the state, but sometimes, he added, "the price is too high." The danger of the present age was "not that the state is not strong enough, . . . but that social claims are in danger of snuffing out any real personal liberty." The ultimate political question of the day, and thus the question for the Human Rights Commission, Malik concluded, was whether the state was for the sake of the human person or the person for the sake of the state. On that note the meeting broke up. Malik had made his point, but he must have gone home feeling more isolated than ever.

On the following morning Mrs. Roosevelt opened the meeting by remarking that she agreed "wholeheartedly" with a number of the points Malik had made the preceding day. She expressed regret that "the representative from Lebanon did not receive the support to which he was really entitled" when he had "come in for a good deal of criticism from two speakers."[22] One imagines Malik looking directly at Tepliakov as he thanked the chairman and took another dig at the Soviet regime: "I hold it to be eminently true that the human person, in his ultimate freedom, is in mortal danger today from the totalitarian state, and that after every allowance is made for full social responsibility, the state in all its functions is for the sake of the free human person, and that this doctrine should be reflected in the proposed Bill of Rights."[23]

Several members of the Human Rights Commission were caricatured in a cartoon of the day showing UN dignitaries as a class of schoolboys, with Mrs. Roosevelt as the teacher, saying, "Now, children, all together: 'The rights of the individual are above the rights of the state.' "[24] Some of the pupils seem bored; many are misbehaving. John Foster Dulles is aiming a slingshot at Andrei Vishinsky, who stands in the corner with a dunce cap on his head. One good little boy, Charles Malik, is standing in front of the class holding an apple for the teacher.

The cartoon captures the disarray that often afflicted UN committees, but the artists, Derso and Kelen, failed to grasp that there was a significant difference between Malik and Roosevelt. She had spoken of the primacy of the "individual," while he preferred to use the term *person* to emphasize the social dimension of personhood and to avoid connotations of radical autonomy and self-sufficiency. ("There are no Robinson Crusoes," he said.)[25] That more capacious notion of personhood, as we shall see, was to have great influence on the Declaration, as would Malik's insistence, to the annoyance of the Soviets, upon the distinction between "society" and the "state."

In retrospect these exchanges precipitated by the young Malik marked a defining moment. Not only did fundamental ideological disagreements become more clear, but the arguments concerning "man" and "society" foreshadowed divisions over what was to prove the most time-consuming subject during the entire period of drafting the Universal Declaration: the formulation of social and economic rights.

The controversy over social and economic rights was not, as many later came to believe, over whether such rights should be included in the document. Eleanor Roosevelt's presence assured that FDR's "four freedoms," which included freedom from want, would be a constant touchstone for all members of the Commission. In a sober newspaper column marking V-E Day, she had written that if "the fortunate countries" desired lasting peace, they would have to lend a hand to peoples whose lives had been devastated by war: "Freedom without bread . . . has little meaning. My husband always said that freedom from want and freedom from aggression were twin freedoms which had to go hand in hand."[26]

The flash points concerned the emphasis such rights should receive in relation to traditional political and civil rights, whether they should be specifically enumerated, how they should be phrased, and, above all, how and by whom they should be implemented. All the Communist countries gave priority to social and economic rights, wanted them to be accompanied by corresponding civic duties, and insisted that the state should be the primary enforcer. Most of the other participants, including Cassin, Chang, Malik, Romulo, Roosevelt, and Santa Cruz, advocated a balance between the traditional political and civil rights on the one hand and the newer social and economic rights on the other. Nowhere was Eleanor Roosevelt's ability to influence U.S. policy more evident than in her success in persuading a reluctant State Department to accept the inclusion of social and economic rights in the Declaration.[27]

The members of the Commission seem to have been sobered by the opening of a great divide between the Soviet-bloc representatives and others at the first meeting. Other divisions were ominous, too—such as those between the philosophically inclined and the more practical-minded members; between representatives of small or weak nations and the major powers; and between proponents of enforceable instruments and supporters of a declaration of principles. Even the normally irrepressible Romulo was somewhat subdued. "For the moment," he observed, "all we can do is try to measure the magnitude of our task, to limit the domain of our inquiry, set up certain reasonable objectives, establish a working procedure, and perhaps, thresh out the basic principles of the proposed bill of rights."[28]

John Humphrey, the distinguished Canadian international lawyer who worked closely with the Commission throughout the entire period of the preparation of the Declaration, was struck by the range of differences among its members. As a member of the UN bureaucracy rather than of the Commission itself, Humphrey had a unique observation post: he was present at nearly every Commission meeting and, as we shall see, played a role as important as that of most commissioners in shaping the Universal Declaration. His memoir provides glimpses of the personalities of the main players as they appeared in 1947 and 1948.

Chang, a big man with a high-domed forehead, struck Humphrey as gruff of manner, but a "master of the art of compromise."[29] Under cover of a quotation from Confucius, "he would often provide the formula which made it possible for the commission to escape from some impasse." Malik was "a tall man with black hair and a nose like an eagle who would have made a good figure dressed as a sheik galloping across the desert." Chang and Malik dominated the Commission intellectually, according to Humphrey, but were usually in disagreement. Humphrey found Chang's "pragmatism" more congenial than Malik's insistence on rigorous thinking, but he said of Malik: "He was one of the most independent people ever to sit on the commission, and he was dedicated to human rights." René Cassin, "a little man with a Vandyke beard," had "a dynamic personality and a sharp and quick mind." He was an excellent public speaker, but "not a particularly effective debater." Hernán Santa Cruz of Chile (like Humphrey himself) was "politically left of center," a close friend from boyhood of the ill-fated future Chilean president Salvador Allende. Like Carlos Romulo, Santa Cruz "had considerable influence with delegations representing the economically developing countries, whose cases he sometimes argued with great energy, a practice that often brought him into conflict with the Western industrial powers."[30]

The memoirs of Santa Cruz show that he shared Humphrey's appreciation for the intelligence of Chang and Malik. The Chilean considered Malik the "most eloquent" of the Commission members and admired the way that Chang, who had been China's ambassador to Chile and Turkey, "combined his Mandarin learning with a broad understanding of Western culture."[31] It fascinated Santa Cruz that when a Commission member came up with what he or she thought was an original idea, Chang could often cite centuries-old antecedents from one or another tradition.

The representative sent by the United Kingdom to the Commission's first session reflected the relatively low priority the Labour government's busy Foreign Office accorded to human rights. Charles Dukes (named Lord Dukeston shortly after the meeting) was a leading trade unionist and had come into government through his friendship with Ernest Bevin, the Labour government's foreign secretary. He was elderly, in poor health, and had no expertise in human rights. He attended only the first and second sessions of the Commission and died before the Declaration was adopted. A British Foreign Office memo on his performance at the Lake

Success meeting was scathing: "[Lord Dukeston] showed at the first meeting of the Commission how absolutely alien all this stuff was to him. So far from being able to take the lead and run the Commission as it is clear any good British representative could have done, he played practically no part at all and I think showed that this is not the sort of stuff that he ever really would be able to handle successfully."[32] Foreign Office officials must have blanched when Dukes answered an interviewer's question whether an international bill of rights would require governments to surrender some of their sovereignty with an unqualified "yes." That, said Dukes, "is the very essence of world justice and that is what makes the whole idea so inspiring."[33]

All members of the Commission were serving as representatives of their governments, owing to the Economic and Social Council's rejection of the recommendation that the Commission be composed of individuals chosen for their expertise. But some members were much more independent than others. The Communist delegates were kept on such a tight rein that the Commission's proceedings were often delayed while they waited for instructions. Most other members had greater latitude. Malik and Cassin, in particular, seem to have been left quite free to exercise their own judgment. Mrs. Roosevelt, though she cooperated closely with her State Department aides, was able to influence U.S. policy at several key junctures, especially by keeping the spirit of the New Deal alive where economic and social rights were concerned.[34]

Early in the first session it became evident that a discussion document could not be produced by the full eighteen-member Commission. The members thus unanimously approved a joint French, Lebanese, and Yugoslavian resolution that a "preliminary draft" of an international bill of rights should be prepared for submission at the Commission's second session by the three officers of the Commission, "with the assistance of the Secretariat."[35] A factor in this decision seems to have been that all those designated (Roosevelt, Chang, Malik, and Humphrey) were based near enough to New York to be available for regular meetings. The resolution also specified that the chairman could "enlist the cooperation of, and . . . receive orally or in writing, any observations and suggestions from any Member of the Commission."

Tepliakov abstained from the decision on the grounds that the drafting committee was too small, while Australia's representative, Colonel Hodgson, maintained that a three-person committee was too large.[36] Hodgson took a dim view of drafting by committee, period. The work, he believed, ought to be carried out by the UN Secretariat (that is, by Humphrey's office) under the supervision of the committee. There was consensus, however, that the drafting committee should take account of the constitutions of UN member states and that the bill, as suggested by Mrs. Mehta, should be short, expressive, and easy to understand.[37]

Shortly after the close of the Commission's first session, Tepliakov gave his assessment of the proceedings to the Soviet Foreign Ministry.[38] The report evokes a certain amount of sympathy for its writer, who must explain to his superiors why he has no good news or concrete achievements to relate. We learn that the reason he kept trying to postpone any action on the bill of human rights was that he had received no instructions from the ministry. Regarding the Commission's decision to press ahead with work on a declaration, he had many excuses. The absence of the Ukrainian and Byelorussian representatives was "extremely unfavorable." Yugoslavia's Ribnikar voted with the USSR but had remained silent except for some general observations on the nature of human rights. The representatives of the Philippines, Uruguay, Lebanon, Egypt, and Iran "blindly followed the positions of the United States while pretending to express their own independent viewpoints." As for Dukeston, he "sometimes expressed decent thoughts" but voted with the United States. Chang "presented himself as independent" but usually supported the United States, too, or "at best abstained when the Soviet Union and the United States had different views." Mrs. Mehta "often displayed indecision, as a result of which she often voted with the United States." "Oddly," Tepliakov reported, "the representative of Australia, Colonel Hodgson, was in most cases supportive of the Soviet viewpoint." Cassin was distinguished by his efforts to reach compromise between the United States and the USSR. Given the composition and "general mood" of the group, and the absence of guidance from Moscow, Tepliakov had had little room for maneuver. It was "vital," he concluded, for the Soviet delegation to come to the next meeting of the Human Rights Commission armed with its own version of an international bill of rights.

Eager to get started, Mrs. Roosevelt invited Chang, Malik, and Humphrey for tea at her Washington Square apartment on the weekend following the Commission's adjournment. As she recalled in her memoirs:

> They arrived in the middle of a Sunday afternoon, so we would have plenty of time to work. It was decided that Dr. Humphrey would prepare the preliminary draft, and as we settled down over the teacups, one of them made a remark with philosophical implications, and a heated discussion ensued. Dr. Chang was a pluralist and held forth in charming fashion on the proposition that there is more than one kind of ultimate reality. The Declaration, he said, should reflect more than simply Western ideas and Dr. Humphrey would have to be eclectic in his approach. His remark, though addressed to Dr. Humphrey, was really directed at Dr. Malik, from whom it drew a prompt retort as he expounded at some length the philosophy of Thomas Aquinas. Dr. Humphrey joined enthusiastically in the discussion, and I remember that at one point Dr. Chang suggested that the Secretariat might well spend a few months studying the fundamentals of Confucianism! But by that time I could not follow them, so lofty had the conversation become, so I simply filled the teacups again and sat back to be entertained by the talk of these learned gentlemen.[39]

Humphrey's recollection of the meeting was similar, down to the detail of Chang's polite and indirect admonition to avoid an excessively Western orientation.[40] "Before the tea party was over," he wrote, "they had decided that I would prepare a preliminary draft." He began working right away.[41] On February 21, 1947, he permitted himself to preen a bit in a letter to his older sister, Ruth: "I am now playing the role of a Jefferson, because it is I who have responsibility for drawing up the first draft of the International Bill of Rights. I have been working on it for three days now."[42]

In later years the scrupulous Humphrey took pains to acknowledge that the Declaration "had no father in the sense that Thomas Jefferson was the father of the Declaration of Independence," because "literally hundreds of people . . . contributed to its drafting."[43] What a pity that Humphrey did not live to learn that the Declaration of Independence had no single author, either! Historian Pauline Maier recently revealed that Thomas Jefferson drew upon many "earlier documents of his own and other people's creation."[44] Maier concludes in her Pulitzer Prize–winning book on the making of the Declaration of Independence that "considering its complex ancestry and the number of people who actively intervened in defining its text, the Declaration of Independence was the work not of one man, but of many."

The decision to entrust the first draft to Humphrey made good sense. He and his multinational staff had been collecting and studying pertinent material from all over the world. Humphrey himself was well grounded in both civil and common law and fluent in French and English. Indeed, it was his linguistic ability that led to his appointment at the UN. During the war years he had befriended Henri Laugier, a French refugee in Montreal who spoke no English. In 1946, when Laugier became the UN's assistant secretary-general for social affairs, he recruited the idealistic Canadian to head the Secretariat's Human Rights Division.

To Humphrey, then a forty-year-old law professor at McGill University, it must have seemed an exciting opportunity. Intelligent and ambitious, he had already built a solid academic reputation as the author of several learned articles on international law and a monograph dealing with the relations among nations in the Americas.[45] Childhood adversity and the Great Depression had given him a lively sense of empathy for the disadvantaged: as a boy of six he had lost his left arm in an accident; then, orphaned at eleven, he was placed in a boys' boarding school, where he learned to detest the abuse of authority. From an early age he had dreamed of helping to "make the world a better place."[46] To Humphrey, as to Eleanor Roosevelt, the new international organization seemed full of hope and promise. Though he had been unable to fight in the war, he could perhaps help to shape the peace.

While Humphrey was plunging ahead with his new assignment, more than one member of the Human Rights Commission was growing dissatisfied with the composition of the drafting committee. Among those who had second thoughts was France's Cassin, who had missed the beginning of the first session, including the election of officers, owing to severe storms that had delayed his Atlantic crossing. Years later Cassin wrote that he had been disappointed to find on arrival that there was "no European" among the officers of the Commission; he noted that many of the commissioners had had no legal training.[47] He seems to have been disconcerted, too, by the fact that the main common language of the commissioners was English. Though Cassin had spent the war years in London as legal adviser to General Charles de Gaulle, his English was shaky.[48] Shortly after his arrival he mistakenly voted in favor of a procedural proposition he opposed, and later in the day he accidentally voted twice. In his memoirs he lamented, "I failed to understand, and thus let pass, proposals and resolutions that did not correspond to my own views."[49]

Cassin had been one of three co-proponents (with Malik and Ribnikar) of the resolution establishing a small drafting committee.[50] But years later in his memoirs, apparently forgetting his own initial position, he described as "deplorable" the decision to entrust the first draft to a small group that included "no European, nor any representative of Latin America, nor anyone from the peoples' republics."[51] What he meant, perhaps, was that there was no French lawyer, one, say, with a Vandyke beard.

Moscow was especially displeased that the USSR was not included in the drafting group. The Soviets took the lead in communicating to the Commission's parent body, ECOSOC, that they were shocked, shocked that there was "no European" on the committee. France joined them in their move for reconsideration.

When Mrs. Roosevelt learned that "considerable opposition to the appointment of so small a committee" had erupted in ECOSOC, she expanded the drafting group on her own initiative, claiming authority under the paragraph of the resolution that authorized the chairman to call on other members of the Commission for advice and assistance.[52] To the original three members she added Australia, Chile, France, the United Kingdom, and the Soviet Union.[53] The new members were Cassin, blustery Colonel Hodgson, Santa Cruz, Geoffrey Wilson of the British Foreign Office, and Vladimir Koretsky of the Soviet Foreign Ministry's Legal Department, one of a succession of Soviet UN delegates whose lexicon did not include the word *compromise*.

The first meeting of the new drafting team was set for June 1947. Humphrey and his staff at the UN Secretariat had spent the previous four months preparing a draft declaration and studying material that had been sent to the UN by various governments and private groups.[54] The Secretariat draft would serve as the basis for discussion in June.

Humphrey and his cadre of assistants were working with an embarrassment of riches: proposals, models, and drafts were continually arriving from governments and nongovernmental organizations far and wide. Roosevelt, Malik, and Chang were taken aback by the sheer volume of this material when they first met with him. Malik later confessed that the commissioners initially felt "completely lost; we had no conception of how to proceed with the task entrusted to us."[55]

The disagreements, misunderstandings, personal quirks, national rivalries, and colonial resentments that surfaced within the Commission were not the only obstacles to effective collaboration: events unfolding in the world outside would further complicate the work ahead.

In February 1947 the British government told the U.S. State Department that it could no longer afford to contribute aid to Greece, where the royalist government was struggling to avert a Communist takeover, or to Turkey, which seemed in danger of becoming a puppet state from which the Soviet Union could dominate the eastern Mediterranean. President Truman decided not only to step into the breach, but that the time had come to take a strong stand against Soviet expansion and subversion. In March he announced the Truman Doctrine, pledging American support to "free peoples who are resisting attempted subjugation by armed minorities or by outside pressures."[56] The House and Senate, by large majorities, approved aid to Greece and Turkey. In June, Truman's new secretary of state, George Marshall, unveiled the Marshall Plan of economic aid to promote Europe's recovery from the devastation of the war.

It was now plain that, in reality, there were not five, or three, but only two "Great Powers" in the world—and both were highly protective of their national sovereignty. Meanwhile the smaller nations resented the power of larger countries and were suspicious of their motives.

Was it really possible for a fledgling organization to produce a document acceptable to delegates from all the countries in a constantly expanding United Nations? By 1948, when the Declaration was put to a vote, the United Nations had fifty-eight member states containing four-fifths of the world's population—twenty-two from the Americas, sixteen from Europe, five from Asia, eight from the Near and Middle East, four from Africa, and three from Oceania.[57] Could any values be said to be common to all of them? What did it mean to speak of certain rights as universal?

Anticipating such questions, the UN's Educational, Scientific and Cultural Organization (UNESCO) recruited some of the leading thinkers of the day for a Committee on the Theoretical Bases of Human Rights. This blue-ribbon panel, chaired by Cambridge political historian E. H. Carr, included University of Chicago philosopher Richard McKeon as rapporteur and French social philosopher Jacques Maritain, who became one of its most active members. In January 1947, as this group was coming together, UNESCO's director, noted scientist Julian Huxley, had sent the poet Archibald MacLeish to the Human Rights Commission's Lake Success meeting to apprise the commissioners of UNESCO's interest in their work and its desire "to be as useful as possible."[58] The philosophers' group began its work in March by sending a questionnaire to statesmen and scholars around the world—including such notables as Mohandas Gandhi, Pierre Teilhard de Chardin, Benedetto Croce, Aldous Huxley, and Salvador de Madariaga—soliciting their views on the idea of a universal declaration of human rights. Meanwhile the drafting process began.

*Eleanor Roosevelt makes her opening remarks at the first
meeting of the drafting committee, June 9, 1947.*

CHAPTER 4

EVERY CONCEIVABLE
RIGHT

The Drafting Committee Begins Its Work

Skeptics must have chuckled when they learned that the drafting committee was composed of eight people representing nations embroiled on either side of the great conflicts of the day. Mrs. Roosevelt and her Soviet-bloc counterparts were certain to be caught up in cold war politics. Chang's relations were tense with both the Soviets and the Americans, for Russia was supporting Mao Tse-tung's Communist insurgents and the Truman administration was cool toward the corrupt Kuomintang military regime. Then there was the controversy precipitated by Britain's decision, in February 1947, to relinquish the Palestinian mandate she had held since the end of World War I. The thorny question of the future of that territory had landed in the lap of the UN, where Charles Malik was emerging as a leading spokesman for the Arab League. This could not but put a strain on his relationship with René Cassin, who had lost twenty-nine relatives, including his sister, in concentration camps.[1] Cassin ardently supported a Jewish homeland, and by 1947 Mrs. Roosevelt did too, her initial reservations overcome by her dismay at the reluctance of many countries, including her own, to accept Jewish war refugees.[2]

Colonel Hodgson was right to be wary of large drafting parties, especially when the members had no common language. More than one person must have been reminded of the old saw about too many cooks or the joke that a camel is a horse drafted by committee.

At its opening session in London, the General Assembly had picked the United States as the site for the permanent headquarters of the United Nations, hoping this decision would encourage America not to withdraw into itself as it had after World War I, when the Senate blocked America's entry into the League of Nations by refusing to ratify the Treaty of Versailles. The choice of location also signaled a desire for a fresh start. Geneva, the former home of the League, was favored by many Europeans, but it was haunted by the memory of the League's failure to avert a second world war. In December 1946 the General Assembly accepted a gift of $8.5 million from John D. Rockefeller, Jr., to buy the tract of land on the East River in New York where the UN building now stands.

The drafting group convened at the UN's temporary headquarters at Lake Success on June 9, 1947. Attending that first session were Roosevelt, Chang, Hodgson, Malik, Hernán Santa Cruz, René Cassin, Geoffrey Wilson (sitting in for Dukes), and the new Soviet delegate, Vladimir Koretsky. The substitution of Koretsky for the relatively junior Tepliakov was a sign that the Soviet Union was beginning to take the human rights project more seriously. Then a legal adviser to the Soviet Foreign Ministry, Koretsky was the USSR's most distinguished international lawyer.

In the months since the first Human Rights Commission meeting, Eleanor Roosevelt had been openly critical of the Truman administration's cold war policy.[3] What mainly disturbed her about the decision to send aid to Greece and Turkey, she explained in "My Day," was that it bypassed the United Nations: "Feeling as I do that our hope for peace lies in the United Nations, I naturally grieve to see this country do anything which harms the strength of the UN. If we could have given help for relief and rehabilitation on a purely non-political basis, and then have insisted that the UN join us in deciding what should be done on any political or policing basis to keep Greece and Turkey free from all outside interference, and to allow her [*sic*] to settle her own difficulties in the way the majority of her people desired to have them settled, I would have felt far happier than I do now."

The Truman Doctrine troubled her for the same reason, especially since it had been announced without advance notice to the United Nations or to the American UN delegates. She sent a stiffly worded note to acting Secretary of State Dean Acheson: "I hope never again that this type of action will be taken without at least consulting with the Secretary-General and with our permanent member on the Security Council beforehand. It all seems to me a most unfortunate way to do things." She feared, she said, that unilateral action by the United States would encourage the Soviet Union to take a similar course: "What if the Russians were to follow U.S. precedent and say, 'Since you have acted alone without consulting the United Nations, we are free to do the same'?" To President Truman, she wrote, "I am afraid that we are apt to lose sight of the fact that if we do not wish to fight Russia, we must be both honest and firm with her. She must understand us, but she must also trust us." Acheson's arguments that the Soviet Union was already acting on its own in Eastern Europe and that the UN was presently incapable of acting with a unified purpose did not entirely satisfy her. Nor did Truman's reply, emphasizing the strategic importance of Greece and Turkey and defending his policy as intended to strengthen democratic forces in Greece.

Roosevelt had been greatly encouraged, however, by the plan for the economic recovery of Europe unveiled by new Secretary of State George Marshall on June 5. On June 9, the day of the drafting committee's first meeting, she replied to a correspondent who feared war would ensue from Truman's decision to send military aid to Greece and Turkey. The Soviet Union, she wrote, "has inaugurated an expansionist program and somewhere it had to be stopped. I do not think it had to be stopped in just that way, and I am very much happier about Secretary Marshall's overall plan."

Roosevelt began the meeting at Lake Success by reminding her colleagues that the draft they were supposed to produce was only a preliminary document. "This Bill will be passed on—and I think it is important for all of us to remember this—six times after this session."[4]

Each step leading up to the final consideration by the UN General Assembly was potentially fraught with difficulty. The draft would first have to be approved by the full Commission on Human Rights, then circulated to all member states for comments. Those comments would undoubtedly require revisions by the drafting committee. The revised document would be returned to the full Commission for final consideration. The Commission would then submit its draft for review by the Economic and Social Council, which would decide whether or not to recommend it to the General Assembly, where it would have to undergo preliminary scrutiny by the Third Committee on Social, Humanitarian, and Cultural Affairs. It was reasonable to hope that the bill might be approved by the General Assembly at its fall 1948 session. But for that to happen, the Commission's draft would have to be ready for ECOSOC within a year.

The drafting group was not, of course, inventing rights out of whole cloth. The Secretariat had provided them with a review of the most fundamental and widely shared principles to have emerged over humanity's long, ongoing process of reflection on freedom. Aiming for comprehensiveness, John Humphrey had instructed his staff at the UN to study all the world's existing constitutions and rights instruments, as well as the suggestions that had poured in to the Secretariat from members of the Commission, outside organizations, and even from various interested individuals.

One such individual was the novelist and science fiction writer H. G. Wells. Wells had been intrigued by the idea of a human rights declaration at least since September 1939, when he submitted one to *The Times* of London in order to satisfy what he perceived to be an "extensive demand for a Statement of War Aims on the part of young and old, who want to know more precisely what we are fighting for."[5] That declaration and several other versions he later produced were curious blends of utopian socialism with the traditional rights of Englishmen. One of these eccentric bills contained a right to work but prohibited "work for the sole object of profit-making." The style of these pieces is well illustrated by the following passage from his 1940 version:

> That he may move freely about the world at his own expense. That his private house or apartment or reasonably limited garden enclosure is his castle, which may be entered only with his consent, but that he shall have the right to come and go over any kind of country, moorland, mountain, farm, great garden or what not, or upon the seas, lakes and rivers of the world, where his presence will not be destructive of some special use, dangerous to himself nor seriously inconvenient to his fellow citizens.

As the author of hugely popular books like *The War of the Worlds* and *Outline of History*, Wells was able to obtain a wide circulation for his thoughts on human rights. But his linkage of human rights to world government and a collectivized global economy did not catch on, and his draft bills do not appear to have influenced the Universal Declaration, except by giving increased public visibility to the idea of human rights.

Humphrey was particularly impressed by two contemporary declarations: the draft of a "Pan American" declaration then in deliberation in Latin America, and the 1944 "Statement of Essential Human Rights" produced on the basis of a study sponsored by the American Law Institute (ALI), a prestigious organization of judges, practitioners, and academics dedicated to the improvement of the law.[6] The Latin American draft, prepared for the predecessor of the Organization of American States, was an interesting document in several respects: it represented a harvest of the main elements of the continental European, as well as Anglo-American, rights traditions; it accompanied its list of rights with a list of duties; it was supranational; and it proclaimed that "the essential rights of man are not derived from the fact that he is a national of a certain state, but are based upon attributes of his human personality."[7] One of its framers, Felix Nieto del Rio of Chile, served briefly on the first UN Human Rights Commission before being replaced by Hernán Santa Cruz.

The group sponsored by the American Law Institute had consulted experts from "Arabic, British, Canadian, Chinese, French, pre-Nazi German, Italian, Indian, Latin American, Polish, Soviet Russian and Spanish" countries and cultures in order to "ascertain to what extent there can be worldwide agreement respecting rights."[8] One of the group's advisers, Panamanian Foreign Minister Ricardo Alfaro, had proposed the ALI statement for inclusion in the UN Charter at the San Francisco conference.

After poring over all this material, Humphrey and his top aide, Émile Giraud, came up with a list of forty-eight items that represented, in Humphrey's view, the common core of the documents and proposals his staff had collected.* "The Secretariat," he said, "has put all this together and included every conceivable right which the Drafting Committee might want to discuss."[9]

Humphrey's draft may not have included every conceivable right, but it provided the drafting committee with a distillation of nearly two hundred years of efforts to articulate the most basic human values in terms of rights. It contained the first-generation political and civil rights found in

---

*Humphrey's draft is set forth as appendix 1.

the British, French, and American revolutionary declarations of the seventeenth and eighteenth centuries: protections of life, liberty, and property; and freedoms of speech, religion, and assembly. It also included the second-generation economic and social rights found in late-nineteenth- and early-twentieth-century constitutions such as those of Sweden, Norway, the Soviet Union, and several Latin American countries: rights to work, education, and basic subsistence. Each draft article was followed by an extensive annotation detailing its relationship to rights instruments then in force in the UN's member states, already numbering fifty-five and rising. All told, the UN Secretariat had prepared over four hundred pages of commentary.[10] The UN proudly announced in its *Weekly Bulletin* that it had produced "the most exhaustive documentation on the subject of human rights ever assembled."[11]

✺

Mrs. Roosevelt took a few minutes at the start of the June 9 meeting to thank Humphrey and his staff for their prodigious efforts. She had scarcely finished her encomium when Colonel Hodgson erupted. "It seems to me there is no order in this document," he complained. In the January-February meeting, Hodgson had wanted to turn over the drafting job entirely to Humphrey and his staff, but now the colonel was in a cantankerous mood. He brusquely demanded to know what "philosophy" had guided the Secretariat's work. "I personally would like some explanation of this monumental document from the Secretariat," he said. "All I would like to know is—and I think we should know—what was the philosophy behind this paper? What principles did they adopt; what method did they follow? Is it their own idea; is it a collection of various principles?"[12] Humphrey replied that he could not oblige Colonel Hodgson "for the simple reason that [the draft] is based on no philosophy whatsoever." As far as he was concerned, he had been asked to compile a list of rights for discussion purposes, and that was what he had done.

Geoffrey Wilson regarded the comprehensiveness of Humphrey's list as a grave defect. Wilson had arrived at the June meeting with instructions from the British Foreign Office to work for a covenant that would impose legal obligations on the states that ratified it, rather than a mere declaration that would have no legal effect.[13] He had been supplied with a concise Foreign Office bill of familiar Anglo-American civil and political rights. The young barrister reported to his superiors in London that the Humphrey draft was "highly unsatisfactory," because many of its provisions, especially those involving social welfare, did not lend themselves to legal enforcement. It "included everything that the Secretariat had been able to cull from previous drafts, from national constitutions, and from their own imagination."[14] The breadth of sources that made the draft so un-British was, of course, an important element of its claim to universality.

At that stage there seems to have been confusion in the minds of some members about the difference between a nonbinding declaration of principles by the UN General Assembly and instruments such as treaties, conventions, and covenants that impose enforceable legal duties on the states that sign and ratify them. Most of the human rights commissioners, after all, were not lawyers. And the precise nature of the document they were about to draft was still an open question.

Confronted with so much heavy reading from the Secretariat, the drafting group decided at the end of its first afternoon to adjourn for two days to give everyone a chance to become familiar with the material. When they reconvened, it soon appeared that the United States and Great Britain had definite, and sharply divergent, views on what kind of document the committee should be preparing. Geoffrey Wilson put forward the Foreign Office bill and urged the committee to prepare a covenant rather than a statement full of high-sounding generalities. Eleanor Roosevelt announced that the United States favored a broad Declaration, to be followed eventually "by conventions on particular subjects which might have the binding force of treaties." The group adopted a compromise satisfactory neither to the United States nor Great Britain: they would work on both types of document at the same time.

Koretsky, like his predecessor, had not received specific instructions from Moscow. Nevertheless he zeroed in on a group of articles in Humphrey's draft dealing with the right to freedom of movement, the right to a nationality, a nation's right to accord asylum to political refugees, and protections against arbitrary expulsion from a country. These rights were not new—Humphrey had found them in various national constitutions and in the Latin American draft—but they had never been internationalized. Koretsky saw their presence in an international declaration as a threat to the principle of national sovereignty. The Secretariat draft, he warned, was pushing the Commission "beyond the limit of international law." It might even lead to "intervention in the affairs of individual countries."[15] Koretsky seemed willing to cooperate, however. He told the group that "the Government of the Union of Soviet Socialist Republics considers this Declaration of great importance," but that it would "need to study the documents closely" and that it reserved the right to submit its own concrete proposals later.

In what was to be but the first of many such clashes, René Cassin responded to Koretsky's view of national sovereignty from the depths of his heart:

> I was very much struck by the statement of our colleague from the Union of Soviet Socialist Republics who several times used the word "interference." . . . I must state my thoughts very frankly. The right of interference is here; it is here in the [UN] Charter. . . . Why? Because we do not want a repetition of what happened in 1933, where Germany began to massacre its own nationals, and everybody . . . bowed, saying "Thou art sovereign and master in thine own house."[16]

When Cassin finished, it was five P.M. and Mrs. Roosevelt adjourned the meeting. The following day, although the Soviet Union had taken the initiative in demanding an expanded committee, Professor Koretsky was the first to acknowledge that little progress was likely to be made by the full eight-member drafting group. He suggested that a small, four-person working party should be appointed to "prepare appropriate drafts" of a Declaration.[17] This proposal was accepted, and the subcommittee, composed of René Cassin, Charles Malik, Geoffrey Wilson, and Mrs. Roosevelt, immediately went to work. The committee invited Koretsky to be a member of this group, but he declined, saying that the Soviet Union's proposals would be made at a later stage.

The working group was instructed to propose a logical arrangement of the articles supplied by the Secretariat, to redraft them on the basis of suggestions from the drafting committee, and to make recommendations concerning what articles should be in the Declaration and what should be placed in the Covenant. The group concentrated on the Humphrey draft, beginning with the problem of structure raised by Colonel Hodgson. Cassin, reviving a proposal Chang had made at the January meeting, suggested that the best way to begin would be to consider not the substance, but the overall "plan" of the bill, beginning with thoughts for a Preamble. Malik agreed a plan was needed but argued that "in the logical sequence of construction" the Preamble should be composed only after the content had been settled.

It did not take long for the four-person working group to conclude that the document would have greater unity if the revisions were handled by a single drafter. Malik, Roosevelt, and Wilson then turned to René Cassin, whom they asked "to undertake the writing of a draft Declaration, based on those articles in the Secretariat outline which he considered should go into such a Declaration."[18] Thus, during a crucial stage, the structure of the Universal Declaration came under the hand of an experienced legislative draftsman.

René Cassin liked to call himself "the man of three frontiers," referring to his birth at Bayonne near the Spanish border, his childhood years in Nice where his father's ancestors had lived for generations, and his frequent visits to his maternal relatives in Alsace. He was French but from his earliest years felt the tugs of Spain, Italy, and Germany.

Cassin had come of age in a society torn in two by the Dreyfus case. At the insistence of his devoutly religious mother, he had received an Orthodox Jewish education, but he was more influenced by his intensely antireligious father, from whom he imbibed the secularist spirit of the French Revolution.[19] As a result of youthful friendships with members of Catholic social action groups, he acquired, he said, "a great respect for religion and for Christian thought."[20] He once told an interviewer that he had concluded as a young man that "though each religion is an absolute, the ensemble of religious movements is very relative. I had no uneasiness on this score, but I had a great curiosity. I have always remained secular."

Though raised in an ardently Dreyfusard family, Cassin had once seriously considered a military career, believing that the army, whatever its faults, was the only means of restoring to France her lost honor and territory.[21] He served in the French army in World War I, suffering a grievous wound that required him to use a cane for the rest of his life. On his return to civilian life he married his university sweetheart, a woman of Protestant background, rose to distinction as a professor of civil law, and became active in veterans' organizations. In 1925 he helped to found an international veterans' organization so that soldiers of former enemies could work together for peace.[22]

In June 1940 Cassin was teaching law in Paris when he heard the news of his country's capitulation to German invasion. He confided his dismay to a friend, who told him about Charles de Gaulle's radio broadcast from London calling all Frenchmen to join the Resistance. Cassin then made a fateful decision. After driving all night, he picked up his wife, Simone, at Bayonne and the couple made their way to the port of Saint Jean-de-Luz, where they managed to catch the last departing English ship. On June 29 the fifty-three-year-old jurist showed up at the Free French headquarters on the bank of the Thames.

To Cassin's surprise, he was escorted directly to the chief. In the presence of the tall young general, the older man was suddenly acutely conscious of his white hair, his limp, his old-fashioned beard, and his lack of military expertise.[23] "General," he said, "I have come to respond to your call of June 18. I know France needs all her sons. I am a disabled infantryman from the war of 1914 to 1918. I have headed a federation of a million veterans and disabled veterans. Do you think my assistance might be useful to you?" Almost apologetically he added that he was also a law professor.

This was what de Gaulle had been waiting for. The British prime minister, Winston Churchill, had just agreed to recognize the Free French, but he had insisted that there must be a legal basis for such recognition. The loose collection of individuals that had gathered around de Gaulle had to be constituted as a legal entity—with a plausible claim to being the "real" government of France. De Gaulle badly needed a lawyer.

"Vous tombez à pic!" he told his visitor. ("You've hit the mark.") Thus began a long collaboration between two men who had little in common beyond their love of country. Cassin later wrote he had the feeling that "everything in my life had mysteriously prepared me for that moment."

In a radio broadcast from London in April 1941, Cassin spoke of his feelings about being Jewish and French. Addressing his remarks to the Jews of Vichy France, he said: "This voice does not come to you from a rabbi nor from one of the chaplains in de Gaulle's army, nor even from one of the faithful followers of your rites. However, certain fellow feelings that slumber in times of prosperity spontaneously reawaken in time of trial. . . . Israelites of France, you know well that the French people are not responsible for the measures the enemy and its collaborators have imposed on you. . . . It is in vain that they strive to break the bonds among the spiritual families of France, the most precious of its strengths." Reminding his listeners that the Jews had been accorded full citizenship by the French Revolution, he concluded: "No sacrifice, none, is too great to partially repay this debt by aiding France to recover her liberty and her greatness."[24] The following month, the Vichy government deprived Cassin of his French citizenship, and the next year a military tribunal sentenced him to death in absentia.

As General de Gaulle's chief legal adviser during World War II, Cassin had been responsible for all the documents governing the internal structure and the external relations of the Free French.[25] When liberation approached, he prepared the ordinances that would ease the transition to republican government. Now, in 1947, Cassin held the most important legal position in France. As head of the Conseil d'État (the central organ of public administration and the highest court for public law disputes), he was responsible for reestablishing the French administrative and judicial systems and restoring the credibility they had lost under the Vichy regime.

Over the weekend of June 14–15, Cassin revised Humphrey's draft with the help of Émile Giraud, the French international lawyer who had assisted Humphrey. His redraft consisted of a Preamble, six introductory articles, thirty-six substantive articles grouped analytically under eight headings, and two concluding provisions on implementation.[26]

Cassin preserved most of the substantive content of Humphrey's draft, but under his hand the document acquired an internal logic and achieved greater unity.[27] Humphrey, a practical man impatient with what he called "philosophical assertions," had deliberately left out any material other than what he considered the key "justiciable" rights gathered from his varied sources.[28] By his own account he "had had practically no experience drafting documents."[29] Cassin, by contrast, was well versed in writing legislation, a craft that has been sorely neglected in the Anglo-American common-law countries but that was brought to high refinement in the code-based continental civil law tradition.

Humphrey had faithfully fulfilled his assignment. But Cassin believed that if people were to make sense of how the various rights fit together, more clarity was needed in their presentation. He added a Preamble, followed by what is known in continental legal terminology as a "general part": six introductory principles to guide the interpretation of each specific provision that followed. Cassin here was imitating the structure of the Code Napoléon, whose six preliminary articles perform a similar function, by providing judges with general directions on how to apply the law.

His Preamble explained the "why" of the Declaration. His introductory provisions affirmed the equal rights of every member of the human family and embodied concepts of man and society that were neither individualist nor collectivist. The rights themselves were arranged according to the logic of the introductory articles or general principles, proceeding from those belonging to the individual to the rights of persons in social and political relationships. The draft that Humphrey had loosely organized by topic began to take on a more organic structure, a beginning, middle, and end. Colonel Hodgson noticed the difference at once. Cassin's first few articles, he commented, "are in a sense, a prelude and a keynote to the actual rights themselves."[30]

Geoffrey Wilson, correctly fearing that work on the Declaration was about to take priority over a binding convention, was not at all pleased. He said little in the drafting committee but wrote London that such a document, if adopted by the General Assembly, "would thereupon become morally, though not legally, binding on all members. The moral obligations it imposed would be very vague and no means whatever would be provided for enforcing them and the whole thing would be a perpetual source of mischief."[31]

A comparison of Cassin's draft with Humphrey's shows that Cassin made very few substantive additions.* One important change was the inclusion of a provision for special care and assistance for mothers and children. A change that did not make it into the final document was the addition of an explanatory principle for economic rights borrowed from the International Labor Organization, stating, "Human labor is not a commodity." (The fate of this addendum may have been affected by the fact that *marchandise* in the original French was awkwardly rendered as "chattel" and "merchandise" in the UN's official translations.) His elaboration of the right to a nationality ("The United Nations, with the member States, have the duty to prevent statelessness, which is contrary to the rights of man and to the interest of the human community") was likewise omitted.

Though the document would undergo many further changes over the next year and a half, most of the ideas in Humphrey's draft ultimately found their way into the Universal Declaration, and the "logical arrangement" contributed by Cassin held firm.

---

*Cassin's redraft is set forth as appendix 2.

A regrettable dispute developed many years later over the question of who had written the "first" draft of the Universal Declaration. It was not exactly a question of paternity, since neither Cassin nor Humphrey ever claimed to be the "author" of the Declaration.[32] But when Cassin was in his seventies, he claimed in a speech that he had had "sole responsibility" for the "first draft" and dismissed Humphrey's contribution as "excellent basic documentary work."[33] This claim, repeated in a 1968 article, was puzzling but not without historical precedent. To this day, no one has been able to explain why Alexander Hamilton, just before his death, claimed authorship of several of The Federalist Papers that were actually written by James Madison![34]

Cassin's more enthusiastic admirers began calling him the "father" of the Declaration.[35] Some of them downplayed Humphrey's role to such an extent that he felt obliged to set the record straight in his memoir.[36] In 1984 the Canadian lawyer, who by then had served with distinction for many years in the important if low-profile post of director of the UN Secretariat's Human Rights Division, presented a straightforward account of the drafting process. "In many cases," he pointed out, Cassin "merely prepared a new French version of the official United Nations translation, and when this was translated back into English the result seemed further removed from the original than it really was."[37]

That Humphrey wrote the first draft, and that Cassin's draft was a revision of Humphrey's, is clear from the official UN records.[38] Some confusion resulted, perhaps, from the frequent use of the term *outline* to describe Humphrey's work. But the records leave no room for doubt. On June 17, 1947, the verbatim transcript finds Mrs. Roosevelt saying, "Now we come to Mr. Cassin's draft, which has based itself on the Secretariat's comparative draft."[39] Cassin himself acknowledged in the drafting committee that "it is always the Secretariat's draft which should be considered the basic source of the Committee's work."[40]

Unfortunately a few careless authors created the impression not only that Cassin had written the first draft, but that he was the principal architect of the Universal Declaration of Human Rights. This error not only scanted the roles of other key individuals such as Humphrey, Malik, and Chang, but it detracted from the universality of the document.

Humphrey felt especially aggrieved when the UN itself helped perpetuate this myth by permitting the French government to organize a display of Cassin's handwritten redraft in the lobby of UN headquarters on the occasion of the Declaration's tenth anniversary. That display, without any accompanying explanation, was wounding to the hardworking and generally self-effacing director of the UN Human Rights Division.

To give each man his due, one might say that Humphrey's work was to Cassin's as Tycho Brahe's was to Johannes Kepler's. Just as Kepler could not have had his paradigm-breaking insight into the movements of the planets without Tycho's meticulous records, so Cassin could not have produced an integrated document of worldwide applicability without Humphrey's distillation of the material he had collected. But just as Tycho was unable to see in his own data what Kepler saw, Humphrey had simply compiled a list of rights, loosely grouped into categories. Cassin's draft illuminated their meaning and relations. No one would suggest that Cassin's revisions yielded a document as elegant as the Code Napoléon, whose lucid style and lapidary phrases were so much admired by the novelist Stendhal that he kept a copy on his bedside table, but they did guarantee that the document would be more than a mere list or "bill" of rights in the Anglo-American sense. It was about this time that the committee began to use the term *declaration* more often than *bill*.

Cassin's Preamble set out to explain why an international bill of rights had become necessary and what it was supposed to do. This proclamation, fragments of which survive in the final Declaration, stated that "[d]isregard and contempt for human rights" had been one of the main causes of human suffering and, in particular, of the massacres that occurred during two world wars; that the four freedoms had been proclaimed as the supreme aims of the recent struggle; that the UN Charter had reaffirmed faith in basic human rights and in the equality of all men and women; and that this Declaration, being "constantly present to all members of the universal society," would "unceasingly remind them of their rights and duties." (Cassin obviously had the 1789 French Declaration of the Rights of Man and Citizen in mind as a model, for the drafters of that document had begun with the proposition that "ignorance, forgetfulness or contempt of the rights of man are the sole causes of public miseries and the corruption of governments." Their Declaration, too, was supposed to "unceasingly remind [citizens] of their rights and duties" by "being ever present to all the members of the social body.")

After the Preamble came a Chapter 1, titled "General Principles." Cassin told the drafting committee that he had taken two leading ideas as "fundamental": "that every human being has a right to be treated like every other human being" and "the concept of solidarity and fraternity among men."[41] Those propositions gained general approval, especially from Koretsky, who stated that in his opinion the nondiscrimination principle was "the most important one to be included in a Bill of Rights."[42]

Cassin also maintained that a declaration purporting to be universal should state a basis for its claim to apply to all people in the world. Though Humphrey's draft had drawn on the legal and political wisdom of many nations, the human rights commissioners were well aware that a large part of the world was not in possession of bills of rights. Cassin therefore reiterated the point upon which he had insisted since the Commission's very first meeting: the Declaration should base universal rights on the "great fundamental principle of the unity of all the races of mankind," a principle that had been shamefully violated in the recent war.[43] In that spirit, his Article 1 proclaimed the unity of the human family and echoed the cherished French themes of liberty, equality, and fraternity: "All men, being members of one family, are free, possess equal dignity and rights, and shall regard each other as brothers."

On June 16, when Cassin presented his draft to the working group, that simple formulation began to fall victim to the hazards of drafting by committee. The working group added the thought that all men are endowed with reason and sent the following text to the full drafting committee: "All men are brothers. Being endowed with reason and members of one family, they are free and equal in dignity and rights." Then P. C. Chang suggested that besides naming "reason" as an essential human attribute, the article ought to include another concept. What he had in mind, he said, was a Chinese word that in literal translation meant "two-man mindedness," but which might be expressed in English as "sympathy," or "consciousness of one's fellow men."[44] The word was *ren* (仁), a composite of the characters for "man" (人) and "two" (二).

A word emblematic of an entire worldview and way of life, *ren* has no precise counterpart in English. To Cassin, it would surely have evoked Rousseau's notion of compassion, but that word, too, fell short of the mark. Chang's suggestion was accepted, but his idea was rendered awkwardly by adding the words "and conscience" after "reason." (That unhappy word choice not only obscured Chang's meaning, but gave "conscience" a far from obvious sense, quite different from its normal usage in phrases such as "freedom of conscience.") The incident was an early warning of the communications difficulties the ambitious human rights project would face.

Koretsky objected to the words *all men.* He was opposed, he said, to "historical atavisms which preclude us from an understanding that we men are only one-half of the human species."[45] Mrs. Roosevelt resisted the criticism, observing that, in English, "when we say 'all men are brothers,' we mean that all human beings are brothers, and we are not differentiating between men and women." She added, "I have always considered myself a feminist but I really would have no objection to the use of the word as the Committee sees it." The language stood for the time being.

The main difficulty in framing the introductory "General Principles," Cassin later wrote, was "to find a formula that did not require the Commission to take sides on the nature of man and society, or to become immured in metaphysical controversies, notably the conflict among spiritual, rationalist, and materialist doctrines on the origin of human rights."[46] The introductory general principles in the Latin American draft, for example, would not do. They recited: "Duties of a juridical nature presuppose others of a moral nature which support them in principle and constitute their basis"; and, "Inasmuch as spiritual development is the supreme end of human existence and the highest expression thereof, it is the duty of man to serve that end with all his strength and resources"; and, "Since moral conduct constitutes the noblest flowering of culture, it is the duty of every man always to hold it in high respect." Those ideas, with their religious connotations, would never have made the cut in the UN.

Yet Cassin's introductory articles (and the Declaration as ultimately adopted) did implicitly take sides against the extremes of capitalist individualism and socialist collectivism. They also implied a position on the nature of man and society. His Article 2, for example, asserted, "The object of society is to enable all men to develop, fully and in security, their physical, mental and moral personality, without some being sacrificed for the sake of others." His Article 3 presented a vision of the human person in community: "Since human beings cannot live and achieve their aims without the help and support of society, everyone has fundamental duties to society: obedience to the law, exercise of useful activity, acceptance of the burdens and sacrifices required by the common good." Article 4, in the same vein, stated, "Everyone's rights are limited by the rights of others."

Cassin's synthesis yielded a whole that was greater than the sum of its parts. By fusing rights from an older tradition of political and civil liberty to those reflecting a more modern preoccupation with social and economic needs, by providing both sets of rights with an interpretive framework, and by declaring that all these rights belonged to everyone, everywhere, the Declaration was bringing something new into the world.

When Cassin turned his draft over to the drafting committee on June 17, he tried to pave the way for a productive use of the week remaining before adjournment with some remarks about what an international declaration could and could not be expected to achieve. Though the French lawyer was one of the staunchest opponents of the Soviet Union's insistence on exclusive national sovereignty, he was also adamant that nation-states would always have to provide the *primary* line of legal defense of human rights and that a "universal" document would therefore have to leave room for an ample degree of pluralism in the understanding and implementation of many of its rights. In deciding how specifically to frame each right, he said, the committee should be mindful of its opportunity "to prove that the coexistence of States which have differing economic conceptions and differing regimes is possible and that it is not necessary for one conception to triumph over another conception."[47]

The following day Mrs. Roosevelt raised the question of priorities. In view of the short time remaining, she said "the Committee might have to choose between a completed draft of a Declaration and a completed draft of a Convention." The United States, she said, supported the preparation of both but did not feel "that anything resembling a generally acceptable Convention could be produced immediately."

The choice was made by default, as the committee continued its review of the Humphrey-Cassin draft. Cassin's Preamble was set aside: the committee agreed with Malik that the task of preparing a Preamble should be postponed until the text was in close to final form. Cassin's provision on the rights of authors was eliminated, too, on the grounds that the subject was one better handled with the detail appropriate to a legal convention. By consolidating some articles, the committee managed to reduce the total number from forty-six to thirty-six.

Perhaps the most consequential decision at this stage was to adopt Malik's proposal that a right to change one's beliefs be added to the religious freedom article. He was moved to make the suggestion, he said, because his native Lebanon had become a haven for people fleeing religious persecution, some because they had changed their religious affiliation.[48] At the time, Lebanon was still known as a cosmopolitan country where many ethnic and religious groups seemed to coexist in relative harmony, though its precarious equilibrium was threatened by the recent influx of refugees from nearby Palestine. Malik's amendment, which survived in the final Declaration, touched a nerve in other states with large Muslim populations, because of the Koranic injunction against apostasy (*murtad*) and the deep resentment of Christian missionary activity. The language was a major factor in Saudi Arabia's decision to abstain from the final vote on the Declaration.

Discussion of the social and economic rights was inconclusive. On June 23, in an attempt to head off disputes, Cassin said: "We must take into account the various possibilities and the circumstances that prevail in various countries. I do not think that within a few years all societies or all states will come to the point where they can put an end to all unemployment and give remunerative employment to everybody, but we are not working here for one year. We are working for the future."[49]

The members quickly staked out divergent positions, however, over the new rights. Regarding the right to work, for example, the American view was that everyone should have the "opportunity" to earn a livelihood, while Humphrey, Cassin, and Santa Cruz favored language saying that everyone has the right and the duty to perform socially useful work. Koretsky seized the moment to remind Mrs. Roosevelt that her late husband's "second bill of rights" (proposed in a State of the Union address that Koretsky "happened" to have with him) had included the right to useful and remunerative work.[50]

On June 25, the day of adjournment, many issues were still unresolved and a number of proposed amendments were still on the table. The drafting committee decided to permit members to insert their proposals as alternate versions next to the draft articles. The result was a rather unwieldy draft, which the committee forwarded, along with Humphrey's documentation, to the full Human Rights Commission for consideration at its second session in December in Geneva.* Some articles were sent for

*The committee's draft is set forth as appendix 3.

comment to the UN Commission on the Status of Women and the Sub-Commission on Prevention of Discrimination and Protection of Minorities. Having made no progress on a convention, they forwarded the United Kingdom's proposal to the full Commission to be considered for that purpose.

On July 1 Koretsky filed his report with the Russian Foreign Ministry.[51] He had participated relatively little in the drafting committee's discussions because he was dividing his time between the Human Rights Commission and a UN international law committee, where the interests of the Soviet Union seemed more immediately threatened. Koretsky had tried, unsuccessfully, to dissuade the Committee on the Progressive Development of International Law from recommending the codification of international penal law, preparing an international agreement based on the Nuremberg Principles, or studying the desirability of establishing a permanent international criminal tribunal with jurisdiction over such crimes. We now know he need not have been quite so concerned.

With regard to the human rights draft, he said he had been unable to make any detailed criticisms because the ministry had not supplied him with its own proposed draft or even with an indication of its basic attitude toward the project. The main problem with the draft, in his opinion, was that it might "make it easier to intervene in the internal affairs of sovereign states." He concluded with two recommendations: 1) that the Soviet Union prepare and submit its own draft no later than August, well in advance of the next Human Rights Commission meeting; and 2) that the USSR should support an international bill of rights in the form of a multilateral convention to which the signers could append any reservations they deemed necessary.

Two days later, on July 3, Eleanor Roosevelt reported to the State Department in a meeting attended by the head of the U.S. mission to the UN, Senator Warren Austin. The Department's memorandum of that conversation indicates that the reason she and her advisers had decided to push for a morally binding General Assembly declaration rather than a legally binding international agreement was that the latter would have had to be approved by the U.S. Senate—where its fate was most uncertain.[52]

Roosevelt related that she had gone along with the proposal to work on both documents because a strong majority favored doing so. She said she was troubled about whether the Senate would accept a human rights convention and asked Austin for his opinion. The senator declined to speculate, saying that it posed "a very difficult problem." Roosevelt, no doubt thinking of Wilson's debacle with the League of Nations, said, "It would be most unfortunate if we were to take the lead in forcing a convention through the General Assembly and then be turned down by the Senate." The group agreed that U.S. policy should be flexible for the time being: open to a convention as well as a declaration, but as to the former, "we must be reasonably certain that the country will back us up."

After a rocky start, the drafting group had made considerable progress. The Soviet representative had shown some disposition to cooperate, and as Chang had predicted in the first meeting, substantial agreement in principle seemed to exist on many items.[53] Though wrangling over the precise formulation of each article would continue for many months, and some new ideas would be added as other nations were heard from, the main features of the Universal Declaration were in place by the end of June 1947.

But had the drafters, drawing on material that was largely Western in origin, produced a document that could be accepted as universal? Reassuring news, on that point, was on its way from UNESCO.

A PHILOSOPHICAL INVESTIGATION

The UNESCO Report

In June 1947, while the drafting committee was embroiled in philosophical debates, the UNESCO philosophers' committee was coming to some very practical conclusions. They had received about seventy responses to their questionnaire asking for reflections on human rights from Chinese, Islamic, Hindu, and customary law perspectives, as well as from American, European, and socialist points of view. The replies included letters from Mohandas Gandhi, French Jesuit paleontologist Pierre Teilhard de Chardin, Italian philosopher Benedetto Croce, and *Brave New World* author Aldous Huxley.[1]

Several respondents from non-Western backgrounds noted that the sources of human rights were present in their traditions, even though the language of rights was a relatively modern European development. The absence of formal declarations of rights in China, said Confucian philosopher Chung-Shu Lo, did not signify "that the Chinese never claimed human rights or enjoyed the basic rights of man." He explained:

[T]he problem of human rights was seldom discussed by Chinese thinkers of the past, at least in the same way as it was in the West. There was no open declaration of human rights in China, either by individual thinkers or by political constitutions, until this conception was introduced from the West. . . . [However], the idea of human rights developed very early in China, and the right of the people to revolt against oppressive rulers was very early established. . . . A great Confucianist, Mencius (372–289 B.C.), strongly maintained that a government should work for the will of the people. He said: "People are of primary importance. The State is of less importance. The sovereign is of least importance."[2]

In a similar vein, Indian political scientist S. V. Puntambekar wrote that great Hindu thinkers had "propounded a code, as it were, of ten essential human freedoms and controls or virtues necessary for good life": five social freedoms ("freedom from violence, freedom from want, freedom from exploitation, freedom from violation and dishonor and freedom from early death and disease") and five individual virtues ("absence of intolerance, compassion or fellow-feeling, knowledge, freedom of thought and conscience, and freedom from fear, frustration or despair").[3]

The Bengali Muslim poet and philosopher Humayin Kabir sounded a universalist note in writing about human rights and the Islamic tradition. Kabir proudly recalled that early Islam had "succeeded in overcoming distinction of race and colour to an extent experienced neither before nor since."[4] In the world today, he continued, "[t]he first and most significant consideration in framing any charter of human rights . . . is that it must be on a global scale. . . . Days of closed systems of divergent civilisations and, therefore, of divergent conceptions of human rights are gone for good." The "fundamental flaw in the Western conception of human rights" was not in the idea, but in the frequent failure to live up to it. "In practice," he remarked, human rights "often applied only to Europeans and sometimes to only some among Europeans."

Shirin Sinnar in a Harvard History Department honors thesis has illuminated the context of India's early and strong defense of universal human rights in international settings.[5] She points out that this stand in part reflected India's long struggle on many fronts against discrimination. The language of universal rights was a powerful weapon for challenging European colonialism and the disparate treatment by South Africa of its minority Indian population. Hindu positions on human rights were also informed by Gandhi's expansive concept of nationalism and his moral message of universal brotherhood. "My nationalism," he once wrote, "includes the love of all the nations of the earth irrespective of creed."[6]

By contrast, India's *internal* discourse on rights was bitter and divisive, owing to acute tensions between the Hindu majority and the minority Muslim communities. That troubled state of affairs was reflected in Puntambekar's response to UNESCO. We should first "be men," he wrote, noting sadly that in India, "There is at present a continuous war of groups and communities, of rulers and ruled, in our body politic and body social, from which all conception of humanity and tolerance, all notion of humility and respect, have disappeared."[7]

The situation was soon to become far worse. Just two months after the UNESCO philosophers' meeting, Muslims achieved their aim of a separate state, Pakistan, that became independent with India in August 1947. The partition, which left large minorities of Muslims in India and Hindus and Sikhs in Pakistan, ushered in an era of violence and unrest. Widespread hostilities broke out between the communities, leaving over five hundred thousand people dead by the end of the year. Some sixteen million men, women, and children, fearing for their safety, fled across the borders.

Most Asian and some European respondents strongly emphasized the importance of including duties in a universal declaration of rights. That was the main advice of Gandhi himself, who jotted down his thoughts in a short letter while traveling by train to New Delhi, where he would be assassinated a year later. He urged those who were thinking about universal rights to remember that respect for rights ultimately depends on ingrained habits and attitudes having more to do with duty than entitlement.

I learned from my illiterate but wise mother that all rights to be deserved and preserved came from duty well done. Thus the very right to live accrues to us only when we do the duty of citizenship of the world. From this one fundamental statement, perhaps it is easy enough to define the duties of Man and Woman and correlate every right to some corresponding duty to be first performed. Every other right can be shown to be a usurpation hardly worth fighting for.[8]

Chung-Shu Lo made a similar recommendation, writing that "the basic ethical concept of Chinese social political relations is the fulfilment of the duty to one's neighbor, rather than the claiming of rights."[9] Infringement of rights could best be prevented, he said, by fulfillment of mutual obligations and by the quality that P. C. Chang had tried to explain to his fellow human rights commissioners as two-man mindedness: "a sympathetic attitude of regarding all one's fellow men as having the same desires, and therefore the same rights, as one would like to enjoy oneself."[10]

Both Humphrey's and Cassin's drafts included duty language drawn from continental and Latin American rights documents, informed by classical, biblical, and socialist thought. Cassin had proposed the following article as one of the general principles: "[E]ach man owes to society fundamental duties which are: obedience to law, exercise of a useful activity, acceptance of the burdens and sacrifices demanded for the common good."[11] Such ideas, in one form or another, had long been a familiar part of the constitutional traditions of many countries, though not explicit in Anglo-American rights documents.

From Teilhard de Chardin, who pioneered in reconciling Christianity with modern evolutionary theory, and social philosopher Salvador de Madariaga, an early proponent of European unity who was teaching at Oxford in exile from Franco's Spain, came recommendations to focus on "man in society" rather than as an isolated individual.[12] That theme, too, could be found in the Cassin draft.

Benedetto Croce advised that the most useful thing for UNESCO to do would be to conduct "a formal, public, and international debate on the necessary principles underlying human dignity and civilisation."[13] Aldous Huxley agreed that a bill of rights could "certainly do something to protect the masses of ordinary, unprivileged men and women against the few who, through wealth or hierarchical position, effectively wield power over the majority," but the well-known author warned that "mere paper restrictions, designed to curb the abuse of power already concentrated in a few hands, are but the mitigations of an existing evil." Prevention, he said, "is always better than cure."[14]

⚊

All in all, the results of the UNESCO survey were encouraging: they indicated that the principles underlying the draft Declaration were present in many cultural and religious traditions, though not always expressed in terms of rights. Somewhat to the UNESCO group's surprise, the lists of basic rights and values submitted by their far-flung correspondents were broadly similar.[15] UNESCO's list of widely shared norms included both political and civil liberties and social and economic rights. There were fifteen in all: the right to live, the right to protection of health, the right to work, the right to social assistance in cases of need, the right to property, the right to education, the right to information, the right to freedom of thought and inquiry, the right to self-expression, the right to fair procedures, the right to political participation, the right to freedom of speech, assembly, association, worship, and the press, the right to citizenship, the right to rebel against an unjust regime, and the right to share in progress.[16]

Finding that several practical concepts constituted "a sort of common denominator" among widely separated ideologies, the philosophers pronounced themselves "convinced that the members of the United Nations share common convictions on which human rights depend."[17] They cautioned, however, that "those common convictions are stated in terms of different philosophic principles and on the background of divergent political and economic systems." Their report explained:

> Varied in cultures and built upon different institutions, the members of the United Nations have, nevertheless, certain great principles in common. They believe that men and women all over the world have the right to live a life that is free from the haunting fear of poverty and insecurity. They believe that they should have a more complete access to the heritage, in all its aspects and dimensions, of the civilisation so painfully built by human effort. They believe that science and the arts should combine to serve alike peace and the well-being, spiritual as well as material, of all men and women without discrimination of any kind.[18]

The UNESCO group concluded that it was possible to achieve agreement across cultures concerning certain rights that "may be seen as implicit in man's nature as an individual and as a member of society and to follow from the fundamental right to live." But they harbored no illusions about how deep the agreement they had discovered went. Maritain liked to tell the story of how a visitor at one meeting expressed astonishment that champions of violently opposed ideologies had been able to agree on a list of fundamental rights. The man was told: "Yes, we agree about the rights but on condition no one asks us why."[19]

Maritain and his colleagues did not regard this lack of consensus on foundations as fatal. The only feasible goal for the UN, he maintained, was to achieve agreement "not on the basis of common speculative ideas, but on common practical ideas, not on the affirmation of one and the same conception of the world, of man, and of knowledge, but upon the affirmation of a single body of beliefs for guidance in action."[20] If there are some things so terrible in practice that virtually no one will publicly approve them, and some things so good in practice that virtually no one will oppose them, a common project can move forward without agreement on the reasons for those positions.[21]

An international declaration of rights would provide a "framework within which divergent philosophies, religious, and even economic, social and political theories might be entertained and developed."[22] The challenge was to make the framework "sufficiently definite to have real significance both as an inspiration and a guide to practice" but "sufficiently general and flexible to apply to all men, and to be capable of modification to suit people at different stages of social and political development."[23]

The UN Charter, despite much evidence to the contrary, had professed the signers' "faith in freedom and democracy." That conviction, according to the Charter, is grounded in another belief that is often sorely tested: "faith in the inherent dignity of men and women."[24] A faith based upon a faith was not much to go on, perhaps. But it was enough, the philosophers concluded, "to enable a great task to be undertaken."[25]

LATE NIGHTS IN GENEVA

The Implementation Debate

"There is always a little excitement about going off to a new job," Eleanor Roosevelt wrote in a column published on the day of her departure for the Geneva meeting of the full Human Rights Commission.[1] "But as I grow older, I find that I regret the things I leave behind. The lovely pink light in the sunrise sky as I awake on my porch at Hyde Park, the morning walks in the woods with a little black dog cavorting happily beside me or dashing off after the squirrels, the beautiful bluebird I saw unexpectedly take wing across my brook the other day, the family and friends I like to have around me, the Christmas preparation which I enjoy—all these are hard to leave." The only thing that made the trip worthwhile, she said, was the hope "of something tangible accomplished that may be of value in the future."

On November 29, 1947, Eleanor Roosevelt set off for Geneva in the company of David Gurewitsch, who had been her doctor since 1945. Gurewitsch, the Swiss-born son of Russian emigrés, had come down with tuberculosis and was headed for Davos to convalesce at the famous sanatorium there. Apprehensive about traveling alone, he had asked Mrs. Roosevelt if he might join her party. She readily agreed. The elegant young doctor, then in his forties, had been recommended by her friend Trude Lash, whose husband Joseph Lash recalled him as possessing "gifts of sympathy and empathy, which, when combined with blue eyes and continental gallantry, had a magnetic effect upon both men and women."[2] Gurewitsch, Lash wrote, "was a stimulating conversationalist, a worldly, cultivated man, and a physician who cared about his patients."

The journey took longer than expected, for, en route, the plane developed engine trouble in Newfoundland and was further delayed by foggy weather at Shannon in the west of Ireland. In a memoir, Dr. Gurewitsch described how a close friendship formed during that "time out" from ordinary routines:

> During the long journey, free of schedules and duties, the contact that had gradually grown between Mrs. Roosevelt and myself became much stronger. On this trip the doctor-patient relationship was reversed, and I was carefully looked after by Mrs. Roosevelt. I began to learn what it meant to have her as a friend. . . . [W]e had long hours of uninterrupted conversation. . . . We discovered although we had come from different parts of the world, from different backgrounds, and were of different ages, we had much in common. We had both grown up fatherless and during our impressionable years had been raised by grandparents. We each had experienced feelings of deprivation. A sense of "service" had been strongly instilled in each of us, and we measured accomplishment in life more in terms of service than in terms of happiness. After these unusual four and a half days and by the time our plane finally landed in Geneva, what had been essentially a professional relationship changed into a friendship that grew with the years and lasted to the end of Mrs. Roosevelt's life.[3]

The extended layover had provided Eleanor Roosevelt with a respite from the demanding schedule she normally imposed on herself. Over the past two years she had thrown herself into the UN work and gained a reputation for being extremely well informed. At Lake Success she was a familiar figure in the employees' cafeteria, where she regularly ate in preference to the delegates' private dining room.

There was a drawback to the UN job, however. When she had accepted the UN assignment, Roosevelt had looked forward to a new life out of the goldfish bowl of the White House. "For the first time in my life," she had told reporters en route to her first UN meeting, "I can say what I want. For your information it is wonderful to feel free."[4] But that was exactly how the State Department did not want her to feel. Durward Sandifer, assigned

Eleanor Roosevelt and John P. Humphrey at the December 1947
Geneva meeting. Humphrey, the director of the UN Human Rights Division,
prepared the first draft of the Declaration.

as one of her advisers, recalled, "I discovered when I began working with her that she had been influenced or contaminated by the attitude of the President [Truman] and his advisers towards the State Department. She had *no idea* that she would have advice and assistance and that if she did it would do any good."[5]

The outspoken Roosevelt soon learned that she was less free to express her own opinions as a representative of the U.S. government than she had been as First Lady, and she accepted the fact with good grace. But she regretted that sometimes she had to disappoint old friends such as Walter White, the president of the National Association for the Advancement of Colored People (NAACP). Not long before the Geneva meeting, White had asked her to accompany him when he presented a petition to the United Nations concerning discrimination against blacks in the United States. "As an individual I should like to be present," she wrote White, "but as a member of the delegation I feel that . . . I should not seem to be lining myself up in any particular way on any subject."[6]

On a day-to-day basis she relied on her State Department advisers to keep her well supplied with briefings and instructions. In that sense she was less independent than delegates such as Charles Malik, René Cassin, and P. C. Chang, who had been given rather free rein by their governments. Her access to President Truman, however, gave her more influence over her country's policy than most other delegates could ever hope to enjoy.

A frank and intimate correspondence had sprung up between Roosevelt and Truman in the first week of his presidency, when the bereaved former First Lady had taken the time to provide him with succinct written evaluations of the men and women who had been FDR's main advisers. A few weeks later, upon receiving from Truman an eight-page handwritten letter describing the surrender arrangements with Germany and his difficulties in dealing with Churchill, she wrote to assure him that she would always respect his confidence: "I will, of course, keep confidential anything which comes to me in any letter from you and I will never mention, and I would not use, a private letter in any public way at any time."[7] As for Churchill, she advised the president, "If you talk to him about books and let him quote to you from his marvelous memory . . . , you will find him easier to deal with on political subjects." Throughout the Truman presidency she remained a sounding board, one who could be trusted not to withhold her honest opinions.

Though she arrived in Geneva a day late, the chairman was determined that the Commission would wind up its work before Christmas. "I have made reservations, and I hope to keep them," she announced to the group assembled in the former home of the League of Nations overlooking Lake Geneva.[8] She had devised a plan to keep eighteen noses to the grindstone. "I immediately laid out a schedule of work that, with night sessions, I believed would enable us to adjourn by eleven o'clock on the evening of December 17." Though the commissioners indulged in good-natured complaining about a chairman who denied them their human rights, they did not object to the grueling pace she set. In fact, this second meeting of the full Commission, by all accounts, represented the high point of harmony for the group.

For one thing, the new Soviet representative, Alexander Bogomolov, was easier to work with than his predecessors. According to John Humphrey, the well-mannered Soviet ambassador to France was the most cooperative of all the men the Soviet Union ever sent to the Human Rights Commission.[9] He also knew how to throw a good vodka and caviar party. Humphrey's memories of Geneva included leaving one of Bogomolov's soirées with Professor Koretsky, both swaying gently as they descended the hotel steps in comradely détente.

This may have been the same evening that Mrs. Roosevelt and General Romulo arrived for an eight P.M. session only to find the meeting room empty. "At eight-thirty," Mrs. Roosevelt recalled, "there was a commotion at the door and the lost sheep began arriving. They were in a happy if unhurried mood, and, I observed, a little shaky on their feet. They took their accustomed places, leaned back in their chairs and gazed at me with pleased, rather foggy, eyes. They were, as one of the younger members of our party put it later, loaded!"[10] After a futile attempt to transact business, she acknowledged "the Russians had me licked" and adjourned the meeting until the next morning.

Despite the eminence of the participants in the UNESCO philosophers' study, their report received little official attention from the Commission. The members probably regarded it as confirming the results of Humphrey's study of the world's rights instruments, even though UNESCO had solicited advice from parts of the world where such documents did not yet exist. The Belgian commissioner and international lawyer Fernand Dehousse complained that UNESCO had invaded their turf.[11] It was nevertheless heartening that the philosophers' list of fundamental rights was so similar to their own.

Before they could turn to the drafting committee's text, the Commission became embroiled in an argument over the problem of implementation. It was the most heated dispute of the Geneva meeting. Several members, led by Colonel Hodgson and Mrs. Mehta, were pushing hard for the establishment of some sort of international tribunal or, alternatively, for amending the UN Charter to include binding rights commitments or, at the very least, for a covenant to make the declaration legally enforceable.

A *declaration* by the UN General Assembly takes the form of a resolution that, like a congressional resolution, has no legal force of its own. *Covenants, conventions,* and *treaties* (more or less interchangeable terms) are agreements by which nations undertake legally binding obligations. Covenants can go into effect only after they have been ratified, which in the United States requires a two-thirds vote of the Senate. After ratification, some covenants are self-executing and take effect right away; others require the further step of being implemented by national legislative or executive action. A nation will often limit the extent of its obligations by entering formal reservations—a technique at which the United States later became adept.

The United Kingdom strongly opposed an international court or Charter amendments but was from the beginning the chief proponent of a covenant. The U.K. Foreign Office had submitted an incomplete covenant—covering only political and civil rights and without implementation measures—to the Human Rights Commission. Though not a major source for the Universal Declaration, this U.K. draft became influential in other contexts. It was an important tributary to the 1950 European Convention for the Protection of Human Rights and Fundamental Freedoms, which established the first international court open to individuals with claims against their own governments. Later it served as a basis for the 1966 UN International Covenant on Political and Civil Rights.

The pursuit by the United States and the Soviet bloc of strategies to avoid or postpone any legal commitments produced an appearance of East-West accord. The USSR took the position that talk of implementation was premature until the content of the rights had been clarified and crystallized. Yugoslavia's Ribnikar agreed that it was inadvisable to prepare a draft Convention at present. The Commission, he said, should proceed instead to prepare "a Declaration to be submitted to Governments for study and comment."[12]

Mrs. Roosevelt, too, argued that all discussion of implementation should be deferred until the Declaration had been completed. She said her government's position had undergone a "slight evolution" since June, when it had agreed to simultaneous preparation of a declaration and covenant. The United States now considered that a covenant should not be drawn up "until it was sure that such Conventions could be accepted and applied in all good faith by the participating states."[13] The reason she gave was that "flagrant, prolonged and repeated violations of these Conventions could not fail to harm the United Nations."

In a "My Day" column cabled home from Geneva, Roosevelt explained the position to her American readers this way:

> In several long sessions there has been careful discussion of whether the Human Rights Commission was to write a bill which would actually be presented to the General Assembly—but which would not have legal weight, since it would not require ratification and implementation from the various nations—or both a convention and a declaration. Our own position as a government has been that on the drafting committee's report we should have sufficient material available to do a fairly finished job as regards a declaration. But many countries like our own would have to consider most carefully the points covered in a convention. For instance, our government must remember the matter of state's rights and decide how far it can go. . . . But we felt it would have a moral value to finish and circulate a declaration.[14]

Bogomolov summed up the difference between the United States and the United Kingdom in his report to Soviet Foreign Minister V. M. Molotov as follows: "The U.S. prefers a Declaration that is as short and empty as possible; the English prefer the same kind of Convention."[15] The USSR, he did not need to add, preferred neither. The main job of its representatives was to protect the Soviet Union from outside meddling in its internal affairs.

Charles Malik, after listening to the discussion on implementation, said he gathered that "the issue of a 'Declaration' or a 'Convention' was a challenge between small and great powers."[16] He could understand the "difficult position of some great powers," he went on, and the problem of "certain representatives" who had received "narrow instructions," but he entreated delegates from such countries to request their governments to rethink the matter. The resolution of the issue of implementation, he said, would be an "acid test" of "whether there was in the world today an international moral sense, whose principles could be incorporated into national law, or whether such an anarchy existed in that field that only a vague proclamation of general principles could be achieved."

Mrs. Roosevelt believed wholeheartedly that a declaration, though not legally binding, would be much more than a vague proclamation. Like the American Declaration of Independence, it would announce the goals toward which all nations would commit themselves to strive. As First Lady, Roosevelt had learned that moral persuasion, publicly exercised, could be a potent force for change. On one notable occasion in 1939, when the Daughters of the American Revolution had refused to let Marian Anderson perform in Constitution Hall in segregated Washington, D.C., the First Lady had resigned her membership in the group and sponsored a free open-air concert by the great black contralto at the Lincoln Memorial. Seventy-five thousand people had attended, and the incident became a symbolic landmark in the struggle to end discrimination. No doubt it fueled Roosevelt's unwavering faith in "soft power."

Unable to reach consensus on which proposals should take priority, the majority of the Commission finally accepted a compromise put forward by Fernand Dehousse. They decided to proceed along all three lines simultaneously, working toward the preparation of a Declaration, a Covenant, and measures of implementation.

Putting the best light on this defeat for the United States, Mrs. Roosevelt wrote in the next issue of *Foreign Affairs* that the United States had thought only a nonbinding Declaration was feasible, but that she had come to see that "[m]any of the smaller nations were strongly of the opinion that the oppressed peoples of the world and the minority groups would feel that they had been cruelly deceived" if the Human Rights Commission did not produce a Convention to be ratified, nation by nation, like any other treaty.[17] "The Government of the United States," she went on, "had never, of course, been opposed to writing a Convention; it simply felt that the attempt would not be practical in these early stages. When it was found that feeling ran high on this subject, we immediately cooperated."

Bogomolov reported to Molotov, "We were outvoted, but my arguments were not useless as most members of the Commission agreed with me that the Declaration is the fundamental document."[18]

The Commission pressed forward in three working groups. The first, chaired by Mrs. Roosevelt, continued work on the draft Declaration. Its membership was composed of Cassin (elected rapporteur of the group), Romulo, Bogomolov, and the representatives of Byelorussia and Panama. The second group, chaired by Lord Dukeston, was to prepare a draft Convention, using the United Kingdom's draft as a basis. Its members were Santa Cruz, Malik, Ribnikar, Dr. C. H. Wu (serving as Chang's alternate), and Omar Loutfi of Egypt. The third group's task was to investigate methods of implementation that might or might not later be incorporated into a Covenant. It was chaired by Mrs. Mehta and included Colonel Hodgson and A. G. Pourevaly of Iran, Michael Klekovkin of the Ukraine, and J. J. C. Victorica of Uruguay. "From this assignment of delegates," Bogomolov wrote Molotov, "you can see a number of differences between the Americans and the English. Roosevelt collected the partisans of a Declaration in the Declaration subcommittee, and the English headed for the Convention subcommittee."[19] The three groups were to prepare reports and reassemble as the full Commission on December 12.

With hindsight, it was a fortunate decision to permit work on the Declaration to go forward independently. It would be nineteen long years before two human rights conventions, one on political and civil rights, the other on economic, social, and cultural rights, were opened for signature by member states and ten more years before those conventions received enough signatures to go into effect, in 1976. The fact was that *all* of the major powers were fiercely protective of their sovereignty, and Britain of its colonial empire.

Washington and London may not have been entirely displeased at Soviet obstructionism in the Human Rights Commission. As historian Brian Simpson has demonstrated, the Foreign Office viewed human rights as basically for export and as a weapon to be used against the Soviet Union.[20] Its Covenant was designed to serve as a way of demonstrating

Britain's own commitment to the short list of rights it was prepared to recommend at that time.

As the United States delegate, Mrs. Roosevelt faced a different sort of problem. Under the U.S. Constitution the president has the power to enter into a treaty but must obtain the concurrence of two-thirds of the Senate. If a president fails to secure Senate approval for a treaty after his administration has negotiated it, the result is an international embarrassment. As Eleanor Roosevelt sized up the situation, a human rights convention could be expected to encounter significant opposition from isolationists and from southern senators. The latter were likely to couch their objections in terms of federal interference with traditional states' rights—a local version of the national sovereignty problem.

Bogomolov, in charging that the United States wanted a Declaration that was as "short and empty as possible," was half-right, but only half-right. Eleanor Roosevelt wanted the Declaration to be concise and knew that there would be a problem domestically with implementation. She did not, however, regard the Declaration as an empty gesture. In a June meeting with State Department officials, she showed her thinking to be far ahead of her time. The "essential in present day consideration of human rights," she had said, was "to secure publicity" in cases of serious violations.[21] She was one of the first people to realize that even a nonbinding Declaration would greatly aid that strategy.

Why, one might wonder, were delegates from less powerful nations so keen on international enforcement mechanisms? The reasons varied. Some countries—Cuba and Lebanon, for example—were struggling to establish constitutional democracies under unstable domestic conditions. France had suffered under a puppet regime run by her own citizens. To men like Charles Malik and René Cassin, the idea of the international community taking an interest in domestic affairs did not seem as offensive as it did to the Americans and British. What Mrs. Roosevelt told her "My Day" readers on December 18 is as true now as it was then: "I think there is more interest in an international bill of human rights over here [Europe] than in the United States. That's largely because, except for a few minority groups, the people of our country don't feel the need for protection."[22]

The working group on the Declaration was able to produce a revised draft in time for discussion when the full Commission reconvened on December 12. The commissioners went over this document during morning, noon, and night meetings that sometimes lasted into the wee hours.

Between sessions, Eleanor Roosevelt kept in touch with David Gurewitsch by phone and took a moment to jot a few lines to her daughter, Anna. "We were much delayed en route," she wrote, but "the two fog bound days at Shannon were peaceful." As for Geneva:

> The work here has been a constant drive & for that reason I will be glad when it is over. The place is beautiful & I find the snow covered mountains even more impressive than in summer. Food here is wonderful but everything except food costs more than at home & even food is not cheap. Bread is rationed & milk is scarce but Switzerland tho' more conscious of surrounding misery than we are is still a little self-centered, complacent & well to do community none too aware of her surrounding nations.[23]

Her growing affection for Gurewitsch was evident in a note she sent to Davos on December 13: "I've always liked you & was drawn to you since we first met & the trip just made me sure that we could be friends. I never want to burden my young friends & with all my outward assurance I still have some of my old shyness & insecurity & that is probably what makes you feel shy. I've really taken you to my heart however, so there need never be a question of bother again. You can know that anything I can do will always be a pleasure for me & being with you is a joy."[24]

The full Commission once again consumed much precious time arguing over Article 1's general statement concerning the human person. Cassin and Romulo, in the working group, had slightly revised the first article to read: "All men are brothers. They are endowed by nature with reason and conscience. They are born equal in dignity and rights." Malik, who had been working with the Covenant group, now proposed substituting the words "by their Creator" for "by nature." He cited the American Declaration of Independence ("endowed by their Creator with certain unalienable rights"). That amendment was opposed by Cassin on the ground that references to God would undermine the universality of the document. Bogomolov moved to drop the entire article, saying that it made no sense to clutter up the document with vacuous assertions, whether they were drawn from eighteenth-century French philosophy or from the Bible.[25]

Hansa Mehta objected to Article 1's use of what would today be called noninclusive language. Mrs. Mehta was particularly vigilant concerning women's rights. During the period of her service on the Human Rights Commission, she was also one of two women advisers on the drafting of the rights provisions of the Indian Constitution, adopted in 1949. She was battling back home against purdah, child marriage, polygamy, unequal inheritance laws, and bans on marriages among different castes, striving to set these ancient customs on a course of extinction.[26] She warned her colleagues in Geneva that the words *all men* would be construed literally in some countries so as to exclude women.[27] Backing her were the Soviet-bloc delegates and representatives of the UN Commission on the Status of Women, who were present as observers.

Mrs. Roosevelt repeated that she personally understood "all men" to include everyone, male or female.

Eleanor Roosevelt's feminism was ardent but pragmatic and subordinate to her broader social concerns. She credited women's suffrage with having forced governments to take more interest in human welfare, and she tried to demonstrate through her own efforts that increased participation by women in political and economic life could make a difference. To her, that chiefly meant lending a helping hand to those who were still politically and economically marginalized—women and men alike, especially blacks in the southern states, the unemployed, the rural poor, and urban slum dwellers. As First Lady she had used the prestige of her position to draw attention to the causes of racial equality and decent housing, health care, and education.

To Eleanor Roosevelt this was women's work—in the sense that she felt these issues would be neglected if women did not push them. It seemed to her that men in power, even men like her husband who sympathized with her goals, had not devoted enough attention to addressing the country's social ills. As her biographer Blanche Wiesen Cook puts it, the First Lady's aim was to reach every woman in America and to convince them that "it was up to them to take charge, to organize and agitate on behalf of social progress."[28] She wanted to see more women working together on an equal basis with men to frame policies within governments and private organizations.[29]

Where women's rights as such were concerned, Roosevelt was completely dedicated to equal opportunities in the workplace and public life.

At times she came close to espousing what today would be called "sameness feminism," writing in a *Good Housekeeping* article, "If women want equal consideration, they must prepare themselves to adjust to other people and make no appeals on the ground of sex. . . . A woman who cannot engage in an occupation and hold it because of her own ability had much better get out of that particular occupation, and do something else, where her ability will count."[30]

But she contended just as firmly that there were certain areas, such as child rearing and military service, where the differences between the sexes ought to be taken into account. Thus she had been opposed to an Equal Rights Amendment in the 1920s because it would have invalidated protective legislation for women. She did not believe that the roles of mother and father were completely interchangeable. She credited mothers, as the main teachers of children, with a special role in shaping the nation's destiny. "It is perfectly obvious that women are not all alike," she conceded, but she believed that most women, mothers or not, shared a special concern for the well-being of children:

> [T]here are certain fundamental things that mean more to the great majority of women than to the great majority of men. These things are undoubtedly tied up with women's biological functions. The women bear the children, and love them before they even come into the world. . . . [W]e find [concern for children] in greater or less degree in women who have never had a child. From it springs that concern about the home, the shelter for the children. And here is the great point of unity for the majority of women.[31]

The home, Mrs. Roosevelt continued, is "one place . . . where sex must be a cleavage in daily activity. . . . [T]his is a part of life in which men and women live as men and women and complement, but do not compete with each other." Women should not "feel humiliated" if they choose homemaking as their first priority, she said, "for this was our first field of activity, and it will always remain our most important one."

In later years, the failure of state governments to move quickly enough on women's rights caused her to change her mind about the Equal Rights Amendment, but she continued to promote a vision of equality that allowed for differences between the sexes. In a 1951 article, while strenuously advocating greater access by women to decision-making roles, she insisted that the "real issue" is whether women's needs and circumstances are recognized fully by those who set the policies of governments.[32] In 1962, after President John F. Kennedy named her to the first U.S. Commission on the Status of Women, she told the readers of "My Day," "The effort, of course, is to find how we can best use the potentialities of women without impairing their first responsibilities, which are to their home, their husbands and their children. We need to use in the very best way possible all our available manpower—and that includes woman-power—and this commission, I think, can well point out some of the ways in which this can be accomplished."[33]

Hansa Mehta left the Geneva session dissatisfied. At later meetings she persisted in her efforts to make Article 1 more inclusive. Her changes were finally accepted at the third and last meeting of the full Commission, in June 1948. They helped to place the Declaration far ahead of most of the world's rights instruments in the clarity with which it affirmed women's equality.

The list of traditional protections for the inviolability of the person occasioned little debate. The Commission decided to retain the general statement "Everyone has the right to life, to liberty and security of person" rather than try to reach agreement on specific issues such as euthanasia, abortion, or the death penalty. This was a defeat for the representatives of Chile and Lebanon, who had pushed for express protection of the lives of the unborn, and for the Soviet-bloc delegates, who had argued for a ban on capital punishment.[34]

The most neuralgic issue for the Eastern bloc concerned the rights to asylum and nationality. The Byelorussian representative returned to a theme that had occasioned a sharp exchange between Roosevelt and Vishinsky at the UN General Assembly's first meeting, arguing that war criminals and traitors should not be given the status of refugees. This time the outcome was more satisfactory to the Soviet Union: provisos were added stating that asylum and nationality would not "be accorded to criminals nor those whose acts are contrary to the principles and aims of the United Nations." Ultimately those limitations survived only in a highly attenuated form in Article 29(3) of the Declaration, which states that none of the enumerated rights may "be exercised contrary to the purposes and principles of the United Nations."

Some important and uncontroversial additions regarding the family were made in Geneva. To Humphrey's draft, which had included a right to marry, Cassin had added protection for mothers and children. Now these ideas were reworked in response to a Byelorussian proposal that originally read: "Marriage and the family enjoy the protection of the State and are regulated by the law on the basis of the equal rights of men and women without distinction of race, religion, or origin. Mother and child have the right to the protection and aid of the State."

At Mrs. Roosevelt's suggestion, the right to marry was followed with the specification that men and women have equal rights when a marriage is dissolved. To the idea of family protection by the state, Cassin proposed adding "and society"—to make clear, he said, that the principle could and should also be implemented by institutions of civil society, such as the churches.[35] When the family article reached the full Commission, Malik suggested that the importance of the family ought to be emphasized even more forcefully. He proposed the following sentence, which the Commission accepted: "The family deriving from marriage is the natural and fundamental unit of society."[36]

During the discussion of the articles pertaining to the rights to work, education, and social security, Bogomolov strove, with some success, to add references to enforcement by the state. His attempt to exempt Fascist propaganda from free speech protection, however, failed to gain any support outside the Eastern bloc.

When the Human Rights Commission voted on the draft, the members approved the document 13–0, with the USSR, Byelorussia, the Ukraine, and Yugoslavia abstaining. The chief problem with the Declaration now, according to Bogomolov, was its vagueness regarding by whom the rights were to be guaranteed. "The Anglo-Americans," he complained to Molotov, "want to leave out all obligations of the State with regard to the provision of human rights like the rights to work, education, social assistance, gender equality, etc. For example, there is a general affirmation of equality without regard to race, nationality or religious belief in both the Declaration and the Convention but without any hint about who is responsible for the actual implementation of equality, especially in colonies and non-self-governing territories."[37] Bogomolov's insistence on references to enforcement by the state was also prompted, no doubt, by his desire to ward off any threats to the Soviet Union's national sovereignty. No one ever asked any of the Soviet representatives to explain why they were working so hard to empower a state that, according to Marxist-Leninist theory, was supposed to be "withering away."

The Geneva draft was now ready to be sent to all member states for their advice and comment by the next meeting of the drafting committee in May.* The text, still lacking a Preamble, had been streamlined and reduced to thirty-three articles. To Mrs. Roosevelt it seemed excessively juridical. She asked the drafting committee to condense the text further before the next Commission meeting and to put it into language "which could be readily understood by the ordinary man or woman."[38]

The discussion of the Declaration had been calm and polite, and significant progress had been made. The Commission's temperature rose, however, when the members turned on December 15 to the next item on their agenda, the report of Mrs. Mehta's working group on implementation.

The implementation group had run into trouble at the outset when the Ukrainian representative, Michael Klekovkin, took the position that the group had nothing to discuss until the contents of the Declaration and the Convention had been decided upon.[39] Other members protested that to do nothing would violate their responsibilities, but Klekovkin was not to be dissuaded. On December 6 he sent Mrs. Mehta a note saying, "I have got a strong opinion during these discussions that it is impossible for me to take my part in them because I am standing on my old position that it is necessary to discuss the question of an implementation at a more late stage of the Human Rights Commission's work." After this he left the working group and took no further part in its discussions.

The implementation group presented the full Commission with a report proposing the creation of an international human rights court and a UN agency to monitor the human rights situation in member states and to receive petitions from aggrieved individuals. Bogomolov dismissed those ideas as completely unacceptable. The working group, he charged, had been motivated not by a desire to devise practical measures for implementing human rights, but by the intention to subject sovereign states to

*The Geneva draft appears as appendix 4.

"fantastic and dangerous" international controls.[40] The Soviet delegation could not accept any of the group's proposals since they constituted "an attempted gross infringement" of the UN Charter's protection of every state's domestic jurisdiction.

Ribnikar (by prearrangement) agreed, describing the report as "a new attempt to transform the United Nations into a kind of world government, placed above national sovereignty."[41] The result would be that "the country that was strongest economically would have complete supremacy and would likewise exert a preponderant political influence." Then, adopting a conciliatory tone, Ribnikar said he continued to have high hopes for "a comprehensive Declaration of human rights." As far as implementation was concerned, he expressed "full confidence in the States parties" who would pledge themselves to enforce such an instrument within their own borders.

Lord Dukeston, on hearing this, wondered aloud whether the Soviet and Yugoslav delegates "were really in touch with reality."[42] He failed to understand, he said, how a state could remain the sole judge of its own compliance with international obligations. The group let pass in silence the Ukrainian representative's reply that "there was no need for a Court of Human Rights to implement the principles of the Declaration in his country, since complete equality between citizens and national groups was guaranteed and respect for human rights assured by the new Stalin Constitution."

The real fears of the Soviet bloc were revealed in Bogomolov's final report to Molotov:

> Instead of working out any kind of plan for the implementation of rights within every state, the center of gravity is shifted to the area of international guarantees of the defense of these rights, a special International Court of Human Rights, the dispatch of U.N. observers to every country, procedures for individuals or groups to petition the U.N. so that these complaints can be used against the violator-state or even to create international scandals, giving a pretext for persecuting any particular country (primarily the USSR or the people's republics).[43]

The arguments made by the Soviet bloc concerning implementation were not too different from those that would be made by the United States when the balance of voting power shifted in the UN in the 1950s—and again in 1998, when the United States was one of the few dissenters from the vote to establish an International Criminal Court.

The Soviet bloc was equally implacable when it came to the report of the working group on the Covenant, which produced a draft international agreement based on the United Kingdom's proposal. It was limited to civil and political rights: equal protection under law, freedom from torture, freedom from slavery, right to a fair trial, right to emigrate, freedom of religion, freedom of information, and the right to participate in government. The Covenant was drafted so as not to be self-executing, and the problem of devising means for its enforcement—reporting requirements, individual petitions, a special commission—was left to be resolved later on.

After the Covenant group delivered its report, Bogomolov explained the Soviet government's position on the question of implementation. The Declaration, he said, was the fundamental document. Work on a Covenant to make human rights binding should not begin until the Commission had achieved a satisfactory definition of human rights. Progress had been made on that front, but the draft Declaration was still too weak, especially where the social and economic rights were concerned. When the draft Covenant was put to a vote, the Soviet Union, joined by Byelorussia, the Ukraine, and Yugoslavia, voted no.

By the close of the Geneva meeting it was clearer than ever that the chief obstacle to unanimous approval of the Declaration was not going to be its content, but its potential for legitimating outside interference in a country's internal affairs. The behavior of the Communist delegates at Geneva suggested that the Soviet bloc might oppose the Declaration when the actual day of decision came. Despite its defects, Cassin argued, the Declaration "contributes something new: the individual becomes a subject of international law in respect of his life and liberty; principles are affirmed, side by side with those already laid down by the majority of national laws, which no national or international authority had hitherto been able to proclaim, let alone enforce."[44] He was referring specifically to three "international" rights—the rights to freedom of movement, to seek asylum, and to a nationality—that the closed societies of Eastern Europe both protested and feared.

On December 31 Bogomolov wrote to Molotov that he thought the new Soviet strategy had been successful:

> In debates, I tried to be reserved, and I refrained from starting fights with colleagues over narrow points. I think that at this point the tactic of reserve, and the search for formulas harmonizing points of view was useful for us, especially since in the voting on specific articles I always abstained, but the Byelorussian and the Ukrainian sometimes voted for this or that correction or even a whole article. This tactic allowed our colleagues to see that we could in the end agree to some kind of general platform. This tactic also allowed them to make some compromises.[45]

For the future, however, Bogomolov urged, as had his predecessors, that it was essential for the USSR to develop its own draft of a Declaration. In view of the voting imbalance in the Human Rights Commission, he recommended against presenting such a draft there. "We should wait," he advised, "until the meeting of the Economic and Social Council where we will have more opportunities to propagandize for our draft." Thus far, he concluded, "the little Anglo-Saxon orchestra has been well organized and harmonious, but not to the degree that our work has been useless. Somehow we will shake that little orchestra apart."

⟋

As the Geneva meeting drew to an end the chairman was far from discouraged. "Participation in discussion has been so much greater in this meeting than before and so much more valuable," she told her readers back home, "that I feel very hopeful of the progress which has been made. However no one can ever tell me that women like to talk longer than men!"[46] She continued to hold out hope for eventual agreement with the Soviets:

> One of the questions I'm most frequently asked is whether I think we can produce a draft on which the Eastern European group and the United States can agree. I think this is quite possible. They like a greater emphasis on the authority of the state, and when it comes to social and economic rights they are most anxious to spell them out in detail. The rights and freedoms of the individual, and religious and

spiritual questions, don't seem to them as important in a draft of this kind. But certainly a balance can be reached.

Impatient by temperament, she had learned to take the long view. Just before leaving Geneva, she wrote again to David Gurewitsch in Davos:

I've been thinking about the meeting here. At first it seemed sad to me to go into that beautiful building built with love & hope by nations who thought they had found the way to peace & understanding. Now I think it gives me encouragement & I wish more meetings could be held here for when you see the present activity you realize that perhaps man's spirit, his striving, is indestructible. It is set back but it does not die.[47]

CHAPTER 7

IN THE EYE
OF THE HURRICANE

The Draft Takes Shape
as the Palestine Crisis Erupts and
the Cold War Intensifies

In the spring of 1948, while work on the Declaration was proceeding more or less according to the schedule laid out by Mrs. Roosevelt, the deteriorating international situation was distracting the attention of its commissioners. Relations between Russia and the United States had become so tense that many expected war to break out between the two superpowers. The odds against the kind of cooperation required to gain unanimous or near unanimous approval were rising rapidly.

Tensions between Russia and the United States had been building over the previous year when Stalin, tightening his grip on Eastern Europe, had ended multiparty government behind the Iron Curtain and established the Communist Information Bureau (Cominform), whose European members would later form the Warsaw Pact alliance.

In March 1948 Truman condemned the Soviet Union for threatening international stability, and Britain, France, and the Benelux countries signed a treaty pledging economic and military cooperation—implicitly against the Eastern bloc. On March 9, after meeting in Washington with State Department officials, Eleanor Roosevelt wrote to Anna, "Everyone is so fearful! News looks worse & war looks nearer & I can't see anyone capable of clearing the atmosphere. Sec. Marshall did not want me to go to Russia. I don't believe I could now."[1]

In the UN General Assembly, diplomatic niceties were increasingly thrown aside. Soviet-bloc delegates repeatedly played their trump card in tirades against the United States: the United States posed as a humanitarian country but permitted flagrant racial discrimination.

Mrs. Roosevelt, whose credentials as a champion of civil liberties were unequaled, was at her calm and devastating best in these debates. She conceded that it was true that racial discrimination still existed in the United States, but progress was being made, she said, and many citizens and groups were working to put an end to it once and for all. To imply the contrary was "hitting below the belt."[2] Perhaps Russia and the United States should exchange experts to study each other's discriminatory practices, she suggested, with a carefully aimed jab at the weak point of a closed society.[3] She issued the same challenge when a Soviet delegate claimed that the health care system in the USSR was superior to that of the United States.

After one particularly vitriolic attack in the General Assembly by a Yugoslav delegate, she delivered an impromptu lecture:

> I think the time has come for some very straight thinking among us all. The ultimate objective that we have is to create better understanding among us all, and I will acknowledge this is going to be difficult. And I will give you the reasons why. I have never heard a representative of any of the USSR bloc acknowledge that in any way their government can be wrong.[4]

Perhaps, she speculated, that posture of self-righteousness was due to the relative youth of the countries concerned. If so, it was time to grow up. Few among her listeners could have suspected how personal was the wisdom of her next observation.

> With maturity we grow much more humble, and we know that we have to acknowledge very often that things are not quite perfect. Because we acknowledge it does not mean we love our country any less. . . . What it does mean is that we know human nature is not perfect and that we hope that all of us can contribute to something better.

The strained relations between America and the Soviet Union were not the only factors casting a shadow over the Commission's work that

*Eleanor Roosevelt conferring with René Cassin and
Charles Malik. In the background are State Department advisers
Marjorie Whiteman and James Simsarian.*

spring. Long-standing hostilities between Chinese Communists and the U.S.-backed government forces of Chiang Kai-shek had erupted into a full-scale civil war as each side moved to seize territories that had been abandoned by the Japanese. The Kuomintang's venality and mismanagement had led to severe inflation, unemployment, and unrest in the war-weakened country. Those conditions, together with the government's harsh measures against protesters, alienated large segments of the population. By early 1947 Mao Tse-tung's guerrilla force, with Soviet support and over a million men under arms, had gained the upper hand.

The United States' efforts to mediate a cease-fire had been a dismal failure. The Communist leaders, confident of eventual victory, were unyielding. President Truman's emissary, General George Marshall, soon to become secretary of state, reported that he was dismayed by the profiteering of Nationalist officials and—though he was a soldier himself—by the dominating influence of the military in the government.[5] When the Human Rights Commission drafting committee met in May 1948, Mao's army was just six months away from consolidating its control over Manchuria, then the country's industrial core.

That spring the Middle East was plunged into conflict as well. In the fall of 1947 an explosive debate had broken out within the United Nations over the fate of Palestine. Four members of the Human Rights Commission—Cassin, Malik, Romulo, and Roosevelt—became deeply embroiled in that issue, which not only divided the Commission, but put Romulo and Roosevelt at odds with their own governments.

On September 1, 1947, a UN commission of inquiry had issued a recommendation that the territory held under British mandate in Palestine be partitioned into an Arab state and a Jewish state, with Jerusalem and its environs cordoned off as a separate entity under UN trusteeship. Most Jewish organizations favored the partition plan because it permitted at last the realization of the dream of a Jewish homeland. The neighboring Arab nations, for their part, were bitterly opposed to the establishment of a Jewish state in a territory where Arabs were in the majority. They argued that Palestine should become a single, independent, democratic state after the departure of the British.[6] The partition plan had given rise to intense lobbying within the UN, as its acceptance required a two-thirds majority in the General Assembly.

Though relations between Russia and the United States were close to an all-time low, one thing upon which the two titans happened to agree was the partition of Palestine. The Soviet Union's interest was strategic: it was concerned about British military bases in the Middle East and hoped that Palestinian Jews would share its aim to banish British presence from the region.

Even though the partition plan had the support of the two major powers, the supermajority requirement placed the outcome in doubt, because several smaller nations were opposed. One of these was the Philippines. "We had a number of reasons for taking this position," General Romulo recalled in his memoirs in 1986, "which I still consider valid. I believed that to carve out a country from an already populated land would create a trouble spot that would continue to fester, which it has."[7] On November 26, 1947, Romulo, with his usual brio, had delivered a speech against partition in the General Assembly.

> We hold that the issue is primarily moral. The issue is whether the United Nations should accept responsibility for the enforcement of a policy which, not being mandatory under any specific provision of the Charter nor in accordance with its fundamental principles, is clearly repugnant to the valid nationalist aspirations of the people of Palestine. . . .
>
> In taking this position, my Government is not unmindful of the sufferings of the great Jewish people who we hold in sincere admiration. . . . During the first dispersal of the Jews from Hitlerite Germany, the Philippines was among the very few countries that opened their doors to Jewish refugees and extended to them a cordial welcome.[8]

After giving this speech, Romulo got into his car and drove to the docks, where he boarded the *Queen Mary,* bound for the December meeting of the Human Rights Commission in Geneva. The Jewish Agency officials, Abba Eban recalled, were glad to see him go: "General Carlos Romulo, who had spoken so brilliantly against partition . . . had left New York and there was a good chance that the Philippine delegation would vote 'yes.' "[9]

Among Romulo's fellow passengers was Czechoslovakian Foreign Minister Jan Masaryk, headed for a martyr's death three months later. When the last democratic elements were forced out of the Czech government, Masaryk either jumped or was thrown from a window. Also on board was Charles Malik. At the end of the crossing he jotted down this account of the massive pressure that had been exerted on Romulo and the president of the Philippines:

Tuesday, Dec. 2, 1947. Southampton, England, in train.

On Wed. Nov. 26, date of our departure from N.Y., Romulo gave a speech in the GA in which he said he was opposed to partition. He left a substitute in his place to vote vs. partition and boarded the Queen Mary.

On board he received a telephone call from Sol Bloom & talked with him for ½ hour; tried to change his mind; told him last sentence in his speech permitted abstention; R told me he promised Bloom nothing.[10]

He received cable also from Norman Cousins, editor of the Saturday Review of Literature, asking him also to change his mind. Rec'd other telephone calls and cables.

In one or two days rec'd telephone call and cable from Phil. Ambassador in Wash. & from his substitute in the UN that Phil. Pres. gave instructions to reverse their stand & vote for partition. . . . R cabled his substitute to stand by his position announced in his speech of November 26 and his pres. to reconsider the reversal of policy. Reviewed in his cable hist. of their position. He showed me both cables & those he received himself.

Later he learned from his substitute or ambassador in Wash. by telephone that Truman got in touch with the ambassador & afterwards by telephone with their pres. in the Phil; that Martin the speaker of the House, Vandenberg, Tydings—who sponsored the Phil. Independence bill, McGrath and many others got in touch with their ambass. He showed me also a cable from his pres. in which he explains his change—U.S. govt intervened, 20 other govts intervened with him, presidents of many Am. univs., many leading Americans etc.—all this led him to change. They all put responsibility for blocking partition on him if he voted against it. He yielded.

The same sort of threat and pressure must have been applied on Liberia and Haiti.

Romulo himself recalled in his memoirs how he had received the cable from President Roxas telling him that the Philippine position was being reversed "in the national interest," which Romulo understood to mean that the United States was threatening to cut off aid to its former colony.[11] Romulo responded by tendering his resignation as Philippine delegate to the UN, but Roxas prevailed upon him to stay on.

On November 29, 1947, the partition recommendation narrowly secured the necessary votes. Under pressure from the United States, Haiti, Liberia, and the Philippines, all of whom Malik had perceived as leaning toward the Arab position, voted in favor of the plan.[12]

The Arab states reacted violently to the partition plan. By May of 1948, with the British mandate about to expire, the Palestine situation had heated up to a point at which armed conflict seemed inevitable.

With war now imminent in the oil-rich Middle East, the U.S. State Department dropped its support for partition. It took the position that partition would be unworkable and that Palestine should be placed under UN trusteeship until a peaceful solution could be found.

This policy reversal outraged Mrs. Roosevelt, who could not understand why the Arabs refused to accept partition and faulted them for defying the UN's authority.[13] Though she herself had once opposed a Jewish state, her views had changed and hardened. Her friend and State Department aide, Durward Sandifer, said of the former First Lady in those days, "She impressed me as having an open mind on every subject other than Palestine."[14]

By March Mrs. Roosevelt's disagreement with the State Department was so profound that she felt obliged to speak out publicly. Though she had derived deep personal satisfaction from her UN work, she was ready to place her job on the line rather than remain silent. Telling President Truman that she did not wish to embarrass him, she tendered her resignation from the U.S. delegation to the United Nations. Her letter to Truman, which she described to her friend Joseph Lash as "very frank and unpleasant," reveals the depth of her disagreement with the State Department, not only on Palestine, but also on its evolving Russian policy.

> I feel that even though the Secretary of State takes responsibility for the Administration's position on Palestine, you cannot escape the results of that attitude. . . .
> We are [also] evidently discarding the UN and acting unilaterally, or setting up a balance of power by backing the European democracies

and preparing for an ultimate war between the two political philosophies. I am opposed to this attitude because I feel it would be possible,
with force and friendliness, to make some arrangements with the Russians, using our economic power as a bribe to obstruct their political advance.

I cannot believe that war is the best solution. No one won the last
war, and no one will win the next war. While I am in accord that we
need force and I am in accord that we need this force to preserve the
peace, I do not think that complete preparation for war is the proper approach as yet. . . .

I realize that I am an entirely unimportant cog in the wheel of our
work with the UN, but I have offered my resignation to the Secretary
since I can quite understand the difficulty of having some one so far
down the line openly criticize the Administration policies.

I deeply regret that I must write this letter.[15]

Mrs. Roosevelt's defection turned up the heat on a man who was already
under a variety of pressures in a controversy where Arab oil, the Jewish
vote, old friendships, and strategic geopolitical considerations were all at
stake.[16]

The beleaguered Truman refused to accept Mrs. Roosevelt's resignation. He implored her to remain, and assured her that her public statements
would not embarrass him. Still, she knew that if the State Department position won out, she was not likely to be reappointed to the U.S. delegation
to the United Nations.

A letter to David Gurewitsch on April 17 reveals that she was, in any
event, taking a hard look at the relationship between her private life and
her calling to public service: "The people I love mean more to me than all
the public things even if you do think that public affairs should be my
chief vocation. I only do the public things because there are a few close
people whom I love dearly & who matter to me above everything else.
There are not so many of them & you are now one of them and I shall just
have to try not to bother you too much!"[17] Her new friendship was to
prove an enduring source of comfort and companionship. For the rest of
her life, wrote Joseph Lash, "there was little she did that she did not share
with David, and, later on, with Edna, his wife."[18]

Charles Malik, meanwhile, was emerging as a major spokesman for
the Arab nations. Shuttling between his embassy in Washington and the

UN, he juggled a hectic schedule of ECOSOC meetings, caucuses among the Arab delegates, and speaking engagements in several American cities, where he tried to explain the mysterious Middle East to social clubs and church groups.

◢

Against this turbulent backdrop, the Human Rights Commission's drafting committee met for the second time, from May 3 to May 21, 1948, in New York. Their task was to prepare the drafts of the Declaration and the Covenant for discussion at the Commission's third meeting, slated to begin on May 24.

Comments on the "Geneva drafts" had been received from thirteen member states: Egypt, Norway, South Africa, Canada, the Netherlands, Australia, the United States, New Zealand, India, Sweden, Brazil, France, and Mexico. Many respondents complained that the Declaration was too long and complicated and urged the Commission to strive for a simpler, more inspirational document. Several wrote short notes expressing concerns about the compatibility of their own national law with parts of the Declaration. Sweden, for example, wanted clarification about the validity of its practices of mandatory blood tests in paternity and drunk-driving cases and reported that its present laws were not in full compliance with the freedom to change one's religion. Those laws, soon changed, forbade any member of the Swedish State Church to relinquish his or her membership, except to become a member of certain other congregations recognized by the state. Egypt wanted the drafters to make clear that the economic and social rights could be exercised only insofar as the economic conditions of each state permitted.

Eleanor Roosevelt opened the meeting by laying down some strict guidelines. "We have had plenty of experience in this Committee," she reminded them, "regarding discussion of general principles. In my opinion we shall gain nothing by discussing general principles further at this session. What we have to do is to confine ourselves to specific drafts. This is not the time for theoretical conjecture. Attention should be given to individual articles, always using the draft declaration and the draft convention produced by the Commission at Geneva as a basis of drafting, and incorporating suggestions of states represented on this committee and other states where appropriate."[19]

She then announced a grueling schedule: "We have nine working days, excluding today. I suggest that we adjourn for study of the comments from various governments and meet again tomorrow; then we take three days on the covenant, three days on implementation and three days on the declaration."

The surrounding circumstances could hardly have been more trying. With the British mandate set to expire on May 14, the crisis in the Middle East was rapidly coming to a head. The Commission's rapporteur was weighed down by responsibilities. Malik's diary entries for the day of the first meeting show a man under terrific strain.

Monday, May 3, 1948
    Had planned to leave early by plane. Didn't sleep well & was so terribly run down and tired that had to cancel early reservation & exchange for plane leaving at 1 p.m. Will make Mrs. Roosevelt's HR Drafting Comm. in p.m., but will miss session on Palestine in the a.m.
    p.m. Arab dels. New Am. plan—4 pts. 10 days uncondtl truce, 10 days extension of mandate. Agreed to cable it to our govts.
    Saw endless people. Eve. Wrote cables—was very tired, could not sleep.

On Tuesday, May 11, after a morning session in which the drafting committee refined the language of the Covenant's antidiscrimination provisions, Malik met with Arab delegates to discuss the statement they would issue a few days later, when their armies would march into Palestine to forcibly prevent the partition plan from going into effect. Malik wrote in his diary, "I stressed 3 pts: abs. protection of Jews & no discrimination whatsoever, abs. protection of holy places and extending hands to every power for pos. cooperation in the maintenance of peace & sec. in the M.E." After lunching with Mrs. Roosevelt and spending the afternoon in the Human Rights Commission, Malik met again with the other Arab delegates in the Waldorf-Astoria. To their final statement, his diary says, "I added one point, a public assurance that there will be no retaliation, no victimization of the Jews."

On Friday morning, May 14, the provisional government of Israel proclaimed a Jewish state. As far as anyone in the UN knew, the United States was still backing the State Department's trusteeship plan. That afternoon, as the Human Rights Commission drafting committee was turning from the Covenant to the Declaration, Malik sent an aide to take his place as rapporteur, arranging to be called if his presence was required. He then went to the General Assembly.

With the British mandate scheduled to end at six P.M., the General Assembly went into session at five o'clock. "Just after 6 p.m.," Malik wrote that night, "rumour started circulating in corridors that U.S. recognized Israel. Did not believe it at all. Colombian asked US Del. formally from rostrum to verify or deny rumor. Sayre [U.S.] got up and said—at about 6:20—true it came on ticker, but his del. had not rec'd any official confirmation. Making sure that it was true, Gromyko and [Cuba's Guillermo] Belt got up and attacked duplicity of U.S. policy. I started to write out a few notes. . . . I got up & said a few things—completely dumbfounded."

Within hours the armies of Egypt, Jordan, Syria, Lebanon, and Iraq moved into Palestine.

One can only imagine the tension the following Monday when Malik sat down with Roosevelt and Cassin for the drafting committee's final week of work. The meeting began with a moment of silence in memory of Lord Dukeston, who had died on May 14. Neither the minutes of the meeting, nor the memoirs of Roosevelt and Cassin, nor Malik's diary, disclose any signs that working relationships among the members were impaired.

Mrs. Roosevelt's column for May 15 contained only a passing reference to the UN. After recounting how she had tried to help a homeless man lying unconscious on the street and ignored by passersby, she noted, "And the next day, at Lake Success, as we argued about human rights at a committee meeting, I wondered how many human rights that poor man had. At heart I imagine I am really a country bumpkin—I like to know my neighbors and to have some sense of responsibility for them."[20]

On Thursday of that week Malik shared a cab with Cassin. They talked about Article 1, and Malik learned, to his disappointment, that France, perhaps in a gesture to the Soviets, was no longer supporting the words *reason and conscience*. From that point on, Malik became the principal defender of the Declaration's expression of faith in human intelligence and fellow-feeling.

That same week, dividing his time between the drafting committee and the Security Council, where Lebanon held a rotating seat, Malik had been struck by the eloquence of a young spokesman for the Jewish Agency, the official voice of the Jewish inhabitants of Palestine. One night he wrote in his diary, "I saw Eban outside and told him, you spoke very well."

The admiration between the antagonists seems to have been mutual. In his memoirs Abba Eban calls Malik "the leading political thinker among Arab scholars"[21] and "our most formidable adversary on the parliamentary floor." Eban speculated that Malik, a member of Lebanon's minority Greek Orthodox community, "was caught up in a tormenting conflict between his Arab patriotism and his Christian and humanistic values." He suspected, too, that while Malik's fellow Arabs applauded his rhetorical skills, they "doubted the authenticity of his anti-Zionist credentials."

It is hardly surprising that, during one of the most troubled periods in the history of the UN, the Human Rights Commission drafting committee was unable to complete its review of the Geneva draft. To make matters worse, the Soviets had sent yet another new man to represent them. Alexei P. Pavlov proved more difficult to deal with than any of his predecessors. It was his bourgeois background, some suspected, that made him go the extra distance to show what a good Communist he was.[22] As the drafting committee was just settling down to business, Mrs. Roosevelt was taken aback when Pavlov ("a big dramatic man with flowing white hair and a bristling black beard") proposed that the committee should scrap the Geneva draft and start all over.[23]

His government could not accept the draft as a basis for discussion, he said, because it was riddled with serious defects, including some provisions "which would violate the principle of sovereignty of states." His other complaints were that it lacked effective guarantees, overlooked the individual's obligations to the state, and "made no reference to the basic democratic principle that every effort should be made to combat fascism, nazism and racial hatred."

Pavlov's proposal to start afresh was shot down by the majority. They had, after all, invested many months in a process in which the Soviet Union had been represented. Mrs. Roosevelt then gently requested the newcomer to help improve the draft, asking him to keep in mind that "the world comprised many states with many forms of government and that they all had to work together."[24] Pavlov showed little disposition to cooperate with what he had pronounced to be a radically flawed project. He delivered several stock tirades on racism in the United States and on the need to deny rights such as assembly or asylum to "fascists or Nazis."

We now know that the obstreperous Pavlov was merely following a highly detailed script. An April 1948 Politburo memorandum instructs the Soviet delegate to declare that because the document does not sufficiently secure human rights, the Soviet Union finds it impossible to build upon it and will submit its own draft at a later time.[25] If that effort should fail, the memo continued, the delegate should propose a general discussion of the issues rather than a detailed article-by-article review of the Geneva draft. If that proposal should fail, the delegate is instructed to criticize the draft, emphasizing respect for national sovereignty, the need to fight against fascism and Nazism, and the need to conform the "half-hearted and false" antidiscrimination article to Article 123 of the Stalin Constitution, which not only condemned discrimination, but prohibited what we would now call "hate speech"—any propagation of racial or national exclusivity, hatred, or contempt. If the draft were put to a vote, the Soviet representative was instructed to abstain.

After rejecting Pavlov's proposal to hold a general discussion, the drafting committee began to go through the Geneva draft articles one by one. They were striving now to make the document clear enough to be readily understandable by men and women everywhere, as well as to achieve a level of generality that would leave each country and culture an appropriate degree of flexibility in interpreting and implementing its provisions. The group wound up its work on Friday, May 21, without having completed its review of the social and economic rights. Thus far, the text did not differ greatly from the Geneva draft. The full Commission met three days later to prepare the draft for final submission to ECOSOC.

The full Commission's last meeting got off to a bad start. The Ukrainian and Byelorussian representatives were not present, their visas having been held up by the United States, apparently in retaliation for the hassling of American diplomats by Moscow officials.[26] Pavlov was furious. At his insistence the meeting was adjourned for two days until the missing members arrived. In the interval, the working group of the drafting committee met to plan their presentation. After one of these sessions, Cassin told Malik that he had heard very good things from Jewish friends about Malik's concern for Jewish minorities in Arab lands.[27]

When the Commission reconvened, the group began to discuss the document article by article. Article 1 was now made expressly inclusive of women in accordance with the recommendations of Mrs. Mehta, the

Soviet Union, and the UN Commission on the Status of Women. Strangely, no one contested the word *brotherhood*. As revised, the article read "All human beings" instead of "All men" and provided that they should act toward one another "in a spirit of brotherhood" rather than "as brothers." Mrs. Roosevelt supported these changes but said she "wished to make it clear that equality did not mean identical treatment for men and women in all matters; there were certain cases, as for example the case of maternity benefits, where differential treatment was essential."[28]

P. C. Chang, with his government about to fall and the Americans seemingly resigned to that fact, was dispirited. He had lost enthusiasm for the statement he had once helped draft that "all human beings are endowed by nature with reason and conscience." He now proposed that they eliminate that "controversial" idea.

Malik was able to convince the group to retain this affirmation of human exceptionalism. He seemed to share James Madison's view of mankind: "As there is a degree of depravity in mankind which requires a certain degree of circumspection and distrust, so there are other qualities in human nature which justify a certain portion of esteem and confidence."[29]

Occasional successes in the Human Rights Commission provided Malik with some consolation in those weeks when, night after night, he returned from discussions of Palestine and wrote in his diary: "Tired, disgusted."

He was in a melancholy mood on Memorial Day, May 31, when he sat down to dinner in a waffle restaurant. His description of the meal reads like a metaphor for his feelings about politics. "The whole thing was disgustingly dirty. The cook in front of us touching everything with his hands—the meat, the potatoes, the bread, the waffle, the pieces of butter, the dollars and silver change, and finally with his dirty hands wiping his face. I ate the waffle."[30]

That same Memorial Day, John Humphrey wrote to his sister about a change in the dynamics of the Commission:

> It is a holiday here today, but I came to the office nevertheless. . . . The Human Rights Commission is in session, but it is working very slowly. . . . We are, of course, in the most difficult stage. In the past, it was largely individuals who were expressing their opinions and making their decisions, now it is governments. The tendency in the past, more-

over, was to slide over difficulties, to put them off; these must now be faced. Another thing is that the Russians are participating more actively. This is significant and even encouraging, but it does not make the work of the Commission any easier.[31]

It soon became apparent that the more active Russian presence was no cause for celebration. As the Commission moved through the draft provisions of the Declaration, Pavlov, adhering closely to his script, proposed amendments to almost every article. To freedom of speech, press, and assembly, he tried (unsuccessfully) to add "except to fascist and anti-democratic elements."[32] Though such a qualifier would strike most Americans as an unacceptable infringement of freedom of expression, it was by no means a uniquely Communist idea. The 1949 German Basic Law, prepared under the watchful eyes of the Allies, contains a ban on anti-democratic political parties and provides for forfeiture of certain basic rights, including freedom of speech, if they are used "in order to combat the free democratic basic order."[33]

Again and again, as political and civil liberties were discussed, Pavlov proposed adding such qualifiers as "in accordance with the law of the State" or "except as determined by national legislation." Several members of the Commission had become concerned since the Geneva meeting, however, about references to the role of the state inserted in response to interventions by the congenial Bogomolov. Cassin, Malik, and Wilson now resisted any language that might foster the impression that the state was the *sole* guarantor of human rights. In a world faced with a tendency toward statism, Malik said, it was important to respect the "intermediate loyalties" to family, friends, and so on from which "real freedom" springs. Cassin agreed. It was essential, he wrote in his memoirs, for human rights to "be envisaged in relation not only to the State, but to the different social groups to which [one] belongs: family, tribe, city, profession, religion, and more broadly the entire human community."[34]

The Commission's repeated rebuffs to Pavlov's attempts to highlight the role of the state probably destroyed whatever small hope there had been of Soviet support for the Declaration. The draft now made clear that responsibility for protecting human rights belonged not only to nation-states, but to people and groups above and below the national level.

The reduced emphasis on the role of the state in enforcing human rights did not mean that the drafters saw supranational or subnational authorities as displacing national ones. This point was so important that Cassin chose to emphasize it in his 1968 Nobel Peace Prize acceptance speech. "There is no room for doubt," Cassin said, "concerning the essential question whether the nations have retained or lost their traditional exclusive jurisdiction over the treatment of their citizens. That national jurisdiction will always be at the base. It will remain primary. But it will no longer be exclusive."[35]

The Soviet fears were understandable. In 1948 the Soviets were outnumbered in the UN, just as the United States would be a few years later when many new nations were granted membership. Faced with a more or less hostile majority, they were in no mood to relax their defense of national sovereignty, which they took to be protected by the domestic jurisdiction language of the UN Charter. The hard-liners they sent to the United Nations showed little disposition, and had no permission, to budge on that point.

Pavlov, even more than the Soviet delegates who preceded him, put a strain on Mrs. Roosevelt's legendary people skills.

From the beginning, one of Mrs. Roosevelt's greatest contributions to the Human Rights Commission consisted of fostering and providing a setting for cross-cultural understanding. Her dinners and teas enabled delegates to get to know one another as human beings and to exchange views off the record.

It was not the food that made her salon a popular gathering place. This, after all, was the woman who had served hot dogs and beer to the king and queen of England when the royal couple had visited the United States. Commenting on a daughter-in-law's concern that the White House meals were "not very good," the First Lady admitted, "As I had never been able to pretend that I knew anything about food, I had to be very humble about her criticisms and try to remedy the defects. Not being conscious of them myself, I'm afraid I was not very successful."[36]

John Humphrey recalled one evening when she served "the toughest roast beef I have ever eaten."[37] On another occasion she beamingly asked René Cassin to uncork a musty bottle of wine that had been in the cellar of her uncle Theodore Roosevelt. Humphrey, who was also there, recounted that Cassin "opened it with great ceremony, proposed a toast and we all lifted our glasses. The wine had turned to vinegar. But none of us flickered an eyelash—and Mrs. Roosevelt never knew what she had given us."[38]

But she had found the Russians resistant to her charm. In her memoirs she reflected ruefully, "My practice of inviting delegates of various nations to tea or to dinner sometimes worked out well with the Russians and on other occasions didn't work at all."[39] Ever the realist, she resigned herself to the fact that the Eastern European delegates, whatever their personal inclinations, were probably not free to engage in informal give-and-take. "It was difficult to know any Russian well and I suppose the Kremlin planned it that way. After a good many attempts, I decided that it was really impossible to have a private and frank talk with Russian officials."

Pavlov succumbed just once, and only briefly. After dinner and a musical evening at Mrs. Roosevelt's Washington Square apartment, Pavlov waited until his assistant had gone to fetch their hats, then whispered to his hostess, "Madame, you like the music of Tchaikovsky. So do I!" That, she said, "was as close as I ever came to getting a frank and confidential expression of opinion from a Soviet official."

The most prolonged arguments of the Commission's third and final session involved the still thorny question of precisely how to frame the social and economic rights, which now included rights to work; education; rest and leisure; an adequate standard of living, including food, clothing, housing, medical care, and social services; and security in unemployment and old age. The disputes centered on their implementation and on their relation to traditional political and civil liberties. Unlike the "older" rights, economic and social rights are more dependent for their realization on a country's economic circumstances, and the means of implementation vary more widely according to each country's political structure. But how were these factors to be taken into account? And how could the articles be drafted without either downplaying or exaggerating the importance of the newer rights in relation to the old?

Mrs. Roosevelt led off with a strong endorsement of the new rights in principle (emphasizing as usual that the Declaration was not legally self-executing). The United States, she said, "favored the inclusion of economic and social rights in the Declaration, for no personal liberty could exist without economic security and independence. Men in need were not free men."[40] The Declaration should not, she went on, try to specify the methods for ensuring the realization of those rights, because methods of implementation "would necessarily vary from one country to another and such variations should be considered not only inevitable but salutary." The Soviet Union was against any language that would appear to relegate social and economic rights to an inferior rank. It filed two draft proposals to emphasize the role of the state as guarantor of social security.

The United Kingdom, seeking to avoid giving the impression that the new rights took priority over traditional political and civil rights, opposed making a detailed list of the new rights. But it was too late in the day to make such a drastic change.

Progress was stalled for days while the commissioners engaged in debates that Cassin recalled as among the most emotional in the Commission's history.[41] Neither of the cold war antagonists wanted to budge on the superiority of their respective approaches. For the two superpowers, it was a face-off between central planning and programs that left substantial room for the free operation of the market. Representatives of developing nations, for their part, feared the political hazards of recognizing a fundamental human right to things their governments could not possibly deliver in the near future. Hansa Mehta and Omar Loutfi reminded everyone that poorer nations such as India and Egypt could hope to move only by gradual steps toward making the new rights a reality. Australia insisted that the differences between the new and the old rights had to be clearly emphasized.

Malik tried to move things forward by proposing a new general article to contextualize the relationship between the new rights and the old: a provision for the right to a social and political order in which all the Declaration's rights and freedoms could be realized. This proposal met with general approval and eventually became the Declaration's Article 28, but it did not resolve the impasse. Loutfi pressed for a "general principle" to introduce the social, economic, and cultural rights. Cassin tried his hand at such a "chapeau," or umbrella provision, affirming "Everyone as a member of society has the economic, social, and cultural rights enumerated below, whose fulfillment should be made possible by the State separately or by international collaboration."[42] But this did not satisfy Loutfi and others who, like Mrs. Mehta, insisted that economic and social rights could be guaranteed only in accordance with the economic and social resources of each country. Loutfi (along with Malik, Cassin, and Roosevelt) also wished to make clear that the state was not the only institution through which these rights might be promoted. With the support of the United Kingdom, he moved successfully to specify that the rights in question would be implemented "in accordance with the organization and re-sources of each State."[43]

This breakthrough enabled the Commission to move forward, though the Soviet-bloc delegates reserved their right to enter objections at the end of the process. The reference to "organization" of the state meant that countries with planned and market economies could proceed in their re-spective ways to make the new rights a reality, and the reference to "re-sources" took much of the pressure off developing nations. The end was in sight. At last the Commission was ready to turn to the long-postponed task of preparing a Preamble.

On Friday, June 11, Malik noted in his diary: "Was asked by Mrs. Roo-sevelt to prepare Preamble over weekend." Malik's diary entry for Mon-day, June 14, permits a glimpse of the taut nerves and frayed tempers that must have affected the commissioners in that tense period when events in the Middle East were weighing heavily on their minds. War had been rag-ing for nearly a month between Israel's defense force, the Haganah, and the united Arab armies, and a refugee crisis had been created by the flight of most Palestinian Arabs from Jewish-held land. Under pressure from the UN Security Council, where both the United States and the Soviet Union had denounced the Arab invasion, a four-week truce had been declared on June 11, but no one expected it to last.

Mon. June 14, 1948
Did not catch my morn. plane for N.Y. Had to take a later one, ∴ Missed morn. meeting. On plane worked & finished preamble.
Arrived late in Lake Success, missing morn. meeting. What a terri-ble man Chang is! Full of hatred and venom and bitterness. My text of the preamble was mainly adopted; there were additions by Cassin. Chang wants to delete the word "inalienable"—just because I had added it. Nor does the independent article I had suggested on the right to a good social and international order seem to have much chance for success.
I feel a bit dizzy today & tired. Went to St. Patrick's this eve.[44]

For the Preamble, Malik put on his philosopher's cap. He began with a statement about why it is important to recognize human rights.[45] That clause gave "dignity" the same prominence at the head of the Declaration as it had been given in the UN Charter.

> WHEREAS recognition of the inherent dignity and the equal and inalienable rights of all persons is the foundation of peace, freedom and justice in the world,

For the next three clauses, Malik drew on Cassin's draft:

> WHEREAS ignorance and contempt for human rights have before and during the last world war resulted in barbarous acts which outraged the conscience of mankind, and
>
> WHEREAS the opening lines of the Charter reaffirm faith in fundamental human rights, in the dignity and worth of the human person and in the equal rights of men and women, and
>
> WHEREAS it is a purpose of the United Nations to achieve international co-operation in promoting and encouraging respect for human rights and for fundamental freedoms for all,

Then the philosopher added the cautionary note:

> WHEREAS this purpose can be attained only on the basis of a common understanding of the nature of these rights and freedoms,

Malik concluded with a proclamation clause based on Cassin's original, with the addition—from a U.S. proposal—of a description of the document as a standard of achievement. The proclamation emphasized the character of the Declaration as a statement of ideals and goals.

> NOW THEREFORE the General Assembly recognizes in the following solemn Declaration the essential rights and freedoms which, constituting the dignity and worth of the human person, should form a common standard of achievement for all nations, and calls upon every individual and every organ of society, national and international, to strive by teaching and education to promote their respect and by progressive measures to secure their universal recognition and observance.

The next day Chang was still getting on Malik's nerves (and presumably Malik on Chang's), but work on the Declaration went forward more smoothly than Malik had expected. To the draft Preamble, the Commission added a reference to the UN Charter's purpose to promote "better standards of life in larger freedom" and an important clause emphasizing the rule of law:

> WHEREAS it is essential, if mankind is not to be compelled as a last resort to rebel against tyranny and oppression, that human rights should be protected by a regime of law, . . .

Malik and Chang had a working lunch that day to prepare the agenda for the forthcoming ECOSOC meeting. Malik was frantically juggling his various duties.

Tuesday, June 15, 1948.
a.m. HR's. Better with Chang today. He agreed to the lifting of the parentheses around "inalienable." I fought for the inclusion of the article on minorities. Suggested a mildest possible form: "Cultural groups shall not be denied the right to free self-development." Was defeated. Americans and Latinos dead against this idea.
Lunch with Chang & Hyde [Louis Hyde, an adviser to U.S. delegation] on agenda ECOSOC & method of procedure. Chang not practical. Also he cannot forget himself.
Spoke for 20 minutes to a crowd of graduate students.
p.m. Security Council. Pal[estine]. Gromyko tried unsuccessfully to have a resolution passed whereby Russia would be able to send military observers to Palestine.

The "article on minorities" for which Malik fought unsuccessfully would have given people belonging to well-defined linguistic, ethnic, or religious minority groups the right to establish their own educational, cultural, and religious institutions and to use their own language in the courts. It had been part of the draft Declaration from the beginning in one form or another and was supported by the UN Sub-Commission on the Prevention of Discrimination and the Protection of Minorities. The principle represented official policy in multicultural nations such as Lebanon, the Soviet Union, and Yugoslavia, but it was so contrary to the American idea of a "melting pot" nation, and to the assimilationist approach to diversity in France, that no common ground could be achieved, even on Malik's mild compromise.

Explaining why the United States was opposed, Mrs. Roosevelt said she thought it was evident that the aim of states in accepting immigrants was "to make them part of the nation."[46] Unless all citizens could speak the same language, she went on, "there was the danger that public order might be disrupted by persons who might not understand their duties as citizens of the country in which they were a minority." It was not, she insisted, "a question of teaching children in a language different from that of the majority, but of adult persons who would be unable to assume their duties as citizens of the larger country."

Egypt's Loutfi supported the United States' position, saying that the Commission was concerned "with a declaration of rights of individuals, and not minorities" and that the rights of the latter could be safeguarded by international conventions.[47] (The idea would return as part of the right of peoples to self-determination recognized in the two 1966 Covenants that, together with the Declaration, became known as the "International Bill of Rights.")

By the end of the week, after an informal subcommittee made a number of stylistic revisions and consolidated some articles, reducing the total number from thirty-three to twenty-eight, the draft was ready for a vote. Pavlov and the socialist bloc continued to insist that the social and economic articles were too weak to be acceptable.

The general discussion on Friday, June 18, the day of the vote, was one long wrangle, with Pavlov complaining bitterly about the document's lack of measures to combat fascism, the absence of provisions for implementation, and the omission of specific references to the obligations of individuals to the state.[48]

Finally, in the early evening, the Declaration was approved by the Human Rights Commission, with twelve votes in favor and none opposed. Pavlov, the Ukraine's Klekovkin, and Byelorussia's Stepanenko, in line with instructions issued before the meeting had begun, abstained and filed a minority report. Though Tito had declared his independence from the Soviet bloc that year, Yugoslavia's representative joined the abstainers.

Under the circumstances, Mrs. Roosevelt must have been heartened that the Eastern bloc at least did not vote against it. To Malik's American assistant, Howard Schomer, it seemed that the face of the chairman after the vote was showing strain as well as relief. "A long day," Schomer commented as they headed for the elevator. "Yes," Mrs. Roosevelt admitted, it was "a bit fatiguing. But worth it!"[49]

A few days later she summed up her reaction to the meeting for the readers of her column. "I think, on the whole, the International Declaration of Human Rights is a good declaration,"[50] she began. It would be adopted as a nonbinding statement of principles by the General Assembly. Later it would be "completed" by a Covenant with implementation provisions to be signed by individual nations. "The Covenant," she explained, "will be a simpler document in one way. It will have to cover fewer rights. But in another way it will be more complicated because the way those rights are to be assured to people throughout the world, under law, must be spelled out, and every nation in ratifying the Covenant—which will have the weight of a treaty—must be prepared to change its domestic laws so that it will be able to live up to its undertakings in the Covenant."

In the course of their June meeting, the commissioners regularly referred to the draft document as a "universal" rather than "international" Declaration, though the change of title did not become official until December 1948.[51] The Declaration was now ready to be forwarded to the Economic and Social Commission.* Those who had signed off on the document were not completely satisfied, but they belonged to a generation that had learned not to expect perfection in human affairs. As they launched their fragile paper boat upon the troubled seas of world politics in the summer of 1948, the civil war in China was nearing its end and fighting was about to resume in the Middle East. The Iron Curtain had descended around Eastern Europe, and the postwar alliance had definitively collapsed on June 24, when Stalin precipitated the gravest crisis since war's end by blockading all land and water traffic in and out of Berlin.

Earlier that year, ECOSOC had elected a new president, a rising young diplomat named Charles Malik.

---

*The Commission's draft appears as appendix 5.

Alexei Pavlov and Charles Malik at the UN Economic and Social Council.

CHAPTER 8

AUTUMN IN PARIS

Charles Malik Takes the Helm

E leanor Roosevelt spent the summer of 1948 at Hyde Park, entertaining family and friends and preparing to present the Declaration to the
UN's third committee in Paris that fall. She invited her eighteen-year-old
grandson, Curtis "Buzz" Dall, to join her on the trip, telling his mother,
Anna, to buy him a tuxedo and have him brush up on his French. Then, in
August, came the shocking news that Buzz had contracted polio. Anna,
who was in the midst of dealing with the failure of a newspaper business
she had begun with her second husband, and with the breakup of that marriage, was distraught. Eleanor, practiced in adversity, wrote to encourage
her daughter:

> What I hope is that with a light case . . . involvement of any muscles
> may be temporary. You remember how badly Father's hands & arms
> were affected & they were normal very quickly. A prayer is in my heart
> for you & for him all the time. . . . If by some marvelous chance he can
> still go with me I will see he gets a rest & good food & not too much
> work. . . . If you need cash there are always "things" I can sell & get a
> few thousand.[1]

"When a child is ill," she added, "you know that the other losses were of
little importance, his life & happiness is all that counts."

The young man's case, to the family's great relief, was a mild one, and on September 13 Buzz was strong enough to board the SS *America* with his grandmother to witness one of her greatest triumphs.

⌁

Sharing that triumph, and equally responsible for it, would be Charles Malik. "The year 1948," Malik recalled in later years, "witnessed the oddest coincidence of my life at the United Nations."[2] In February Malik, the rapporteur of the Commission on Human Rights, was elected president of the Economic and Social Council, to which the Commission had to submit its draft Declaration. That fall he was elected chairman of the UN's third committee (the Social, Humanitarian, and Cultural Affairs Committee), which had to present the Declaration for approval by the General Assembly at its December meeting in Paris. Thus Malik found himself "as Rapporteur submitting to myself, as President of the Economic and Social Council at its summer session in Geneva, the draft of the declaration prepared by the Commission, and then submitting, as President of ECOSOC, again to myself as Chairman of the Third Committee, the draft text as passed on by ECOSOC." The delegate from tiny Lebanon was wearing three big hats as the Declaration moved through its crucial final stages in the fall of 1948. By the time he finally returned to his native Lebanon, he would also be elected president of the General Assembly (in 1958) and would serve on the powerful UN Security Council.

How can one explain this meteoric rise of a man who felt himself profoundly unsuited for politics? This was the man who had written to his old teacher Alfred North Whitehead after the San Francisco conference, "My interest in politics and diplomacy is only temporary. My heart lies definitely in teaching and speculation to which I shall return as soon as I find my mission reasonably fulfilled."[3] This was the philosophy professor who had alternately despaired of mastering political skills and despised himself for trying to play the game. Malik's diaries disclose that the sense of being an alien in the world of politics caused him much internal torment. How did he become the suave diplomat elected by secret ballot to so many key UN positions? How had he come so far in a mere three years?

Charles Habib Malik was the son of the village doctor in Bitirram, a town of five hundred surrounded by mountains and olive groves. The Lebanon of his youth was a unique blend of Islamic, Christian, Arabic, and French cultures, its population about equally divided between Christians and Muslims. The Maliks were Greek Orthodox Arabs. Their gifted son, Charles, whom they sent to an American Protestant mission school, grew up speaking Arabic, French, and English and loving to read the Bible.

At the American University of Beirut he studied mathematics and physics and developed a passionate interest in the philosophy of science. "My reading of the works of Alfred North Whitehead fired me with an ambition to study under him at Harvard, so I became determined to go there," he told E. J. Kahn in a *New Yorker* interview.[4] Whitehead responded encouragingly to Malik's application.

Howard Schomer, who later served as an aide to Malik at the UN, was a graduate student at Harvard when the striking foreigner arrived in the fall of 1932. Charles Malik, he recalled, "could have modeled for Michelangelo as Jeremiah. Enormous head, immense arc of a nose, burning black eyes, bristling curly black hair and bushy black eyebrows."[5]

Malik flourished in the new environment, quickly finding intellectual companionship. As Schomer described him in that first year:

> Malik was quite impecunious, always wearing the same outfit—a ridiculous greenish tweed jacket and knickers—and he lived off-campus sharing a quite cheap room with a budding atomic physicist. He invited a few students from various disciplines to drop in Tuesday nights for free-wheeling exchanges of ideas and concerns. Before our brainstorming ended toward 2:00 A.M. we usually had consumed quantities of oranges or other fruit. Charles launched the evening's talkfest by reading a brief provocative passage from some current theologian, philosopher, scientist, or intellectual historian.

In these discussions Malik displayed the turn of mind that at first impeded his progress as a diplomat, for, according to Schomer, "he was clearly out to get to the bottom of any serious issue. Hating bland smoothing over of significant disagreements, he was single-mindedly in search of the truth."

The studious foreigner impressed his teachers enough to win one of Harvard's coveted traveling fellowships, which he used, in 1935, to study with Martin Heidegger at Freiburg University. "While there," he told E. J. Kahn, "I realized I couldn't remain where Whitehead had remained. If I may so put it, I outgrew him."[6]

But after being beaten up on the streets of Freiburg on account of his Semitic looks, Malik also realized that he could not remain in National Socialist Germany. On his return to Harvard before the term of his fellowship was over, he tried to explain what he had seen:

What can I say to impress on you the absolute ubiquity of the Hitler spirit? SA and SS uniforms everywhere. Hitler youth, Hitler girls, Arbeitsdienst, the new army. Swastika flags sticking out of every window on official occasions. Columns of uniformed men—strong, healthy, hopeful, confident—marching, marching; singing, singing. National-socialist papers the same everywhere; the same controlled news, the same terrible hatred against communists, the French, the Jews and what they call the colored races. The Professors at the University beginning their classes with the Nazi salute to which the students respond. On the southern side of the University inscribed lately "Dem ewigen Deutschtum"—to the eternal German race—, to counterbalance what had been for a long time inscribed on the western side, "Die Wahrheit wird euch freimachen"—the truth shall make you free.[7]

Back at Harvard, Malik finished his doctoral thesis, "The Metaphysics of Time in the Philosophies of Whitehead and Heidegger," and returned home in 1937 to teach at the American University of Beirut.

From 1937 to 1945 Malik was happily settled in what he believed to be his life's work: "mediating the things of the mind and the spirit to the youth of the Arab world."[8] When Schomer visited him in Beirut, he found his old schoolmate "had already gathered a group of young professors of diverse backgrounds—Christian, Islamic, Jewish, Marxist, radical secularists—for fortnightly evenings, striving to build a strong bridge between Middle Eastern and Western cultures and future leaders."

As Lebanon moved toward independence from the French mandate imposed at the end of World War I, Malik's intelligence, his fluency in many languages, and his following among Muslim and Christian students alike did not go unnoticed among the power elite in that country of fewer than a million inhabitants. One summer evening in 1944, Malik and his wife, Eva, were invited to a party at the home of President Bechara El-Khoury. It was a gala affair, attended by a hundred or more of the new nation's political and economic leaders. The young academic did not enjoy his first outing with the rich and famous. In his diary he described it as a "terrible, awful, horrible" evening.[9] "I do not belong in this crowd of unreality and untruth," he wrote. He was repelled by the atmosphere of "snobbishness, ruthlessness, commercialism and sensuality." Though completely at ease in any kind of intellectual gathering, he felt "a complete foreigner" among businessmen and politicians.

The new country's leaders, however, had apparently decided that the Harvard-educated professor might do as their envoy to the United States. They soon made overtures along those lines, appealing to his patriotism. A man reputed to be the owner of one of the finest stables of Arabian horses in the world told him, "I love my horses, but I have put them aside for a time. You must put aside your books."[10] His letters and journal do not reveal what finally swayed him—love of country, intellectual curiosity, the thought of future regrets about a path not taken, desire to make a difference at a historic moment—but on Christmas Eve 1944 Malik confessed ruefully to his diary that he had "fallen to political worldly seduction."

His outsider status now filled him with anxiety of a different kind. Other political men have "followers, supporters, parties, comrades who stand by them. But I am all alone." "I can still refuse going," he wrote. Then, a few days later, he told himself that it was only a temporary job. On April 6, 1945, Charles and Eva Malik set out on the long journey by propeller aircraft from Beirut to Washington. There, on April 19, he presented his diplomatic credentials to President Truman, who had taken office upon the death of Roosevelt just a week earlier. Immediately thereafter the new envoy took off for his first assignment: to represent Lebanon at the founding conference of the United Nations in San Francisco.

When the UN created the Economic and Social Council, Lebanon was given one of ECOSOC's eighteen seats. This important post forced Malik to travel back and forth frequently between the embassy in Washington and UN meetings in New York. ECOSOC was established by the UN Charter, along with the Security Council, as one of the organization's principal organs. Its duties included investigating and making recommendations to the General Assembly on international economic and social questions and supervising more specialized bodies, such as the Human Rights Commission.

During his early days at the UN, Malik felt almost as much out of place as he had at El-Khoury's party. He was isolated, without allies or intellectual companions. In notes scribbled to himself during ECOSOC's fall 1946 meeting, Malik agonized about the role of his small, newly independent country: "When Lebanon was under the wing of France, France was our friend. But then we had no chance to sit in international councils. Now France is weak; we have a chance to sit in such councils. But who is our friend? Who is our politico-socio-ideological friend? Who can give us counsel, friendship, guidance, support in the cold international plane? France is impossible. England doesn't care, it only 'uses.' Russia will never answer to our deep needs. America believes in the United Nations—that is the extent of her interest in others. The Arab world is more lost than we are; it is not a support, it must be supported. The loneliness, the unutterable loneliness of Lebanon."[11]

Those reflections were prompted, Malik fully understood, by "a deeper existential loneliness in my heart." Sitting in the dining room of his New York hotel one evening, he wrote: "I went to the Council room this morning in the car alone. I sat there at the Council table alone. I almost sat at lunch alone, but for the kindness of the Yugoslav delegate who asked me to sit with him. Last evening I was all alone back at the hotel. When I returned this afternoon I returned in the car alone. I am now all alone eating at the restaurant of the hotel. A feeling of void and blankness overtakes me. I must bear my loneliness. Drink and sex can never relieve it. On the contrary, they cover it up, for a time only. Then it comes back with added force. It cannot be evaded, it must be faced." His Christian faith, far from easing his mind in this period, intensified his dissatisfaction with himself. The diaries reveal an intensely prayerful man, who endured long periods of seeking without finding spiritual consolation.

Over the months that followed, Malik gradually turned his loneliness into a source of strength. He gained a reputation for independence, for which he was respected even by those who opposed his positions. Instead of dining alone, he began to invite others to join him. He was discovering by trial and error what Eleanor Roosevelt knew in her bones about the political importance of personal relationships.

Early in 1948 the *New York Herald Tribune* reported that Malik was the leading candidate for the presidency of ECOSOC and that his popularity was "based on his personal U.N. record and is maintained despite criticism from some sources that Lebanon, as a member of the Arab bloc defying the U.N. decision to partition Palestine, should not be singled out at this time for one of the U.N.'s highest honors."[12] In February 1948, in the midst of the Palestine crisis, Malik was elected by secret ballot to the presidency of ECOSOC.

He had become one of the best-known figures in the UN, and one much sought after by journalists, perhaps because he never lost his love of explaining, arguing, and analyzing. His striking appearance made him a favorite of political cartoonists such as Alois Derso and Emery Kelen, who described him puckishly in the introduction to their book of United Nations caricatures: "Malik of Lebanon is a tall, broad-shouldered giant, with a formidable nose that would make Durante, Fields, and Cyrano tremble together. His curly hair is as untameable as his passion for debate. When he talks, his strong body waves like a palm tree in a storm, and his voice is thunder."[13]

That Malik should be president of ECOSOC in 1948 was fortuitous for the fate of the Declaration. As the Human Rights Commission's parent body, ECOSOC had to decide whether the Declaration was ready to be presented to the General Assembly's Third Committee on Social, Humanitarian, and Cultural Affairs, where Mrs. Roosevelt had received her baptism by fire at the first UN meeting. The third committee would scrutinize the document in open deliberations before turning it over to the General Assembly for final approval. Owing to the deterioration of the international situation, most observers believed that if the Declaration was not adopted at the General Assembly's fall 1948 meeting, it would be tabled indefinitely.

ECOSOC's most influential members were hard-nosed politicians. As a group they were, in John Humphrey's words, "not distinguished by their sympathy for the Human Rights Program."[14] This was the case with representatives of the major powers who had not been part of the human rights process—men such as Willard Thorp, the American assistant secretary of state for economic affairs; Hector McNeil, the British Labour government's minister of state for foreign affairs; and French socialist leader Pierre Mendès-France. To make matters worse, the USSR's representative in ECOSOC was the redoubtable Pavlov. No doubt that was why Bogomolov had advised the Politburo after the Geneva meeting that Soviet efforts to water down the human rights program would fare better in ECOSOC than in the Human Rights Commission.

It was a gloomy John Humphrey who traveled to Geneva for the Economic and Social Council meeting beginning on July 19, 1948. The draft

Declaration was but one of many items on a crowded agenda that had to be covered before the six-week session ended. Humphrey, present in his capacity as director of the Secretariat's Human Rights Division, became increasingly nervous as days and weeks passed with no action on the item he deemed to be most important. In his diary he let off steam over what he saw as utterly inept leadership on Malik's part. Humphrey complained that the president kept the draft Declaration in a subcommittee that he insisted on chairing himself and where he "invites debate, does little to direct the discussion, and tries to be everybody's friend."[15] To Humphrey it seemed that Malik was allowing the delegates to "ride off furiously in every direction." He could not understand why Malik had allowed many precious days to be taken up with women's issues or why he permitted Pavlov to talk "ten times at least as much as any other delegate."

Malik was distracted by the situation in Palestine, where the Arab armies had suffered a series of resounding defeats between the end of the June 11 truce and the commencement of a second UN-imposed truce on July 18. He seems, however, to have known what he was doing. On August 26, unable to complete the human rights part of its agenda, ECOSOC voted unanimously and without discussion to transmit the draft Declaration without changes to the General Assembly's third committee for the next round of scrutiny. It was, as Cassin later put it, "an implicit vote of approval."[16] Malik had been inept like a fox.

PARIS, SEPTEMBER 1948

The UN General Assembly chose to hold its fall 1948 meeting in Paris in order, it was said, to conduct its business at a sensible remove from the final weeks of the American presidential election, in which Harry Truman was engaged in a close race against New York's Republican governor, Thomas E. Dewey.

The tension between Russia and the United States may have played a role in the decision, too. In June, after Stalin attempted to force the Western occupational forces out of Berlin by blockading all land and water traffic, Truman had ordered a full-scale airlift. Since then American and British transport planes laden with food and supplies had been flying across Soviet-occupied East Germany into Berlin twenty-four hours a day. That same month, covert action by American agents was stepped up after the National Security Council instructed the CIA to conduct "propaganda, economic warfare, preventive direct action, including sabotage, antisabotage, demolition and evacuation measures; subversion against hostile states, including assistance to underground resistance movements, guerillas and refugee liberation groups, and support of indigenous anti-communist elements in threatened countries of the free world."[17] With the Berlin blockade, Mrs. Roosevelt's hopes for cooperation with the Soviets had dimmed. Stalin's tactics, she wrote in "My Day," "explain why we no longer seem to consider the Russians are our Allies."[18]

Another dangerous situation was brewing in Korea. After the war, the Allies had promised independence to that former Japanese protectorate but had "temporarily" divided it into a Soviet zone in the north and an American zone in the south. In 1947 the UN General Assembly had voted to establish a commission to supervise elections leading to the formation of an independent government in a unified Korea, but the Soviet-dominated regime in the north refused entry to UN officials. In May 1948, at the insistence of the United States, the UN went ahead with elections in the south, and on August 15 the Republic of Korea was declared. Ten days later North Korea held its own elections and constituted itself as the Democratic People's Republic of Korea. With each republic claiming to be the sole legitimate government of Korea, the stage was set for war.

⚓

Paris beckoned. The French capital was beginning to revive as the City of Light, and the delegates enjoyed a round of dinners in fine restaurants, gay parties, concerts, and theater evenings. Mrs. Roosevelt nonetheless observed the toll the war had taken on the inhabitants of Paris—the straitened circumstances of her French hosts and the pale, drawn faces of men and women in the streets.

> The French people are badly off. If you walk around on a Sunday or watch them going down into the Metro you very quickly realize that most of the people you see look tired and listless. . . . The older people uniformly look badly.
>
> The French have done their best to receive their guests with warmth and with their customary hospitality. When we have gone to their apartments they tried to warm them up for us and to give us all kinds of food in the lavish ways of days gone by. Only now and then by a casual sen-

tence do you realize what they have gone through. . . . [One woman] said, rather sadly, "It takes a long time to restore the soul of a conquered country. You are free, but you know that you have been beaten. You cringe because you have known the conqueror's touch."[19]

John Humphrey recalled the political atmosphere that fall as "charged to the point of explosion by the Cold War with irrelevant recriminations coming from both sides."[20] The officers of the Human Rights Commission, Roosevelt, Chang, Malik, and Cassin (now a second vice president of the Commission), gathered early in Paris. All were convinced that, given the state of East-West relations, it was now or never for the Declaration. The team, in their different ways, worked to smooth the progress of their draft through the third committee.

René Cassin was still living on the Boulevard Saint-Michel in the same apartment he had occupied on the day he had decided to join de Gaulle in London. As a reminder of the death sentence delivered against him during the war, he kept on his door a black seal placed there by the Gestapo. In his memoirs Cassin wrote that "on a number of occasions" in the fall of 1948, "I received discreet personal encouragements from the Papal Nuncio Roncalli."[21] Angelo Roncalli was then a popular mediator between conservative churchmen and a younger, more socially active, clergy. Ten years later, at age seventy-seven, he would be elected pope. As John XXIII he remained an advocate of social reforms to improve the lot of workers and the poor and convened the Second Vatican Council in 1962 to consider measures for renewal of the church in the modern world. There were many correspondences between his own thoughts on peace and justice and the Universal Declaration, which he praised in his encyclical *Peace on Earth* as "an act of the highest importance."

P. C. Chang arrived in Paris suffering from heart disease and disappointed by the West's apparent indifference to the fate of China. Born into a mercantile family in 1893, Chang was a young boy when seething resentment of foreign influence in China had erupted into the Boxer Rebellion of 1898. After that uprising was put down by the armies of Britain, France, Russia, the United States, Germany, and Japan, this formidable consortium of nations aroused further ill feeling among the Chinese by exacting huge financial reparations. The United States alone chose to return some of those funds in the form of scholarships for advanced study in the United States by Chinese students. The precocious Peng-chun Chang was one of the beneficiaries of that gesture, earning a doctorate under John Dewey at Columbia University in 1921.

Though Chang's intellectual odyssey took him far afield, like Malik, he knew how to come home. By the time Japan attacked and invaded China in 1937, Chang was one of China's most respected educators, well known also as a playwright and literary critic. He joined the anti-Japanese resistance at Nankai University near Beijing, and when the Japanese closed in on the area, he fled for his life, disguised as a woman.[22] Upon reaching safety, he was recruited by the Chinese government to help make Europeans and Americans aware of wholesale massacres such as the infamous "Rape of Nanking," in which three hundred thousand Chinese civilians were said to have been killed by Japanese soldiers.

When Chang was called to full-time diplomatic service in the 1940s, he brought to his first ambassadorial posts in Turkey and Chile a genuine curiosity about other societies and an almost missionary zeal to promote understanding of Chinese culture abroad. In 1942, for example, while serving in Turkey, Chang accepted an invitation to Baghdad, Iraq, where he delivered two lectures: the first on reciprocal influences and common ground between Chinese and Arabic cultures; the second on the relation between Confucianism and Islam.[23]

A 1947 State Department memorandum describes Chang as "one of China's outstanding liberals . . . probably not a member of the Kuomintang and, in any case, not an active party man." By September 1948 Chang must have been close to despair. His government was in a shambles, due largely to its own malfeasance. And the West, which had once turned a deaf ear to reports of Japanese atrocities, was now standing by again as the Red Army moved toward Beijing. Chang put his shoulder to the wheel, however, and used his talents to good effect in the coming debates.

The occasional skirmishes between Chang and Malik in the Human Rights Commission had been partly clashes between two strong personalities, partly a confrontation between religious and secular worldviews, and partly disagreements about how far one could go in the direction of pragmatic compromises without putting truth, and therefore universality,

up for grabs. Malik believed the Declaration should be anchored more ex-
plictly in "nature," Chang thought it better to leave it up to each culture to
supply its own account of the philosophical underpinnings of human
rights. Both men's ideas had been unsettled by the "transvaluation of values" in the post-Nietzschean, postwar world, but neither was ready to give
up on values altogether.

In the third committee, putting their rivalry aside, Malik and Chang
made a formidable duo when they joined forces. Later, viewing that turbulent time through the soft lenses of memory, Malik wrote, "Those were
great days twenty years ago when we were in the throes of elaborating for
final submission to the General Assembly of the United Nations the draft
Universal Declaration of Human Rights. Mrs. Roosevelt, M. Cassin, Mr.
Chang, Mr. Santa Cruz and I, together with our respective advisers and assistants, soon achieved a fairly close identity of views on aims and objectives. We worked more or less as a team."[24]

The American delegation, which included Secretary of State George Marshall, traveled to Paris on the *America* and set up their headquarters in the
Hotel Crillon on the Place de la Concorde. They immediately began putting the full court press on other delegates in advance of the opening
session. State Department aide Durward Sandifer described the process—
and Eleanor Roosevelt's intensity—in a letter to his wife:

> Mrs. Roosevelt is quite a different person from what she was in London
> [in 1946]. She has been around and likes negotiating and wants to be
> kept busy all the time. . . . For the first time I feel she is driven by some
> inner compulsion that will never let her come to rest. We have already
> had conferences with Malik, chairman of Committee III, [Hector]
> McNeil, Santa Cruz, Dehousse and Evatt, the President of the Assem-
> bly. I have been busy arranging meetings and lunches with other Dele-
> gates. Tomorrow we have six Latin Americans, Chile, Brazil, Peru,
> Venezuela, Uruguay, Panama. Today we had lunch with Romulo, Tues-
> day we had lunch with the Canadians, Monday with three French dele-
> gates, Cassin, Grumbach (Chairman of the French Senate Foreign
> Relations Committee and about as much of a character as Senator Con-
> nally) and a well polished diplomat, Ordonneau of the French Delega-

tion in New York. We have conferred with any number of others including Madame Pandit.[25]

Humphrey recorded in his diary that Mrs. Roosevelt called him to her suite at the Crillon to discuss with some members of the U.S. delegation how to get the draft through the third committee and into the General Assembly as quickly as possible.[26] Later he wrote of that summons, "I was always embarrassed when Mrs. Roosevelt asked me to come to this kind of meeting. The Americans assumed that the Secretariat necessarily shared their objectives. In this particular case I did share them personally; but as a [UN official] I knew there were other delegations whose objectives were quite different."[27]

Secretary Marshall gave a strong endorsement to the Universal Declaration in a speech to the General Assembly on September 23: "Let this third regular session of the General Assembly approve by an overwhelming majority the Declaration of Human Rights as a standard of conduct for all; and let us, as Members of the United Nations, conscious of our own shortcomings and imperfections, join our effort in good faith to live up to this high standard."[28] He went on to acknowledge the social and economic dimension of human rights:

Our aspirations must take into account men's practical needs—improved living and working conditions, better health, economic and social advancement for all, and the social responsibilities which these entail. The United Nations is pledged in the Charter to promote "higher standards of living, full employment, and conditions of economic and social progress and development."

The architect of the U.S. plan for European recovery next turned to current affairs. He looked forward to "an early and just peace settlement so that Japan and Germany may exist as democratic and peaceful nations . . . and so that they may in due course demonstrate their qualification for membership in the United Nations." Then, addressing the matters uppermost on the minds of most of his listeners, he said, "[T]ension in the past year has increased." He alluded briefly to Palestine, Korea, Greece, violent anticolonial uprisings in Indonesia, the dispute between India and Pakistan over Kashmir, the arms race, the need for control of atomic en-

ergy, and the "deep rift" between the Soviet bloc and the West. He urged
UN members to "redouble our efforts to find a common ground" and reminded them of their pledges in the UN Charter, written "while the
tragedy of war was vividly stamped on their minds." Now, "Three years
later, we are confronted with the need to save not only succeeding generations, but our own." Marshall concluded by assuring the General Assembly that the United States did not wish to increase current world tensions
and by affirming once more America's commitment to human rights.

> It is [the United States'] wholehearted desire to alleviate that tension.
> But we will not compromise essential principles. We will under no cir-
> cumstances barter away the rights and freedoms of other peoples. We
> earnestly hope that all Members will find ways of contributing to the
> lessening of tensions and the promotion of peace with justice. The peo-
> ple of the earth are anxiously watching our efforts here. We must not
> disappoint them.

Four days later Charles Malik prepared the way for the Declaration
with a speech to the General Assembly that Humphrey called "important
and good."[29] Malik acknowledged that there were many pressing items on
the agenda—the reunification of Korea, the control of atomic energy—
but no issue was more important than human rights. "Unless this issue is
rightly settled," he said, "there is no meaning to any other settlement. Do
not tell me you are going to settle Korea, and Germany, and Palestine, and
atomic energy, and leave *this* central issue unsettled!"[30]

Before the General Assembly could vote on the Declaration, the document had to pass the scrutiny of "Committee Three." The General Assembly's third committee was now larger and more diverse than when Eleanor
Roosevelt had won her UN spurs there in early 1946. It was composed of
delegates from each UN member state, many accompanied by a retinue of
advisers.[31] The presence of a number of women on the third committee,
Mrs. Roosevelt always suspected, was an indication of the low priority
most governments gave to social and humanitarian concerns. She once remarked to an American audience, "I imagine you know that is a good
committee on which to put women! . . . I think some of the members of

our delegation believe we might not do so well if we were put in the political or legal committees."[32]

When the third committee convened on September 28, a crisis erupted almost immediately. The first item of business was to elect the officers who would preside over the group's review of the Declaration. Most of the Latin American delegates (a large contingent comprising more than a third of the Committee's membership) were backing Émile Saint-Lot, a Haitian senator and lawyer. Chile's Hernán Santa Cruz admired Saint-Lot (he called the Haitian "*el Danton negro*," the black Danton, on account of his imposing presence and fiery oratory), but he was worried about what might happen if the chairmanship went to someone who was neither closely familiar with the document nor experienced in conducting UN debates.[33] He feared that this would play into the hands of the Soviets, who were expected to try to draw out the proceedings until the General Assembly adjourned, thus defeating the Declaration without having publicly to oppose it.

Fortunately Santa Cruz was able to persuade his fellow Latin Americans to accept a compromise under which Malik was made chairman; Saint-Lot rapporteur; and Mrs. Bodil Begtrup of Denmark, a former chairman of the UN Commission on the Status of Women, vice chairman. "That election," Santa Cruz wrote in his memoirs, "I honestly consider to have been one of the factors that assured the successful final result."

Santa Cruz may well have been right, but the rainbow bureau displeased Humphrey, who had favored nominees from Belgium and New Zealand for the vice chair and rapporteur positions. He complained in his diary that the elections of Begtrup and Saint-Lot "completely disregarded competence and qualifications." Despite his negative evaluation of Malik's performance in Geneva, Humphrey added: "One can only hope that Malik's health remains good!"[34]

That evening Mrs. Roosevelt went to the Sorbonne to deliver a speech that had been drafted in the State Department and preapproved by Secretary Marshall.[35] A huge crowd turned out to see and hear the woman who had become one of the best-known and most admired public figures of her time. Secretary Marshall and his wife were seated in the front row. After a few words about the Declaration and its importance to humankind, she devoted the bulk of her address to an anti-Communist tirade. "We must not be deluded," she said in her clear, high-pitched voice, "by the efforts of the forces of reaction to prostitute the great words of our free tradition and thereby to confuse the struggle. Democracy, freedom, human rights have come to have a definite meaning to the people of the world which we must not allow any nation to so change that they are made synonymous with suppression and dictatorship."[36] Her uncharacteristically harsh remarks included a criticism of the behavior of the socialist bloc in the Human Rights Commission. Their numerous proposed amendments, she charged, had been designed to cripple the Declaration, and they had abstained from the draft that was now before the General Assembly.

As an example of the "basic differences that show up even in the use of words between a democratic and a totalitarian country," she cited the "right to work."

> The Soviet Union insists that this is a basic right which it alone can guarantee because it alone provides full employment by the government. But the right to work in the Soviet Union means the assignment of workers to whatever task is given to them by the government without an opportunity to participate in the decision that the government should do this. A society in which everyone works is not necessarily a free society and may indeed be a slave society. . . . We in the United States have come to realize [the right to work] means freedom to choose one's job, to work or not to work as one desires.

She made clear that Americans, as a result of the Great Depression, had also come to realize "that people have a right to demand that their government will not allow them to starve because as individuals they cannot find work of the kind they are accustomed to doing." But, she continued, "we would not consider in the United States that we had gained any freedom if we were compelled to follow a dictatorial assignment to work where and when we were told."

Sandifer wrote his wife that Mrs. R. had done "a perfect job."[37] The Soviet press was less impressed, calling her a "hypocritical servant of capitalism."[38] Some of her UN colleagues were disappointed. The audience that had come to hear words of wisdom from a great lady, wrote Humphrey that night, "heard a speech that had obviously been written by the State Department and ninety percent of which was devoted to an attack against the U.S.S.R."[39] In Humphrey's view, the speech had "seriously shaken" Mrs. Roosevelt's position as "a symbol that stood above this quarrel around which reasonable men and women could have rallied in a final effort to find a basis not for compromise so much as for an understanding." After the speech, when Humphrey joined UN Assistant Secretary-General Henri Laugier and others for a drink, "We all agreed that Mrs. Roosevelt's international position had been compromised."[40]

THE PRELIMINARY GENERAL DEBATE

The morning after the Sorbonne speech, Malik announced that the floor would be open for general debate before proceeding to the substance of the draft Declaration. He then turned the podium over to Mrs. Roosevelt, who, as chairman of the Human Rights Commission, presented the draft.[41] To reassure those who had wanted enforceable legal obligations rather than a declaration of principles, she stressed that the document they were about to consider was only a first step in the UN's human rights program. The Commission's work on the other two parts of the program established at Geneva, the Covenant and measures for implementation, was going forward but was still incomplete. Then, with an eye toward those states wary of any intrusion upon their national sovereignty, she emphasized that the Declaration would not be legally binding. It was a statement of principles, she said, which set up "a common standard of achievement for all peoples and all nations." Though without legal force, it would carry considerable moral weight.

Eleanor Roosevelt appealed to the third committee members not to be distracted "by a search for absolute perfection." Her own delegation, she said, was aware that the Declaration could be improved upon.

[The U.S. delegation] did not think, for instance, that article 14, which dealt with marriage, should be included in the declaration at all. . . . The United States government did not feel that it was infringing any basic human right by excluding individuals with subversive ideas from its civil service. It did not believe that the economic, social and cultural rights listed in the latter part of the declaration implied the need for direct governmental action, except as stated in the covering article. Nevertheless, the United States delegation considered the declaration, as a whole, a good document and was prepared to accept it in its existing form, without further amendment, if the majority so agreed.

In a vain effort to forestall prolonged discussion of each article, she reminded the members of the third committee that the draft had already undergone minute scrutiny, that the original version of the Declaration had been circulated to all member states for comments, and that the current draft reflected feedback from that process. She urged the delegates not to endanger the chance of adopting a good document by insisting on perfection.

Buzz Dall's health had by now improved to the point where he was well enough to accompany his grandmother at times on her busy rounds. On October 3 Eleanor reported his progress to Anna:

> Buzz is taking a French lesson daily from one of the "girls" (she is now at least seventy-four) where I stayed as a student. . . . He's heard most of the important speakers once but done little sightseeing as he gets tired so easily. I think the illness slowed him mentally & physically & only rest will bring him back. . . . He is such a dear & I love having him & Tommy [Mrs. Roosevelt's secretary, Malvina Thompson] would be lost without him.[42]

The preliminary general debate in "Committee Three" lasted for several days. First there was an unsuccessful effort, spearheaded by New Zealand, to postpone consideration of the Declaration until a binding Covenant was ready. This would, in effect, have tabled the Declaration for the indefinite future.

No sooner was that hurdle passed than what John Humphrey called "the Bogotá menace" arose. On October 3, Humphrey wrote, "The greatest danger the declaration has to face at the moment, apart from Russian opposition, is the South American move to set up a subcommittee to compare our text with the Bogotá declaration" (the American Declaration of the Rights and Duties of Man, adopted earlier that year by the Conference of American States).[43] This process would have been so time-consuming as to cripple the Declaration's chances for adoption in the current session. The Soviets praised it as a capital idea.

Santa Cruz again came to the rescue. The Pan-American Declaration, grounded as it was in Western philosophies and political ideas, was not suitable, he pointed out, for a more diverse conglomerate of nations.[44] A document of universal application needed to concentrate on a few essentials. Besides, he explained, a draft of the Bogotá Declaration had been a major source for the drafters of the Universal Declaration, and many of its provisions had found their way into the final document. The proposal was dropped.

The Latin American representatives were also concerned about the relationship between rights and duties. Cuban delegate Guy Perez Cisneros expressed disappointment that the draft did not sufficiently emphasize the responsibilities corresponding to many rights. Pavlov hastened to agree, taking the opportunity to speak of the duties that citizens owe to the state, and the state's obligation to provide for the material needs of its citizens. Chang, too, welcomed the opportunity to reopen a question he had raised in the drafting committee. The aim of the United Nations, he said, should not be to ensure the selfish gains of the individual, but to try to increase man's moral stature. The Declaration should proclaim man's duties, because it was through consciousness of his duties that man reaches a higher level of moral development.[45] Cassin quieted those concerns by reminding everyone that a general reference to duties covered the entire Declaration.

E. H. Louw, a member of the South African delegation, expressed his fear that the Declaration would produce legal or moral obligations with which "certain countries might not be able to comply."[46] South Africa, then preparing to codify its apartheid system, was unwilling to be associated even in a nonbinding way with principles of equality. "It was a strange speech," Mrs. Roosevelt reported to the readers of her column back home. "When you looked around the table where 58 nations are represented you wondered how any nation could live in the world of today and hold such a philosophy."[47]

Two themes raised in these general debates were to bedevil the Declaration for years to come. Jamil Baroody of Saudi Arabia claimed that the parts of the draft relating to marriage and religious freedom were based largely on "Western" concepts, which were frequently at variance with patterns of culture in other parts of the world.[48] Pavlov, on instructions from Molotov, reiterated his government's complaint that the Declaration lacked sufficient regard for the national sovereignty of states.[49] The Russian delegate was in full form. "He was an orator of great power," Mrs. Roosevelt recalled, "the words rolled out of his black beard like a river, and stopping him was difficult indeed."[50]

Chang and Santa Cruz joined forces to rebut Baroody's "Western" accusation. Chang pleaded once again for "two-man mindedness," the ability to see things from another's standpoint as well as one's own particular point of view. "As only he can do," wrote Humphrey, Chang reminded his fellow delegates that each culture's contributions had to be made with a view toward producing a document "meant for all men everywhere."[51] As the debates proceeded, Chang's position received some support from delegates representing nations with large Islamic populations.

Santa Cruz told his fellow Latin Americans that they were right when they said the draft was "not perfect," but he asked them to consider how difficult it had been to arrive at an acceptable text, one that could apply to different economic, social, and legal systems and to cultures at varying stages of development.[52]

Charles Malik, in the chair, listened attentively and seldom intervened. Weeks later he would eloquently state the case for the universality of the Declaration when he presented it to the General Assembly. His case would rest in part on the broad participation of third committee members as they now turned from general debate to discussing the Declaration's articles, one by one.

CHAPTER 9

THE NATIONS
HAVE THEIR SAY

Chang and Malik Navigate

the Shoals

W hen the third committee turned from its general discussion to the specific provisions of the Declaration, Mrs. Roosevelt was dismayed to find that the members of that large group seemed determined to debate "every single word of that draft declaration over and over again."[1] There was hardly any issue that the human rights commissioners had not thoroughly considered, yet the third committee, she complained, was treating each article "exactly as though it was all an entirely new idea and nobody had ever looked at it before."[2]

To a bored and impatient John Humphrey, most of the speeches and proposed amendments seemed inspired by considerations of national prestige. He found the silent role of an international civil servant increasingly frustrating. "Sitting next to the Chairman, and both professionally and emotionally involved, I wished at times that I were a delegate. . . . There were times when I felt that I must speak if only to set the record straight."[3]

Perhaps only someone like Malik, from a small, newly independent country, could understand how important it was for every member state to have a sense of ownership with respect to the Declaration. Malik was heartened by the fact that though amendments were flooding in from many countries, no nation thus far had rejected the Declaration outright. The debates might be lengthy and tedious, but he knew it was essential to clear up the misunderstandings that were bound to occur among delegates who were not as familiar with the draft as the human rights commissioners. Most important of all was the need to assure broad participation in what everyone felt to be a great historical event. The process took time, but it was well gauged to smooth the Declaration's path to adoption and to improve its chances of reception among many cultures in the long run.

Not that Malik was less determined than any of his fellow commissioners to get the Declaration to the General Assembly before its adjournment in December: when some speakers went on for too long, he reminded them in the language of the draft itself that everyone's rights are limited by the rights of others. In the case of flagrant offenders, he did not hesitate to gavel them down; but he took pains to give everyone a hearing. Humphrey began to revise his estimate of Malik's skills as a chairman, noting that "Malik is doing better . . . and shows much more energy and leadership than at Geneva."[4]

Two years of verbal sparring with P. C. Chang had paid dividends. When Mrs. Roosevelt expressed her impatience with the committee's progress, Malik blandly answered her, Chang-like, with a Chinese proverb: "Matters must be allowed to mature slowly free from sharp corners."[5] In fact, Malik seems to have been moving things along in the only way they could be if the Declaration was to win broad-based support.

Even Malik's heart must have sunk, however, when it took six days to get through Article 1. That much-revised draft article at this stage read:

> All human beings are born free and equal in dignity and rights. They are endowed by nature with reason and conscience, and should act towards one another in a spirit of brotherhood.

South African representative C. T. Te Water produced a brief show of solidarity among the rest of the delegates when he moved to replace "dignity and rights" with "fundamental rights and freedoms."[6] While everyone was equally entitled to certain "fundamental" rights, he explained, the principle of equality could not be extended to *all* rights listed in the Declaration. Nor, he insisted, was there any universal standard of dignity. Te Water's motion "so electrified the meeting," Humphrey wrote, that everyone there, including Mrs. Roosevelt and Pavlov, "united in protest."[7] Malik reminded Te Water that the word *dignity* had been inserted in the UN Charter on the suggestion of Field Marshal Jan Smuts, who had led the

P. C. Chang and Charles Malik in conversation. By most accounts,
the two philosopher-diplomats were the intellectual leaders
of the Human Rights Commission.

South African delegation to the San Francisco conference. The next day Te Water stated that he wished to clarify his government's position: The Declaration ought to be devoted to statements of fundamental rights, and since "dignity" was not a "right," South Africa questioned the advisability of the reference to "dignity" in Article 1.[8]

Mrs. Roosevelt, when her turn came, said that the word *dignity* had been considered carefully by the Human Rights Commission, which had included it in order to emphasize that every human being is worthy of respect.[9] In the scheme of the Declaration, Article 1 did not refer to specific rights because it was meant to explain why human beings have rights to begin with.

Next, a proposal was made by a Greek delegate to move the second sentence of Article 1 into the later article dealing with duties. Chang, who understood and appreciated the holistic character of the text, quickly stepped in. He had apparently repented the position taken in his black mood the previous spring, for he now argued that it was essential to keep the injunction to act "in a spirit of brotherhood" in the first article. Otherwise the rights that followed would appear too individualistic.

Controversy then broke out over the words *by nature.* The Belgian delegation wanted to eliminate them, while a Brazilian amendment would have added that "all human beings are created in the image and likeness of God." It was Chang, again, who carried the majority by reminding everyone that the Declaration was designed to be universally applicable. His own country, he pointed out, comprised a large proportion of humanity, and its people had ideals and traditions different from those of the Christian West. Chinese ideals included good manners, decorum, propriety, and consideration for others. Yet he, as the Chinese representative on the Human Rights Commission, had refrained from proposing those ideals for inclusion in the Declaration. He hoped his colleagues would show similar consideration. Article 1 as it stood, Chang said, struck just the right note by calling upon all men to act toward one another in a spirit of brotherhood. That was consistent with the Chinese belief in the importance of considerate treatment of others—and also with the ideals of eighteenth-century Western thought. The first line of the article, therefore, should refer neither to nature nor to God. Those who believed in God, he suggested, could still find the idea of God in the strong assertions that all human beings are born free and equal and endowed with reason and conscience.[10]

Mrs. Roosevelt must have been impressed with Chang's argument, for she later adopted it when she explained to an American audience why the Declaration contained no reference to the Creator. Consciously or not, she also echoed the UNESCO philosophers:

> Now, I happen to believe that we are born free and equal in dignity and rights because there is a divine Creator, and there is a divine spark in men. But, there were other people around the table who wanted it expressed in such a way that they could think in their particular way about this question, and finally, these words were agreed upon because they . . . left it to each of us to put in our own reason, as we say, for that end.[11]

Chang was also supported by Mrs. Lakshmi Menon of India and by Salomon Grumbach, a French representative, who reminded the group of Jacques Maritain's conclusion (in the UNESCO philosophers' committee) that the nations should and could reach practical agreement on basic principles of human rights without achieving a consensus on their foundations.[12] The Belgian motion to eliminate "nature" was adopted, and the Brazilian delegate withdrew his amendment.

Chang played a mediating role time and again throughout the third committee debates in the fall of 1948. The Chinese ambassador to the UN was uniquely suited for his role as explainer of the Declaration to the committee's diverse membership.[13] Then in his fifties, he had spent much of his adult life trying to make China better understood in the West and familiarizing his own countrymen with ideas from other traditions. As ambassador to Turkey from 1940 to 1942 and to Chile from 1942 to 1945, Chang had developed an interest in Islam and a sympathetic appreciation for the problems of South American countries. A lover of Chinese high culture, he had pioneered in making the riches of Chinese literature and theater accessible to Western audiences. It was scholarly P. C. Chang, not the Disney Corporation, who first introduced Americans to the story of Mu Lan, the brave girl who dressed as a boy, took her aged father's place in the army, and rose to the highest rank. His English dramatization of the Chinese folk tale, performed at the Cort Theatre on Broadway in 1921 to raise money for famine relief in China, was well reviewed by the *Christian Science Monitor* and *The New York Times*.

Chang's earlier career as an educator and his long-standing avocation as a man of letters now stood him and the Declaration in good stead. As a poet and playwright he intuitively grasped the relations among the parts of the text and, like the good teacher he was, could explain them to many different sorts of listeners. As the discussions wore on, he was able to clear up misunderstandings, allay anxieties, promote consensus, and engineer compromise on many occasions.

THE LONG MARCH THROUGH THE ARTICLES

The discussion of Article 1 continued for almost a full week. A number of delegates questioned the wisdom of beginning a Declaration of rights with an article that contained no rights. Soviet-bloc representatives attacked the article's affirmations as hypocritical, meaningless, or patently false. Pavlov scoffed at the brotherhood language. The relations between the United Kingdom and Malaya, between the Netherlands and Indonesia, between different groups in Spain, between the rich and the poor everywhere, could not be described as brotherly, he commented wryly, unless the brothers referred to were Cain and Abel.[14] Jamil Baroody, the Lebanese Christian Arab who represented Saudi Arabia, took issue with the statement that all human beings are endowed with reason and conscience. That, he said, was not, and never had been, true.[15] Iraq's A. Abadi argued, as philosopher Robert Nozick would years later, that it is logically impossible for human beings to be both free and equal since inequality is the inevitable result when people are free to develop all their latent talents.[16]

Several members suggested that the content of Article 1 be transferred to the Preamble, at which point an alarmed Cassin intervened.[17] The Declaration was designed to begin with a statement of the framework within which all of its rights were contained, he said. Article 1, together with Article 2 on the nondiscrimination principle and the article on limits and duties (later moved over Cassin's objections to the end of the document), constituted that framework. It was essential, he urged, for the United Nations to proclaim to the world the basic principles of freedom, dignity, equality, and responsibility that had come so close to extinction during the preceding ten years.

Finally, on October 12, the third committee voted to adopt Article 1, deleting only the words *by nature.*

The committee then turned to Article 2, whose blanket principle of nondiscrimination made it unacceptable to South Africa. The article then read: "Everyone is entitled to all the rights and freedoms set forth in this Declaration, without distinction of any kind, such as race, color, sex, language, religion, political or other opinion, property or other status, or national or social origin."

The debates on this language produced some awkward moments for the United States. "Mr. Pavlov lectured the U.S. for its sins for about a half hour in Committee III this morning," Durward Sandifer wrote his wife, "lumping us with South Africa. To which the South African delegate retorted that his only consolation was that he was placed in the distinguished company of the United States, which put us in our place as South Africa is virtually a pariah in this Conference."[18]

Yugoslavian representative Vladimir Dedijer inquired why the United States had kept silent when it was revealed that South Africa was preparing new, severely discriminatory legislation—referring to the apartheid system that went into legal effect in 1950. The reason, he charged, was obvious: The United States itself legally condoned racial discrimination.[19] Mrs. Roosevelt replied, as usual, that the position of Negroes was improving in the United States, though it still had far to go. She pointedly called Dedijer's attention to the fact that Article 2 condemned *political* as well as racial discrimination.

Dedijer then trained his sights on the European colonial powers, proposing a new article to state that the rights proclaimed in the Declaration apply to people in non-self-governing territories. Representatives of Belgium, France, the Netherlands, and the United Kingdom objected, saying that this specification was unnecessary in view of Article 2's general ban on discrimination. Mrs. A. M. Newlands of New Zealand shot back that "a vague line or two" was not enough, in view of entrenched discriminatory practices in colonial territories. Those who opposed the proposal, she said, "had little idea of the feeling of exasperation and despair generated in peoples living under colonial regimes." Dedijer's motion passed by a narrow vote. Later the new language was moved into Article 2 as a second paragraph: "Furthermore, no distinction shall be made on the basis of the political, jurisdictional or international status of the country or territory to which a person belongs, whether it be independent, trust, non-self-governing or under any other limitation of sovereignty."

One might have expected Article 3 ("Everyone has the right to life, liberty, and security of person") to require little discussion. It was, in fact, approved without changes, but not before the committee had spent most of a week debating the Soviet Union's proposal to abolish capital punishment (legally banned in the USSR since 1947). At its Geneva meeting, the Human Rights Commission had rejected a Soviet amendment to that effect, along with proposals by Chile and Lebanon to specify that the right to life includes unborn life. Different countries had different laws on those subjects, and the decision had been made to avoid specificity.

Now Pavlov renewed the plea for a ban on the death penalty, taking the occasion to decry the lynchings mentioned in the petition the NAACP had submitted to the UN in the fall of 1947. Eleanor Roosevelt was becoming exasperated with the Russian's windy and repetitious speeches. "I would remind my Soviet colleague," she said, "that since we are dealing with [human rights], we should try not to attack each other or our Governments, but since he has in his speech again chosen to repeat many things which I have heard many times, I would suggest to him that he has used the petition of the NAACP . . . that is over a year old, and that lynching in the United States is deplorable but that it is against the law and when it takes place it is a violation of the law and exceptional."[20]

Two full days of cold war polemics then ensued, with Soviet-bloc denunciations of racism and colonialism and Western attacks on the Communist regimes for limiting personal freedoms. René Cassin said that he personally favored the abolition of capital punishment, but that if it were included, it would have to be carefully defined, "so as to cover the practice of sending prisoners to concentration camps where a lingering death awaited them."[21] Party man Pavlov commented, startlingly, "Under proper administration, concentration camps and penal institutions did not lead to death but rather to reform of the persons temporarily deprived of their liberty."[22] The United Kingdom's Christopher Mayhew then accused Russia of having "erected within its borders a system which made slaves of millions of human beings." Pavlov said the British representative had shown complete ignorance of the real situation in the USSR and must have been reading books written by persons the Soviet Union considered "traitors."

At that point Mexico's Pedro De Alba protested in vain that the major powers were reducing "countries of lesser importance" to the role of "worried and helpless spectators to their verbal duels."[23] Chang offered some ancient wisdom addressed to no one in particular: "Sweep the snow in front of your own door. Overlook the frost on another's roof tiles."[24] But the bickering continued.

John Humphrey, bored to distraction, used some of the time to catch up on his correspondence. He wrote to his sister on October 14:

> I am writing this letter during a session of the Third Committee of the General Assembly. I suppose I should be listening to the South American gentleman who is expounding on Article 3 of the Declaration of Human Rights, but I have heard so many of these speeches that it is only in revolt that I can hope to find sanity. We have been on this thing for 3 weeks now and have adopted 2 out of the 28 articles. When we will finish the Lord only knows. But I am really very happy about the way things have gone so far and fully expect that the General Assembly will adopt the declaration substantially as it was drafted by the Human Rights Commission. . . . A sense of duty calls me back to work. They also serve who only stand and wait.[25]

During breaks Eleanor Roosevelt relieved the monotony with sightseeing and Christmas shopping. On the first Sunday in October, she, Dr. Gurewitsch, Durward Sandifer, and Malvina Thompson attended an afternoon performance at the opera, followed by a drive out to Versailles for a view of the formal gardens and fountains. A few days later, on October 11, friends and coworkers gave her a sixty-fourth birthday party at the Crillon. "The party was gay," she wrote in her column, "and I proceeded to cut my birthday cake and feel duly grateful for having reached the advanced age of sixty-four. One should be grateful for the accumulated experience and knowledge that goes with the years. At least, one knows, in addition, that one must say one's prayers daily that what one has acquired in knowledge may translate itself into wisdom and tolerance which can make old age useful to rising generations."[26]

On October 20, after six days of debate, Article 3 was at last adopted. The Soviet Union's amendment was defeated, with only three countries besides the Soviet bloc voting in favor—Cuba, the Dominican Republic, and Mexico. Though many representatives had expressed sympathy for abolishing capital punishment, and several of their own countries had done so, most agreed with the Human Rights Commission's decision to state the general principle without taking an explicit position on abortion, euthanasia, or the death penalty.

Later that day the third committee had to suspend its discussion of the Declaration to listen to UN mediator Ralph Bunche's report on the plight of the half million Arab refugees who had been forced by hostilities to leave Jewish-held territory and seek refuge in neighboring countries. When Bunche had finished his report, the Iraqi delegate commented that the third committee would do better to take up this concrete case of human rights violation than to spend hours debating human rights in the abstract.[27] But the committee moved on. The sands in the hourglass were running.

On Saturday, October 23, Eleanor Roosevelt made a quick trip to Stuttgart, where she gave a speech under the auspices of a German women's group. Her main emphasis was on the importance of democratic institutions. Noting that women now outnumbered men in war-ravaged Germany, she encouraged her listeners to be in the forefront of rebuilding a free and democratic society. Before returning to Paris, she visited some of the refugee camps to which over fourteen million displaced persons had fled from Eastern European countries. "Human misery is widespread over here," she wrote Anna.[28]

MALIK'S STOPWATCH

Malik, at this point, adopted a more aggressive strategy against the Soviet bloc's stepped-up delaying tactics. "We were alerted to this danger," Malik later recalled, "by many signs, even intimations, both in and outside the Committee."[29] Ulla Lindstrom of Sweden moved to limit the length of interventions to three minutes.[30] This motion, fiercely opposed by the long-winded Pavlov, was adopted (though not until the committee had spent most of an afternoon arguing about it). Malik took two more steps. With a whole month elapsed and only three articles approved, he announced that the committee would begin holding night sessions, and he bought himself a stopwatch.

Malik later wrote that he had used the stopwatch "mercilessly, warning each speaker by a stroke of the gavel 30 seconds before the end of the time allotted to him. Now and then I used my judgment about the 3-minute limitation, but as I recall, I never allowed more than 5 minutes, be the speaker Mrs. Roosevelt or Cassin or Pavlov or Santa Cruz or Chang or Azkoul of Lebanon. The Committee cooperated splendidly."[31]

The committee began to average one article a day as it moved through the political and civil liberties, often meeting morning, afternoon, and late into the evening. One night, as Mrs. Roosevelt and Sandifer returned to their Paris hotel together at three A.M., she joked, "If we don't keep earlier hours we are going to lose our reputations here."[32] On November 3 the news came from the United States that Harry Truman, contrary to most predictions, had defeated Thomas Dewey in their close race for the presidency. "President Truman," Eleanor Roosevelt commented, "only had the people with him."

The Palestinian refugee crisis prompted discussions that led to two significant changes. Fighting between Israeli and Arab forces had resumed in October, and some of Israel's neighbors had become concerned about the burden on their societies posed by the continuing influx of refugees. On the motion of Lebanon, the "right to return" to one's own country was added to Article 13, and on the motion of Saudi Arabia, the right to be "granted" asylum from persecution was diluted to become the right to "enjoy" asylum in Article 14. Delegates from many countries, including the United States, were persuaded to vote for the latter change after Mrs. Corbett, the United Kingdom delegate, pointed out that a right to be "granted" asylum would conflict with the immigration laws of nearly every country.

A more controversial change was made in Article 16's right to marry, when the committee decided, on the motion of Mexico, to add "without any limitation due to race, nationality or religion." That article, with its bold proclamation of equal rights for men and women in marriage, was already problematic for some delegates representing countries with predominantly Islamic populations. In an unsuccessful attempt to replace "equal rights" in marriage with "full rights as defined in the marriage law of their country," Saudia Arabia's Baroody charged that the authors of the draft Declaration had adopted Western standards for family relations and "had ignored more ancient civilizations, which were past the experimental stage, and the institutions of which, for example marriage, had proved their wisdom through the centuries."

The Saudi reaction cannot have come as a surprise to Eleanor Roosevelt. Upon FDR's return from Yalta, he had told her that his "one real failure" had been with King Ibn Saud, whom he had arranged to meet there.[33] On Palestine, "Franklin got nowhere." When the American president tried to discuss the possibility of irrigating the desert for agricultural development, the Saudi monarch curtly replied that his people were nomads. Roosevelt's impression, he told his wife, was that the warrior king "did not want his people changed and he felt contact with Europeans would be bad for them." Ibn Saud had even declined American coffee, politely offering the services of his own coffeemaker.

The Muslim nations, however, were not of one mind on the question. Shaista Ikramullah of Pakistan said her delegation would accept the "equal rights" in marriage language, with the understanding (also shared by Mrs. Roosevelt) that equal rights did not mean identical rights.[34] The Saudi amendment, she noted, might condone discrimination against women. Egypt's Dr. Wahid Raafat announced that his country would vote for the marriage article, but that candor required him to express his delegation's view that religious limitations on the freedom to marry did not "shock the universal conscience, as did, for instance, the restrictions based on nationality, race or colour, which existed in certain countries and which were not only condemned but unknown in Egypt."[35] At the time, an Allied commission was purging such restrictions from German law, and miscegenation bans were still in effect in several American states.

The Muslim delegates were also divided on Article 18's freedom to change one's religion. Though that right was arguably implicit in the general principle of religious freedom, Malik's insistence that this be spelled out had made the article controversial. Baroody was again the most outspoken critic. His delegation supported freedom of conscience and religion but objected to the right to change one's religion because proselytization historically had caused so much bloodshed and warfare. Saudi Arabia's vigorous opposition to the marriage and religion articles in the third committee foreshadowed that country's abstention from the Declaration. A Muslim delegate from India, Mohammed Habib, took a different view, supporting the right to change one's religion and pointing out that the new Indian Constitution guaranteed the right to convert or be converted. And Egypt's Rafaat said that his delegation, though "not entirely" in agreement with the right, would vote for the Declaration and that his country "intended to apply and execute it in all honesty."[36]

On November 11 the committee took up the right to participate in government. A consensus rapidly developed that it was desirable to be more specific about how that right was to be exercised. As suggestions for amendments began to accumulate, Malik requested the proponents to get together and try to reach agreement. The result was an amendment that greatly strengthened the article by adding, "The will of the people shall be the basis of the authority of government: this will shall be expressed in periodic and genuine elections which shall be by universal and equal suffrage and shall be held by secret vote or by equivalent free voting procedures."

Pavlov, after fulminating against the denial of voting rights to American blacks, had participated actively with Chang and several Latin American delegates in framing the new language. Durward Sandifer, sitting in temporarily for Mrs. Roosevelt, had objected, commenting only that while he agreed with the principle, he found the details "unsatisfactory." In the event, however, he voted in favor of the joint product. The revised article was overwhelmingly approved, with only one dissenter—the Haitian representative, who said he thought it might lead to restrictions on voting by illiterate people.

In mid-November the provisions on social and economic rights predictably slowed the committee down. The debate was not over the principle of including these rights, but on their scope and details. John Humphrey, listening silently for the past two years, felt he had heard it all before. Though he was tired of the debate, he admitted to his diary that his socialist views had changed. "[M]oral bankruptcy is the reason for our failure to organize peace. I once thought that socialism could fill this moral gap; but now, although I still remain a socialist, I know better. For socialism is a technique and nothing more. What we need is something like the Christian morality without the tommyrot."[37]

René Cassin temporarily took the chair on November 18 to handle questions about the "new" rights. Humphrey was bemused to note that Cassin, with "one of the quickest minds that I have ever seen," was a poor chairman.[38] "He sometimes forgets indeed that he is in the chair," Humphrey wrote in his diary, "and the meeting goes on merrily without leadership." General de Gaulle had been similarly disappointed in Cassin's administrative skills in the summer of 1941 when he had left his legal aide in charge of the Free French operations in London while he traveled to the Middle East for talks with leaders of British and Turkish

forces. The general had told Cassin to use a firm hand, but when he returned he found the office in chaos. That one incident marked a change in
the relationship between the two men. From that time on, according to
historian Jean-Louis Crémieux-Brilhac, "René Cassin, secure in the
honor of being a founding father of Free France and its republican conscience, would never again be entrusted with first-rank political responsibilities."[39] Despite the high legal positions he had achieved after the war,
Cassin always resented his exclusion from the innermost circles of
power.[40]

In his own sphere of expertise, though, Cassin excelled. Throughout
the third committee sessions, and especially in connection with the social
and economic rights, he reverted to his old role of law professor, patiently
explaining each article in relation to the structure of the whole document—the connections among various articles and the way the different
parts of the Declaration worked to amplify or limit other parts.

P. C. Chang, with his love of language, was also adept at these *explica-
tions de texte*. Chang seemed to enjoy pointing out how "perfectly clear
and logical" the document was and calling attention to the relations
among its parts. Leo Beaufort, the Dutch delegate, chimed in from time to
time, appealing to the delegates not to lose sight of the document as a
whole when they submitted their amendments to individual articles, and
the Norwegian delegate Frede Castberg gave a little lecture on the interpretation of texts.

The struggles over the social and economic articles were mainly between representatives of liberal democracies such as the United States
and the United Kingdom, who wanted to leave more room for individual
initiative and collective bargaining, and delegates who thought the state
should play a greater role in regulating wages and working conditions.
The latter group was sizable, for it included social and Christian democrats from Latin America and Western Europe, as well as the Communist
representatives.

Pavlov, one of the first to speak, praised this group of rights, which, according to him, "had not appeared in any of the previous declarations of
the rights of man; their inclusion was a result of the social progress
achieved in the nineteenth and twentieth centuries."[41] That was not quite
accurate, since the Bogotá declaration, from which Humphrey had drawn
some of this language, had been adopted earlier that year. Pavlov, however, proposed an amendment to the introductory "chapeau" article to

stress the need for the state "to insure every individual a real opportunity to enjoy" these rights. Cassin said that he did not think "a special guarantee" should be included in the chapeau, because a general pledge to honor all the rights and freedoms in the Declaration was included elsewhere.

Santa Cruz and several others expressed concern that the term *social security* in the chapeau's opening sentence ("Everyone has a right to social security . . .") was apt to be misconstrued. In some states it had a technical sense, limited to the situations of persons unable to work because of incapacity, whereas its function here was to introduce a series of articles aimed at protecting individuals against a variety of social and economic risks including unemployment. Syria proposed to replace "social security" with "social justice." Mrs. Roosevelt, though conceding the term *social security* might not be perfect, said she hoped the chapeau would be adopted without modifications. She opposed the Soviet amendment because her government did not believe that the obligations of the state should be specified in a Declaration, as distinct from a Covenant, and because a special guarantee by the state in this article would suggest that the economic and social rights were more important than political rights.

The Soviet and Syrian amendments were both rejected, and the committee moved on to consider a Cuban proposal to give the "new" rights parity with the "old" by stating that the "new" rights are "indispensable" for the dignity and free development of the individual. The chapeau, with that amendment, was adopted by an overwhelming majority (39–1, with three abstentions). The article, in its final form, reads:

> Everyone, as a member of society, has the right to social security and is entitled to realization, through national effort and international cooperation and in accordance with the organization and resources of each State, of the economic, social and cultural rights indispensable for his dignity and the free development of his personality.

The only nay vote was cast, curiously, by Lebanon. Karim Azkoul, sitting in temporarily for Malik, seems to have been confused about the article's meaning. After the vote, Jamil Baroody of Saudi Arabia explained his abstention. He had been disappointed by the failure of the Syrian motion to substitute "social justice" for "social security." The former term conformed better to the Saudi system, where "*zaka,* a voluntary tax levied for the purpose of assisting the poor and unemployed, was one of the five pillars of Islam. Social security was a recent historical development in western society, while *zaka* had been an article of faith in actual operation in Moslem communities for almost fourteen centuries." This and other Islamic institutions, he said, "were not only the equivalent of a social security system, their machinery was simpler, their administration less costly and their effectiveness had stood the test of time."[42]

The committee then turned to the article on the right to work. There, controversy centered on Soviet amendments to include a right to protection against unemployment and a right to equal pay for equal work without discrimination as to race, sex, or nationality, and a Cuban proposal to add the right to a level of pay suitable for a worker and his family. The United States opposed all three changes: the first implied too great a role for the state, the second was already covered in Article 2, and the third was objected to on the grounds that it was undesirable to take the needs of a worker's family into consideration, other than by way of a minimum wage for everyone. All three amendments were adopted.

Then a crisis developed. When Malik, now back in the chair, put the right-to-work article to a vote, paragraph by paragraph, each paragraph was approved, but when the committee voted on the article as a whole, the votes were evenly split, which meant that the article had been rejected. The Soviet bloc, with Denmark and several Latin American countries, had voted in favor; the United States, China, India, and most European countries had voted against. Mrs. Begtrup of Denmark called the situation "ridiculous," and Pavlov said it was "disgraceful," charging the United States and the colonial powers with bad faith.

Malik invited those delegates who wished to do so to explain their votes. Cassin began by saying that it was "unthinkable" that the Declaration should not contain a right to work, but that he had voted against the article because the clause forbidding discrimination on the basis of race, sex, or nationality seemed to limit the protection afforded by Article 2's broader ban on discrimination. Mrs. Roosevelt said that she agreed on the need to include the right to work, but she, too, was unable to vote for a provision that, by omission, might appear to condone discrimination on the basis of religion or political opinion.

Chang pointed out that the favorable votes on each paragraph were a sign that the draft needed only to be improved. Santa Cruz agreed, commenting that many seemed to have voted against the article only because the wording was inadequate. In that spirit, Fernand Dehousse of Belgium proposed to eliminate "without distinction as to race, sex or nationality" after the prohibition on discrimination in employment and moved that the article be reconsidered. His motion was adopted unanimously, and a drafting subcommittee was instructed to prepare a revised text, taking all suggestions into account.

Meanwhile the committee moved on. In the article on education it made an important change, influenced directly by recollections of the National Socialist regime's efforts to turn Germany's renowned educational system into a mechanism for indoctrinating the young with the government's program. The draft already contained a paragraph, based on a proposal submitted by the World Jewish Congress, that said education should promote tolerance, understanding, and respect for human rights.[43] In the third committee, after Beaufort of the Netherlands recalled the ways in which German schools had been used to undermine the role of parents, a third paragraph was added: "Parents have a prior right to choose the kind of education that shall be given to their children."

In the subcommittee on work, Dehousse's proposal to remove the limitation on the nondiscrimination clause was accepted. Now the problem was the family wage, which Mrs. Roosevelt unsuccessfully opposed again. On November 22 she wrote to Anna, "our working hours are getting bad as they do at the end of the Assembly."

When the article on work came back to the third committee on Thanksgiving Day, November 25, Roosevelt said the article was now acceptable to the United States, except for the provision that the needs of a worker's family should be considered in determining wages.[44] Several countries, including the United States, she said, had learned from experience that the scale of wages should be fixed by assessing the work done, and not on the basis of considerations foreign to the idea of labor proper. Social protection for the family, she pointed out, was covered in the article on the right to a minimum standard of living. Her position was overwhelmingly rejected. The rest of the third committee was now ready to suppress their differences in order to approve the article. When the vote was taken, the only negative vote was that of the United States.

The article, in its final form, reads:

(1) Everyone has the right to work, to free choice of employment, and to just and favorable conditions of work and to protection against unemployment.

(2) Everyone, without any discrimination, has the right to equal pay for equal work.

(3) Everyone who works has the right to just and favorable remuneration ensuring for himself and his family an existence worthy of human dignity, and supplemented, if necessary, by other means of social protection.

(4) Everyone has the right to form and join trade unions for the protection of his interests.

Explaining her vote, Mrs. Roosevelt said that "it would be a matter for long and difficult discussion to decide exactly what was meant by a decent existence."[45] She predicted that the principle in paragraph (3) would prove extremely difficult to implement, noting that different countries had different methods of giving social protection to the worker who needed more than he was able to earn. "To assess a worker's wages by his needs rather than by the work he performed" was, in her opinion, "a false principle."

Thanksgiving dinner for the Americans that day had to be held between the first and second of three committee meetings, but Mrs. Roosevelt was determined not to let the holiday pass unobserved. She invited sixteen guests to the Crillon, instructing the hotel to prepare a dinner from two large turkeys she had obtained from the American Embassy commissary. That special order seems to have posed a challenge to the chef. Durward Sandifer described himself as "startled" when the turkeys were brought to the table with their feet still on and "sticking high in the air."[46]

For the remaining days of the third committee's work, the Soviets replaced Pavlov with Ambassador Bogomolov. Gone was the genteel, cooperative Bogomolov who had given such fine parties in Geneva. Now it was no more Mr. Nice Comrade. Humphrey was disappointed in the change but wrote in his diary, "I do not think this necessarily means the Soviets will not vote for the declaration. . . . But whatever Mr. Bogomolov's motives are I am sure they are not dictated by personal interest. I can therefore respect him."[47]

On November 26 the Soviet Union, Yugoslavia, and Denmark made one final attempt to revive the issue of protection of minority groups. Once again the Americans, North and South, successfully resisted. In her November 30 "My Day" column, Mrs. Roosevelt explained the U.S. position to her readers in terms of an assimilationist ideal that most Americans in 1948 took for granted:

> So far as I was concerned, the point brought most clearly before us was the fact that this was not a subject on which a general article could be written for a universal declaration. All of the Americas' delegates declared that this problem did not exist with them because people who come to our shores do so because they want to become citizens of our countries. They leave behind certain economic, religious and social conditions that they wish to shed and prefer to be assimilated into the new country that they are adopting as their own. They are accepted by us with that understanding, and from our point of view we would like to see the committee recognize the fact that the European problem should be handled differently.[48]

When the third committee took up the Preamble as its final item, a last vain effort was made (by the Netherlands) to insert a mention of the deity. Malik, who earlier in the drafting process had proposed a reference to "the Creator," seems to have come round to Chang's and Mrs. Roosevelt's view. Arguments about the use of words like "God" and "created," he later wrote, "are often concluded silently by sheer sensing that the prevailing climate of opinion will never admit such terms."[49]

As soon as the committee wound up its review of the draft Declaration, a subcommittee on style chaired by Cassin began to put everything into final form. At this stage a few changes were made in the sequence of articles, and the title was officially changed to the "Universal Declaration of Human Rights" from "International Declaration of Human Rights." The new title had been in casual use for some time, but Cassin, who proposed the official change, rightly considered the name to be of the utmost significance. The title "Universal," he later wrote, meant that the Declaration was morally binding on everyone, not only on the governments that voted for its adoption. The Universal Declaration, in other words, was not an "international" or "intergovernmental" document; it was addressed to all humanity and founded on a unified conception of the human being.[50]

At last, on December 4, the Declaration was ready for the final vote in the third committee. Remarkably, after more than eighty third-committee (and numerous subcommittee) meetings, during which nearly 170 amendments had been proposed, the structure of the document had survived relatively intact, and its content, though further qualified and refined, was roughly similar to the draft that had emerged from the Human Rights Commission in June 1948. That was due in large part to the fact that the members of the Human Rights Commission, except for the Soviet bloc, were committed to the draft that had emerged from their deliberations. Roosevelt, Malik, Cassin, Chang, and Santa Cruz presented a united front most of the time, resisting the temptation to reopen old debates.

Most of the changes made by the third committee consisted in drawing out the implications of, or extending, principles already present in the draft. The general nondiscrimination clause of Article 2, for example, was made specifically applicable to non-self-governing territories and to the freedom to marry. Special mention was made in the Preamble of the equal rights of men and women, thanks to Minerva Bernardino of the Dominican Republic. Cuba was largely responsible for strengthening the link between new and old rights and for reviving Cassin's original inclusion of a reference to the special needs of families in the article on the right to an adequate standard of living. On the motion of Ecuador, the article guaranteeing that no one shall be subject to arbitrary arrest or detention was amended to include arbitrary exile. At Mexico's behest the committee added a new article adopting the Latin American institution of the *amparo* (the right to a hearing for acts in violation of fundamental rights under national law).

With the end in sight, Chang's patience and composure began to erode. On December 4 Humphrey wrote in his diary, "P. C. Chang was less helpful than usual. His emotional outbursts have become more frequent and he has made some personal enemies. I am told however that he has not been well and he must be disturbed by events in China."[51] Within a month Beijing would fall, and the world's most populous nation would come under Communist rule.

On December 7 at three A.M. the draft was approved by the third committee for submission to the General Assembly. There were no votes against it, but seven countries recorded abstentions—the six members of the Soviet bloc (including Yugoslavia) and, to the surprise of many, including an indignant John Humphrey, Canada. The Canadian position, ostensibly having to do with federal-provincial relations, was quickly reversed, but not before Canada had taken a considerable public relations hit for its abstention.[52] Humphrey stated in his memoirs, "I had no doubt whatsoever that this quick change in position was dictated solely by the fact that the government did not relish the company in which it found itself."[53] Saudi Arabia and South Africa did not vote.[54]

Over the course of the fall, Humphrey had upgraded his estimate of Malik's political skills. "We were fortunate in having Charles Malik in the chair," he conceded in his memoirs. "Presiding over a much more turbulent body—perhaps the most turbulent in the United Nations, he conducted the proceedings with a firmness that at first surprised me. There were indeed times when he approached arrogance, even losing his temper, and with a bang of his gavel refusing the floor to delegations. But my respect for him grew as the session progressed, and he got the Declaration through the committee."[55] Durward Sandifer commented with awe that Malik "was the only person I ever knew who succeeded in holding a stopwatch to Pavlov."[56]

THE ADOPTION OF THE DECLARATION

As the day of decision in the General Assembly approached, the climate among the delegates was as chilly as the December weather. Relations between the Soviet bloc and the North Atlantic powers had never been worse. British and American planes were flying supplies into Berlin around the clock at the incredible rate of a planeload every three and a half minutes. The atmosphere in the UN was tense, the mood cynical. Mrs. Roosevelt wrote to her aunt Maude that she thought they would be lucky to get the required two-thirds vote. "The Arabs and Soviets may balk—the Arabs for religious reasons, the Soviets for political ones."[57]

It was a good sign therefore when the General Assembly adopted the Genocide Convention on December 9 unanimously and without debate. When ratified, the convention would require its signers to prevent and punish acts of genocide, defined as acts "committed with intent to destroy, in whole or in part, a national, ethnical, racial, or religious group, as such." Australia's Herbert Evatt, president of the General Assembly, urged all member states to ratify as soon as possible. It marked, he said, "an epoch-making development in international law":

> Intervention of the United Nations and other organs which will have to supervise application of the convention will be made according to in-

ternational law and not according to unilateral political considerations. In this field relating to the sacred right of existence of human groups we are proclaiming today the supremacy of international law once and for-ever.[58]

At eight-thirty P.M. on December 9 Charles Malik took the podium to introduce the Universal Declaration. Now one of the most respected fig-ures in the General Assembly, the tall, striking Arab showed no trace of the insecurities that had plagued him in his early UN days. The crowd of delegates, reporters, and onlookers fell silent as the philosopher-diplomat began to speak. Flanked by fifty-eight brightly hued flags, Malik tailored his plea to the public and posterity as much as to delegates caught up in the play of power and interest. Unlike previous declarations of rights that had sprung from particular cultures, he said, the Universal Declaration was something new in the world.

Thousands of minds and hands have helped in its formation. Every member of the United Nations has solemnly pledged itself to achieve respect for and observance of human rights. But, precisely what these rights are we were never told before, either in the Charter or in any other international instrument. This is the first time the principles of human rights and fundamental freedoms are spelled out authoritatively and in precise detail. I now know what my government pledged itself to promote, achieve and observe when I had the honor to sign the [UN Charter]. I can agitate against my government, and if she does not ful-fil her pledge, I shall have and feel the moral support of the entire world.[59]

He described the Declaration as a "composite synthesis" of all existing rights traditions, and of much Asian and Latin American wisdom. Such a synthesis had never occurred before in history.

Malik pointed each country to places in the Declaration where it could either find its own contributions or the influence of the culture to which it belonged. The Latin American countries had brought to the process the ideas and experience gained in preparing the Bogotá Decla-ration on the Rights and Duties of Man. India had played a key role in advancing the nondiscrimination principle, especially with regard to women. France was responsible for many elegancies in drafting. The

United Kingdom and the United States had shared the wisdom acquired in their long experience with traditional political and civil liberties. The Soviet Union, with broad support from many quarters, had championed the newer social and economic rights in the interest of "improving the living conditions of the broad masses of mankind." The importance of remembering that rights entail duties had been emphasized by participants from China, Greece, Latin America, the Soviet Union, and France. Many countries had contributed to the articles on freedom of religion and the rights of the family. Due to the immense variety of its sources, the Declaration had been constructed on a "firm international basis wherein no regional philosophy or way of life was permitted to prevail." In a last-ditch effort to win Soviet support, Malik mentioned each of the Russians who had served on the Human Rights Commission by name, praising them for their "unrelenting efforts to lift the Declaration from being a mere catalog of hopes and aims into something directly and materially bearing on material life."

It would be impossible, he said, to name and thank all the individuals who had been involved in the process leading up to this day, but he made another exception for his old rival, P. C. Chang, who had "never failed to broaden our perspective by his frequent references to the wisdom and philosophy of the Orient and who, by a special drafting gift, was able happily to rectify many of our terms."

Malik closed by reviewing the history of the document, its "negative roots" in the atrocities of the recent war and its "positive roots" in the common aspirations summed up so well in Franklin Roosevelt's four freedoms. The Declaration represented delivery on the promise of the UN Charter, which had mentioned human rights seven times but had not specified what they were or how they were to be protected. The Declaration would now need to be supplemented with binding conventions and an enforcement machinery. But even without these, he concluded, it would "serve as a potent critic of existing practice. It will help to transform reality."

Of Malik's speech, Santa Cruz later wrote: "He gave a detailed account of the whole long process of elaboration of the instrument that was being discussed. No one was able to do it with such authority, not only because of the responsibilities he had assumed in the process, but also by virtue of his lucid intelligence and his extraordinary talent for explanation."[60]

Others were then given the opportunity to speak. Cassin harshly rebuked the Soviets for their criticism of the Declaration as an incursion on national sovereignty. He reminded them that in 1933 Hitler's representatives had used the same argument in the League of Nations to justify their actions against their own countrymen.[61]

The speeches continued on December 10. P. C. Chang told the General Assembly that over the course of the long debate on the Declaration, "representatives had reached agreement whenever they were concerned first and foremost with the defense of human rights." Their disagreements had been due to "preoccupations of a purely political nature."

The effort of the Chinese delegation, he said, had been to promote a spirit of sincere tolerance of the different views and beliefs of one's fellow men. He blamed "uncompromising dogmatism" for accentuating disputes, saying that there was at the present time "a tendency to impose a standardized way of thinking and a single way of life." With that attitude, he concluded, "equilibrium could be reached only at the cost of moving away from the truth, and employing force. But however violent the methods employed, equilibrium achieved in that way could never last." Mrs. Lakshmi Menon made a plea for tolerance, too, and took the occasion to recall Mahatma Gandhi's insistence that all rights are born of obligations. From the very fact that it proclaimed rights, she said, the Declaration should be understood as a "declaration of obligations."

When her turn came, Mrs. Roosevelt, in a simple, long-sleeved blue dress, stepped up to the bank of microphones and donned her reading glasses. The golden brooch at her neck, resembling a fleur-de-lis, was a replica of the three-feathered Roosevelt crest that FDR had given her on their wedding day. In a high, clear voice, she announced:

> We stand today at the threshold of a great event both in the life of the United Nations and in the life of mankind, that is the approval by the General Assembly of the Universal Declaration of Human Rights recommended by the Third Committee. This Declaration may well become the international Magna Carta of all men everywhere. We hope its proclamation by the General Assembly will be an event comparable to the proclamation of the Declaration of the Rights of Man by the French people in 1789, the adoption of the Bill of Rights by the people of the United States, and the adoption of comparable declarations at different times in other countries.[62]

She praised the Declaration as an important step in the unfinished task of lifting human beings everywhere "to a higher standard of life and to a greater enjoyment of freedom." It was based, she said, "upon the spiritual fact that man must have freedom in which to develop his full stature and through common effort to raise the level of human dignity." In passages that were probably written by the State Department, she emphasized that the document was not legally binding and explained why most of the amendments proposed by the Soviet bloc had been rejected. She concluded with her characteristic blend of idealism and realism about human nature, "Let this session of the General Assembly approve by an overwhelming majority the Declaration of Human Rights as a standard of conduct for all; and let us as Members of the United Nations, conscious of our own shortcomings and imperfections, join our efforts in good faith to live up to this high standard."

It was not one of Roosevelt's best speeches. Santa Cruz wrote that her "intervention disappointed me a little. I did not hear the spontaneous expression of her personal fight for human rights that was present on previous occasions. On the other hand, one sensed the caution of someone who was speaking on behalf of a State that does not forget the political implications of the practical application of human rights instruments."[63]

The Soviet-bloc delegates made one last effort to have the matter put over to the next session of the General Assembly on the grounds that, while it had "many good features," the Declaration was still seriously defective. The bases for their objections were somewhat inconsistent. The project was mostly empty words, but it was also a threat to national sovereignty. They called it "overly juridical" but complained that it lacked effective legal guarantees.

Stung by Cassin's charge that the doctrine of national sovereignty had led to crimes against Germany's own people and against human rights, Soviet Deputy Foreign Minister Andrei Vishinsky took the occasion to deliver a blast in return.[64] The French representative, he said, had forgotten the real reasons for the Second World War. Those reasons were not to be found in the violation of the human rights of the German people, but in the policies of the leading European statesmen of the day, namely Daladier and Chamberlain, supported by the United States. Their 1938 Munich agreement (permitting Germany to occupy the Sudetenland of Czechoslovakia) had encouraged the reestablishment of Germany's military power, in order to direct German aggression toward the Soviet Union and the East. (The 1939 Soviet-German nonaggression pact that had enabled Hitler to invade Poland apparently slipped his memory.) The principle of national sovereignty, Vishinsky concluded, was the sole protection of small, weak countries against the expansionist aims of more powerful states.

In the end, the controversial religious-freedom article caused only one defection. All the states with large Muslim populations except Saudi Arabia voted yes when the whole draft Declaration was presented for approval by the third committee. The main speaker on the issue in the General Assembly was Muhammad Zafrulla Khan, the foreign minister of Pakistan and head of its UN delegation. A member of the minority Ahmadi Muslim sect, Kahn told the delegates that the article on religious freedom would have the full support of Pakistan, then the UN member with the largest Muslim population. The issue, he said, "involved the honor of Islam."[65] He cited a passage from the Koran for the proposition that faith could not have an obligatory character: "Let him who chooses to believe, believe, and him who chooses to disbelieve, disbelieve." Moreover, he pointed out, Islam was a proselytizing religion that strove to persuade others to change their faith and to alter their way of living. It recognized the same right of conversion for other religions, though it had objections to Christian missionary work when that work assumed a political character. The freedom to change beliefs, he concluded, was consistent with the Islamic religion.

Syria's Abdul Rahman Kavaly rose to defend the Declaration against those who complained of its imperfections. There had been many human rights declarations throughout history, he began. Those earlier declarations had not been perfect, nor had they been perfectly observed. Civilization had progressed slowly. As for the present Declaration, "It was not the work of a few representatives in the Assembly or in the Economic and Social Council; it was the achievement of generations of human beings who had worked towards that end." Now the task was to put its principles into effect—through education, national legislation, and forms of government.[66]

⚊

In all, thirty-four delegates expressed their views. There was a "great solemnity, full of emotion" in the Palais de Chaillot, Santa Cruz recalled, as one speaker after another offered his or her appraisal of the value the document was likely to have.

> I perceived clearly that I was participating in a truly significant historic event in which a consensus had been reached as to the supreme value of the human person, a value that did not originate in the decision of a worldly power, but rather in the fact of existing—which gave rise to the inalienable right to live free from want and oppression and to fully develop one's personality. In the Great Hall . . . there was an atmosphere of genuine solidarity and brotherhood among men and women from all latitudes, the like of which I have not seen again in any international setting. Sincerity and a sober eloquence free of bombast characterized most of the interventions.[67]

When the speeches were over, the General Assembly polled the members on each article separately, with an impressive result: twenty-three of thirty articles gained unanimous approval. A few scattered abstentions were recorded on Articles 1 and 2—as well as on the articles dealing with freedom of movement, freedom of religion, freedom of opinion and expression, the right to education, and the article stating that everyone has a right to a social and international order in which the Declaration's rights can be fully realized. There were no nays except on the nondiscrimination article (one vote); the article on the family (six votes); and the article on freedom of opinion and expression (seven votes).

With the Declaration certain of adoption at that point, the question uppermost in the minds of the framers must have been whether any of the nays on certain articles would carry over into votes against the Declaration as a whole. Roosevelt seems to have expected the Soviet bloc might vote against it, while Humphrey was still desperately hoping until the last minute for the "miracle" of their approval.[68] Neither her fears nor his hopes were realized.

At four minutes before midnight the president called the roll and drew by lot the name of the country to vote first, Burma. After Burma voted yes, Byelorussia, next in order, abstained, as did the other members of the Soviet bloc when their turns came up—Czechoslovakia, Poland, the Ukraine, the USSR, and Yugoslavia. It had been clear from the beginning that South Africa would be unable to accept the Declaration, but she too abstained rather than voting against it. So did Saudi Arabia, breaking

ranks with the other Muslim nations that had voted yes. The final tally
was forty-eight in favor, eight abstentions, and none opposed. Two countries, Honduras and Yemen, were absent. The Soviet abstention, Mrs.
Roosevelt believed, was attributable mainly to one article that "they
couldn't possibly accept": Article 13, which provides that everyone has
the right to leave his country.[69]

Herbert Evatt, president of the General Assembly, closed the session
by paying tribute to Eleanor Roosevelt: "It is particularly fitting that there
should be present on this occasion the person who, with the assistance of
many others, has played a leading role in the work, a person who has
raised to greater heights even so great a name—Mrs. Roosevelt, the representative of the United States of America."[70] As the General Assembly
rose to give her a standing ovation, a radiant smile illuminated her weary
face.

Now that her efforts on the Declaration had been brought to a successful conclusion, Eleanor Roosevelt was uncharacteristically pensive. "It
was after midnight when I left the Palais de Chaillot," she wrote. "I was
tired. I wondered whether a mere statement of rights, without legal obligation, would inspire governments to see that these rights were observed."[71] The mood soon passed, however. Throughout her life she would
treasure the memory of December 10, 1948, when her most important
work came to fruition.

Charles Malik seems not to have been in a triumphal mood, either. His
diary, after draft notes for his speech, contains only one cryptic, Heideg-
gerian note: *"Wir sind zu spät für die Götter, zu früh für das Sein."*[72]*
René Cassin was more sanguine. He had gone out to celebrate with some
English and American reporters. "That night, with so many martyrs in my
memories," he later mused, "it was my good fortune to be seated next to
the great dancer, Katherine Dunham, whose modern dance troupe was
then enjoying acclaim in Paris."[73] He took the African American woman's
companionship as a sign that a new age of brotherhood was perhaps
dawning.

The absence of any nays enabled the framers of the Declaration to proclaim a great victory. Less emphasized at the time, but equally significant,
was the fact that twenty-three of thirty articles were approved without

---

*"We are too late for the gods, too early for Being."

nays or abstentions when votes on each article were taken separately. For the first time in history, the organized community of nations had issued a common declaration of human rights and fundamental freedoms. With its claim to universality, the Declaration marked a new stage in humanity's quest for freedom. But what could that claim to universality mean in a world so divided along political, cultural, and ideological lines?

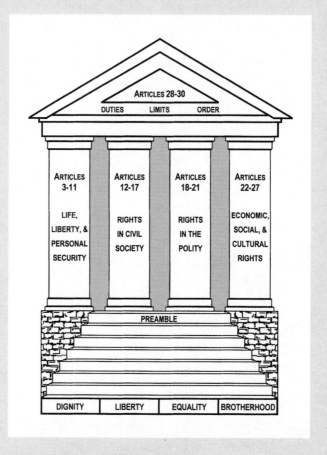

"Cassin's Portico."

CHAPTER 10

THE DECLARATION OF
INTERDEPENDENCE

A Close Look at the Declaration

In her speech urging the adoption of the Declaration, Eleanor Roosevelt had expressed the hope that it would take its place in the pantheon occupied by the Magna Carta, the French Declaration of the Rights of Man and Citizen of 1789, and the American Bill of Rights. Potentially the document she had nurtured into being would touch even more lives than those earlier milestones on humanity's long struggle for freedom, for it aspired to affect every man and woman on earth. England's Magna Carta had asserted rights of barons and prelates against absolute monarchs. The American Declaration of Independence, with its ringing affirmation of equality, had justified a break with the mother country on the ground that the colonists had been denied the rights of Englishmen. The Bill of Rights and the French Declaration of 1789 claimed certain political and civil rights for all citizens. The Universal Declaration harvested the wisdom of these and other declarations, but it reflected the growing modern conviction that fundamental freedoms included "freedom from want" and that these freedoms must not be conditioned on membership in a particular nation, class, race, or gender.

The Universal Declaration heralded a new moment in the history of human rights. With its emphasis on dignity, and its insistence on the link between freedom and solidarity, the document epitomized the spirit of the prolific constitution and treaty-making activity that followed World

War II. When read as it was meant to be, namely as a whole, it is an integrated document that rests on a concept of the dignity of the human person within the human family. In substance, as well as in form, it is a declaration of interdependence—interdependence of people, nations, and rights.

René Cassin compared the Declaration to the portico of a temple.[1] He chose the word carefully, for he knew that the Declaration could never be more than an entryway to a better world. In Cassin's image, the Preamble, with its seven stately clauses, represented the *courtyard steps* of the portico. The general principles of dignity, liberty, equality, and brotherhood (proclaimed in Articles 1 and 2) were the portico's *four foundation blocks*. The main body of the Declaration consists of rights arranged in *four columns:* rights pertaining to individuals as such (Articles 3 through 11); the rights of the individual in relation to others and to various groups (Articles 12 through 17); the spiritual, public, and political liberties (Articles 18 through 21); and the economic, social, and cultural rights (Articles 22 through 27). The Declaration is crowned by a *pediment* (Articles 28 through 30) linking the individual and society and placing the enumerated rights in the context of limits, duties, and the social and political order in which they are to be realized.

Let us stroll through the portico, noting the relations among its parts and some of the more interesting architectural details.

THE COURTYARD STEPS

The Declaration's Preamble and Proclamation, together with Articles 1 and 2, belong to what in civil-law terminology is called the "general part," setting forth the premises, purposes, and principles that apply to what follows.

PREAMBLE

Whereas recognition of the inherent dignity and of the equal and inalienable rights of all members of the human family is the foundation of freedom, justice and peace in the world.

Whereas disregard and contempt for human rights have resulted in barbarous acts which have outraged the conscience of mankind, and the advent of a world in which human beings shall enjoy freedom of speech and belief and freedom from fear and want has been proclaimed as the highest aspiration of the common people.

Whereas it is essential, if man is not to be compelled to have recourse, as a last resort, to rebellion against tyranny and oppression, that human rights should be protected by the rule of law.

Whereas it is essential to promote the development of friendly relations between nations.

Whereas the peoples of the United Nations have in the Charter reaffirmed their faith in fundamental human rights, in the dignity and worth of the human person and in the equal rights of men and women and have determined to promote social progress and better standards of life in larger freedom.

Whereas the Member States have pledged themselves to achieve, in cooperation with the United Nations, the promotion of universal respect for and observance of human rights and fundamental freedoms.

Whereas a common understanding of these rights and freedoms is of the greatest importance for the full realization of this pledge.

Now, Therefore, THE GENERAL ASSEMBLY proclaims

THIS UNIVERSAL DECLARATION OF HUMAN RIGHTS as a common standard of achievement for all peoples and all nations, to the end that every individual and every organ of society, keeping this Declaration constantly in mind, shall strive by teaching and education to promote respect for these rights and freedoms and by progressive measures, national and international, to secure their universal and effective recognition and observance, both among the peoples of Member States themselves and among the peoples of territories under their jurisdiction.

This prologue establishes the Declaration's membership in the large family of dignity-based rights instruments that were adopted after the Second World War.[2] Like other members of this family, the Declaration joins ideas associated with liberty-based constitutionalism to a strong commitment to social justice. Like them, it embodies a vision of ordered liberty, grounded in an understanding of human beings as both individual and social. And like them, it traces its legitimacy to fundamental characteristics of human nature: human dignity is said to be "inherent"; human beings are said to be "born" free and equal and "endowed" with reason and conscience.

The Preamble begins by linking freedom, justice, and peace and by asserting that these goals *depend* upon the recognition of human dignity and rights. The proposition that human rights are *universal,* belonging to "all members of the human family," challenged the traditional view that the relation between a sovereign state and its own citizens was that nation's own exclusive business. Equally noteworthy in the first clause is the word *recognition.* Prior to World War II, legal positivism (the view that there are no rights other than those granted by the laws of the state) flourished in the United States and Europe and was dogma in the Soviet Union. But legally sanctioned atrocities committed in Nazi Germany had caused many people to reevaluate the proposition that there is no higher law by which the laws of nation-states can be judged. The Declaration implicitly rejected the positivist position by stating that fundamental rights are recognized, rather than conferred.

The second clause evokes in general terms the circumstances that give rise to the need for universal standards: "[D]isregard and contempt for human rights have resulted in barbarous acts which have outraged the conscience of mankind." This clause, taken from Cassin's draft Preamble, originally mentioned the atrocities of World Wars I and II, but the reference was removed at the third committee stage in order to avoid giving the impression that the Declaration was merely a response to specific historical circumstances.[3] Cassin himself came to believe that this decision was wise. In later years he wrote approvingly that "the United Nations refused to lower the Declaration to the rank of an act of resentment turned toward the past."[4] The clause speaks of hopes for a better world where human beings may enjoy what many readers of the day would have recognized as Franklin Roosevelt's four freedoms: "freedom of speech and belief and freedom from fear and want."[5] Roosevelt's articulation of the aims of the war had been a touchstone for the framers of the Declaration, from Humphrey's draft onward.

The third clause gives prominence to a key concept: the importance and the fragility of the rule of law. Echoing allusions to the right to revolt in the U.S. Declaration of Independence and other documents, this clause reminds the nations that they ignore human rights at their peril. Both Humphrey and Cassin had included a right to resist tyranny and oppression in their drafts, but the Human Rights Commission, balancing that venerable notion with the hope that the Declaration would promote peaceful resolution of grievances, decided not to proclaim a fundamental human right to resistance.[6] If people are not to resort to violence against oppression, "human rights should be protected by the rule of law."

The fourth and fifth clauses anchor the Declaration firmly in the UN Charter. By expressly including women, by alluding to freedom from want, and by evoking the UN Charter's commitment to better standards of life, the Preamble signals that the Declaration is not just a universalization of the eighteenth-century "rights of man," but part of a new stage in the history of human rights.

The last two "whereas" clauses recite the pledge to promote respect for human rights and fundamental freedoms and implicitly acknowledge the hurdles ahead by stating that "a common understanding of [the Declaration's] rights and freedoms is of the greatest importance for the full realization of this pledge."

The Preamble concludes with a proclamation clause, announcing the nature of the document. The clause makes clear that the Declaration is not a binding treaty. Eleanor Roosevelt had insisted on this point in her December 9 speech:

> In giving our approval to the declaration today, it is of primary importance that we keep clearly in mind the basic character of the document. It is not a treaty; it is not an international agreement. It is not and does not purport to be a statement of law or of legal obligation. It is a declaration of basic principles of human rights and freedoms, to be stamped with the approval of the General Assembly by formal vote of its members, and to serve as a common standard of achievement for all peoples of all nations.[7]

As Roosevelt noted, the Declaration is not addressed merely to nations. It is "a common standard of achievement for all peoples and nations" toward which "every individual and every organ of society" should "strive" and by which the conduct of nations and peoples can be measured.

The term *declaration* has since been officially defined by the UN Secretariat as "a formal and solemn instrument, suitable for rare occasions when principles of great and lasting significance are being enunciated."[8] Though not legally binding, a declaration "may by custom become recognized as laying down rules binding upon States." In the case of the Universal Declaration, most of its rights already had the force of law in 1948 in many states and have since been incorporated into the domestic legal systems of most countries.[9] Several parts are regarded as having become part of "customary international law," though the extent to which this has occurred is much disputed.[10]

THE FOUNDATION STONES

The Declaration proper begins not with a right, but with two introductory articles that, together with the Preamble, were meant to set the tone for the entire Declaration.

> Article 1. All human beings are born free and equal in dignity and rights. They are endowed with reason and conscience and should act towards one another in a spirit of brotherhood.
>
> Article 2. Everyone is entitled to all the rights and freedoms set forth in this Declaration without distinction of any kind, such as race, colour, sex, language, religion, political or other opinion, national or social origin, property, birth or other status.
>
> Furthermore, no distinction shall be made on the basis of the political, jurisdictional or international status of the country or territory to which a person belongs, whether it be independent, trust, non-self-governing or under any other limitation of sovereignty.

If Cassin had had his way, Article 29 on duties and limits would have been a third article in this sequence. But Chang prevailed on this point by arguing that it was more "logical" to deal with limitations on rights after the rights themselves had been stated.

For the precise formulation of Article 2, the Human Rights Commission relied heavily on the advice of the UN Sub-Commission on the Prevention of Discrimination and the Protection of Minorities. The first paragraph, reinforcing the principle of universality, makes clear that "Everyone" in the Declaration really means everyone—"without distinction of any kind." To the UN Charter's nonexclusive list of forms of discrimination based on race, sex, language, and religion, Paragraph 1 adds color, opinion, national or social origin, material circumstances, and birth. The second paragraph—adopted, as we have seen, over the objections of the colonial powers—left no room for doubt that "Everyone" includes persons under colonial rule, foreign occupation, or otherwise deprived of self-government.

COLUMN ONE

The Declaration devotes its first column (Articles 3 to 11) to familiar individual rights that had received a significant degree of recognition in principle, if not necessarily in practice, in the constitutions of many nations, including the Soviet Union: rights to life, liberty, and personal security; bans on slavery and torture; rights to legal recognition, equality before the law, effective remedies for violation of fundamental rights and freedom from arbitrary arrest and detention; guarantees of fair criminal procedures, presumption of innocence; and the principle of nonretroactivity in criminal law.[11]

Article 3. Everyone has the right to life, liberty and security of person.

Article 4. No one shall be held in slavery or servitude: slavery and the slave trade shall be prohibited in all their forms.

Article 5. No one shall be subjected to torture or to cruel, inhuman or degrading treatment or punishment.

Article 6. Everyone has the right to recognition everywhere as a person before the law.

Article 7. All are equal before the law and are entitled without any discrimination to equal protection of the law. All are entitled to equal protection against any discrimination in violation of this Declaration and against any incitement to such discrimination.

Article 8. Everyone has the right to an effective remedy by the competent national tribunals for acts violating the fundamental rights granted him by the constitution or by law.

Article 9. No one shall be subjected to arbitrary arrest, detention or exile.

Article 10. Everyone is entitled in full equality to a fair and public hearing by an independent and impartial tribunal, in the determination of his rights and obligations and of any criminal charge against him.

Article 11. (1) Everyone charged with a penal offense has the right to be presumed innocent until proved guilty according to law in a public trial at which he has had all the guarantees necessary for his defense. (2) No one shall be held guilty of any penal offense or any act or omission which did not constitute a penal offense under national or international law at the time when it was committed. Nor shall a heavier penalty be imposed than the one that was applicable at the time the penal offense was committed.

These articles, aimed at protecting individuals from aggression and assuring fair procedures, are at the heart of the most widely publicized human rights disputes in the world today. They had abundant antecedents in existing constitutions, provoked little controversy in the drafting process, consumed the least time in the third committee, and were approved unanimously without abstentions by the General Assembly. They are also the most tightly drafted sections of the Declaration, leaving far less room for local variation than the rights set forth in subsequent articles. As P. C. Chang suggested in the third committee debates, this whole series of rights is probably best understood as progressively enlarging the principles set forth in Article 3.

Article 11, though easily approved, provoked some discussion within the Commission of the question of whether the Nuremberg trials had violated the ex post facto principle. Telford Taylor, who served on the U.S. prosecution staff, wrote in his history of the trials, "There is no likelihood that this particular clash of opinions will ever be resolved."[12] He pointed out, however, that Nuremberg did set a precedent for the *future,* a precedent formally ratified by the UN General Assembly in December 1946, when it "affirmed the principles of international law recognized by the charter of the Nuremberg Tribunal and the judgment of the Tribunal."

American readers will note the absence from this list of such familiar elements of the U.S. Bill of Rights as the requirement of a grand jury indictment, the right to a trial by jury in criminal cases, and the prohibition of double jeopardy. The omission of these protections illustrates the Human Rights Commission's aim to present a framework containing only the most basic ideas, to be supplemented and elaborated (the commissioners hoped) by different nations in their own ways.

COLUMN TWO

Articles 12 to 17 are concerned primarily with the rights of people in civil and political society. They include the right to be free of arbitrary interference with one's "privacy, family, home, or correspondence" and from arbitrary attacks upon one's "honor and reputation"; freedom of movement and the right of return; the right to seek and enjoy political asylum; the right to a nationality; provisions on marriage and the family and the right to own property. American readers will note, again, the omission of such specifics as requirements for search warrants, the prohibition on peacetime quartering of troops in private residences, and the requirement of just compensation for the taking of private property for public use.

Article 12. No one shall be subjected to arbitrary interference with his privacy, family, home or correspondence, nor to attacks upon his honour and reputation. Everyone has the right to the protection of the law against such interference or attacks.

Article 13. (1) Everyone has the right to freedom of movement and residence within the borders of each state. (2) Everyone has the right to leave any country, including his own, and to return to his country.

Article 14. (1) Everyone has the right to seek and to enjoy in other countries asylum from persecution. (2) This right may not be invoked in the case of prosecutions genuinely arising from non-political crimes or from acts contrary to the purposes and principles of the United Nations.

Article 15. (1) Everyone has the right to a nationality. (2) No one shall be arbitrarily deprived of his nationality nor denied the right to change his nationality.

Article 16. (1) Men and women of full age, without any limitation due to race, nationality or religion, have the right to marry and to found a family. They are entitled to equal rights as to marriage, during marriage, and at its dissolution. (2) Marriage shall be entered into only with the free and full consent of the intending spouses. (3) The family is the natural and fundamental group unit of society and is entitled to protection by society and the state.

Article 17. (1) Everyone has the right to own property alone as well as in association with others. (2) No one shall be arbitrarily deprived of his property.

The three articles on freedom of movement, asylum, and nationality represented, as we have seen, an important innovation: they were rights with an international dimension. The article on freedom of movement, in particular, was a sore point for the Soviet Union. In its instructions to Pavlov in April 1948, the Politburo called special attention to the fact that the draft "contains articles proclaiming the utmost freedom of citizens toward their country, state and people." Pavlov was told to oppose the freedom of movement article because it established "the right of an individual to leave his country and to acquire citizenship of any other country, irrespective of the laws of the mother country and its interests."[13]

Article 16, dealing with marriage and the family, is a blend of old and new ideas with varying genealogies. It went far beyond most national legislation of the day with its affirmation of the principle of equal rights between spouses both during marriage and at its dissolution. The idea that the family "is entitled to protection by society and the state," on the other hand, was familiar in many countries as legislative policy, had already appeared in several constitutions, and would shortly appear in many others.[14] Though Article 16 has no counterpart in the U.S. Constitution, the freedom to marry found a secure place in American constitutional law in 1967, when the Supreme Court struck down laws banning interracial marriages, saying, "The freedom to marry has long been recognized as one of the vital personal rights essential to the orderly pursuit of happiness by free men."[15]

Article 17 on property rights occasioned much debate. The United States strongly supported a right to own private property and to be protected against public taking of private property without due safeguards. The United Kingdom's Labour government representatives, however, took the position that the article should be omitted, arguing that regulation of property rights was so extensive everywhere in the modern world that it made no sense to speak of a right to ownership. Many Latin Americans took an entirely different tack: they wanted the article to specify a right to enough private property for a decent existence. The Soviets, for their part, objected to the idea that a decent existence should be grounded in private property and insisted that the article should take account of the different economic systems in various countries. The compromise above was achieved by omitting the word *private* and, as characteristically happens in difficult negotiations, by escaping to a high level of generality.

The rights in column two are significantly more open-ended than the protections against violent and arbitrary treatment in column one, thus leaving larger scope for variation in different social and political contexts. Individuals everywhere have the right to be free of torture, but different countries may, within limits, legitimately come to different conclusions about the conditions under which private property may be taken for public use.

COLUMN THREE

Articles 18 through 21 contain a group of rights in which representatives of liberal democracies took special pride: freedom of religion and belief in Article 18; freedom of opinion, expression, and communication in Article 19; freedom of assembly and association in Article 20; and the principle of participation in government in Article 21.

Article 18. Everyone has the right to freedom of thought, conscience and religion; this right includes freedom to change his religion or belief, and freedom, either alone or in community with others, and in public or private, to manifest his religion or belief in teaching, practice, worship and observance.

Article 19. Everyone has the right to freedom of opinion and expression; this right includes freedom to hold opinions without interference and to seek, receive and impart information and ideas through any media and regardless of frontiers.

Article 20. (1) Everyone has the right to freedom of peaceful assembly and association. (2) No one may be compelled to belong to an association.

Article 21. (1) Everyone has the right to take part in the government of his country, directly or through freely chosen representatives. (2) Everyone has the right of equal access to public service in his country. (3) The will of the people shall be the basis of the authority of government; this will shall be expressed in periodic and genuine elections which shall be by universal and equal suffrage and shall be held by secret ballot or by equivalent free voting procedures.

The Soviets, in keeping with Marx's theory that human freedom was possible only in the collective, labeled the rights in Articles 18 through 20 hollow words. According to Andrei Vishinsky's textbook, *Soviet Public Law,* these so-called freedoms posed a danger to struggling people's republics and were "the most false and hypocritical department of law."[16] The USSR's delegates did not openly oppose these "bourgeois" rights in the Human Rights Commission but proposed to make them more compatible with the Soviet Constitution, where they were accompanied with qualifying phrases to the effect that they must be exercised in conformity with the interests of working people and used to strengthen the socialist system. Socialist-bloc representatives repeatedly submitted amendments to deny such rights to "fascists and nazis." These proposals were always defeated after some member of the Commission, usually Chang or Cassin, pointed out that this group of rights, like other rights, was already limited by the general language in what are now Articles 29 and 30.

Absent from Article 18 on religious freedom is a distinctive feature of the American Bill of Rights, the language regarding religious establishment in the First Amendment: "Congress shall make no law respecting an establishment of religion or prohibiting the free exercise thereof . . ." The article also contains a more elaborate description of religious freedom: it includes "freedom, either alone or in community with others, and in public or private, to manifest his religion or belief. . . ." As we have seen, the decision to specifically mention the freedom to change religion (already implicit in freedom of religion) was a deal breaker for Saudi Arabia.

The differences between democratic and Communist regimes, and between planned and market economies, were so great that agreements regarding the right to participate in government and to own property could be reached only by leaving much room for local variation. In the Human Rights Commission, representatives of liberal democracies had tried hard to include a reference to political parties in Article 21, on the ground that, as Belgium's Fernand Dehousse had argued, two or more parties are necessary for a truly democratic system. But Pavlov had energetically defended the Soviet system of one "completely representative" party, and Dehousse, for the sake of consensus, had withdrawn his amendment. In the third committee, Communist regimes, colonial powers, and monarchies alike joined in the overwhelming vote of approval for the principles of Article 21 that would one day transform their world.

COLUMN FOUR

The same political differences that made compromise difficult on Articles 17 and 21 also had to be bridged in framing the last group of rights in the Declaration, the "new" social, economic, and cultural rights. Contrary to later belief, the countries within the Soviet sphere of influence were neither alone nor the most vigorous in pushing for the inclusion of social and economic rights. Though the details of these provisions were a continuing source of controversy within the Commission, no nation opposed them in principle. On the drafting committee it was the Chilean Hernán Santa Cruz, a social democrat of upper-class background, who was their most consistently zealous promoter. Chile had been hard hit by the Depression of the 1930s, and labor, education, and housing reforms were high on the agenda of its democratic-left coalition government. Leftist governments were then in power in England and France, too. Clement Attlee's Labour Party had defeated Churchill in 1945, and de Gaulle had resigned as provisional president in 1946, when the Fourth Republic was established by a socialist, Communist, and centrist coalition.

P. C. Chang was also a strong backer of the social and economic articles. He liked to let Westerners know that economic and social justice, far from being an entirely modern notion, was a 2,500-year-old Confucian idea. In one speech to ECOSOC, Chang informed his colleagues:

> When the Ta Tao or Grand Way prevails, the world is for the welfare of all. . . . People regard not only their own parents as parents, nor only their own children as children. Provisions are made for the aged, employment is provided for the able-bodied and education is afforded to the young. Widows and widowers, orphans and the childless, the deformed and the diseased, are all cared for.[17]

The Declaration's provisions on social and economic rights from Humphrey's draft onward were similar to those already in effect in many countries. Some of these were long-standing, with ancestors in early continental constitutions such as Frederick the Great's Prussian General Code (which provided that the state was obliged to provide food, work, and wages for all who could not support themselves and relief for the poor who were unable to work); the Norwegian Constitution of 1814 (obliging "the authorities of the State to create conditions which make it possible for every person who is able to work to earn his living by his work"); and various French constitutions from the revolutionary period to the 1946 Constitution of the Fourth Republic. Several articles in the Bogotá Declaration, inspired in part by Christian social thought and in part by the Mexican socialist revolution, dealt with rights to education, work, and social security. Sponsored by social democratic, socialist, and Christian political parties, comparable rights had appeared or would soon appear in most modern constitutions, where (though not directly enforceable) they lend a presumption of constitutionality to social legislation.[18] At the international level, similar principles had been recognized by the International Labor Organization.

The eighteenth-century U.S. Constitution was silent on such matters, but similar ideas had been embodied in New Deal legislation, such as the National Labor Relations Act and the Social Security Act. Articles 21 through 25 contained more than an echo of FDR's economic program, a legacy that Mrs. Roosevelt "through her very name," according to Malik, had "imported into our council chambers."[19] In 1944 Franklin Roosevelt had even proposed a "second bill of rights," in a State of the Union speech summing up the social and economic goals of his administration. His list included rights to "a good education"; "a useful and remunerative job"; a wage adequate for basic needs; "adequate medical care"; "adequate protection from the economic fears of old age, sickness, accident, and unemployment"; and the "right of every family to a decent home."[20]

With regard to the economic, social, and cultural rights, Eleanor Roosevelt told the General Assembly on the eve of the Declaration's adoption that her government gave its "wholehearted support" to those articles. The United States did not, however, consider them to "imply an obligation on governments to assure the enjoyment of these rights by direct governmental action."

Where this group of rights was concerned, the devil, as Mrs. Roosevelt knew, was in the details. She had written in a 1940 essay:

It would seem clear that in a Democracy a minimum standard of security must at least be possible for every child in order to achieve the equality of opportunity which is one of the basic principles set forth as a fundamental of Democracy. This means achieving an economic level below which no one is permitted to fall, and keeping a fairly stable balance between that level and the cost of living. No one as yet seems to know just how to do this without an amount of planning which will be considered too restrictive for freedom. The line between domination and voluntary acquiescence in certain controls is a very difficult one to establish.[21]

Unlike Articles 3 through 20, which refer primarily to what must not be done *to* people, Articles 22 through 27 sometimes refer to what ought to be done *for* people. Representatives of Western liberal democracies were concerned not to dampen private initiative or to give too much power to the state, while Soviet-bloc representatives maintained that these rights were meaningless without a strong state in charge of health, education, and welfare.

All the rights in column four are introduced by Article 22, the chapeau or mini-Preamble that describes them as "indispensable" and connects them to traditional protections of the individual.

Article 22. Everyone, as a member of society, has the right to social security and is entitled to realization, through national effort and international cooperation and in accordance with the organization and resources of each State, of the economic, social and cultural rights indispensable for his dignity and for the free development of his personality.

Article 23. (1) Everyone has the right to work, to free choice of employment, to just and favorable conditions of work and to protection against unemployment.

(2) Everyone, without any discrimination, has the right to equal pay for equal work.

(3) Everyone who works has the right to just and favourable remuneration ensuring for himself and his family an existence worthy of human dignity, and supplemented, if necessary, by other means of social protection.

(4) Everyone has the right to form and to join trade unions for the protection of his interests.

Article 24. Everyone has the right to rest and leisure, including reasonable limitation of working hours and periodic holidays with pay.

Article 25. (1) Everyone has the right to a standard of living adequate for the health and well-being of himself and of his family, including food, clothing, housing, medical care and necessary social services, and the right to security in the event of unemployment, sickness, disability, widowhood, old age or other lack of livelihood in circumstances beyond his control.

(2) Motherhood and childhood are entitled to special care and assistance. All children, whether born in or out of wedlock, shall enjoy the same social protection.

Article 26. (1) Everyone has the right to education. Education shall be free, at least in the elementary and fundamental stages. Elementary education shall be compulsory. Technical and professional education shall be made generally available and higher education shall be equally accessible to all on the basis of merit.

(2) Education shall be directed to the full development of the human personality and to the strengthening of respect for human rights and fundamental freedoms. It shall promote understanding, tolerance and friendship among all nations, racial or religious groups, and shall further the activities of the United Nations for the maintenance of peace.

(3) Parents have a prior right to choose the kind of education that shall be given to their children.

Article 27. (1) Everyone has the right freely to participate in the cultural life of the community, to enjoy the arts and to share in scientific advancement and its benefits. (2) Everyone has the right to the protection of the moral and material interests resulting from any scientific, literary or artistic production of which he is the author.

The reference in the chapeau to the "organization" of each state is key, because it leaves room for choice among a range of *means* of striving toward the common social and economic goals—state programs and policies, international initiatives, market dynamics, voluntary action, or various combinations of approaches. The reference to "resources" is equally crucial—a response to the fears of Egypt, India, and other poor countries about arousing unrealistic expectations. They needed to clarify that the right to social security could be implemented gradually as resources permitted.

Much of the language on work in Articles 23 and 24 was already the common stuff of social legislation in the liberal democracies (decent working conditions, including paid vacations and limits on working hours; protection against unemployment; the right to form and join unions; maternal and child protection). Less widely recognized, however, were Article 23's "right to work" and its "right to equal pay for equal work" without discrimination; Article 25's right to a decent standard of living for the worker "and his family"; and Article 26's right to education. The last sentence of Article 25—on children born outside marriage—was an important specification of Article 2's nondiscrimination principle. It was one of the earliest acknowledgments of a principle that would eventually transform national legislation nearly everywhere.

The Human Rights Commission's desire for consistency of style—specifically, to use the formulas "Everyone has the right to . . ." or "Everyone is entitled to . . ."—ruled out a common alternative approach to this group of issues. At the national level, welfare principles are sometimes framed as obligations of society and the state rather than entitlements of individuals. With hindsight, it is perhaps regrettable that the framers, in dealing with these provisions, did not adopt the obligation model. To couch the social security and welfare principles in terms of a common responsibility might have resonated better than rights in most of the world's cultures and would still have left room for experiments with different mixes of private and public approaches.

Article 26 on education is one of the few articles in the Declaration directly influenced by the European holocaust. There was relatively little discussion of Nazi atrocities in the Human Rights Commission, probably because the members saw the business of punishing war criminals as belonging to the law of war (the Nuremberg Principles and the Genocide Convention) and regarded their own task as setting conditions for peace. There was consensus on the Commission that education was crucial to the aim of establishing "freedom, justice, and peace in the world," and the first paragraph of Article 26 was drafted to reflect that belief. The second paragraph was added at the Geneva meeting after an observer from the World Jewish Congress noted that the article "provided a technical framework," but "contained nothing about the spirit governing education." Claiming that lack of attention to that essential matter in Germany "had been the main cause of two catastrophic wars," he proposed the language that in substance became Article 26 (2). The reference to the activities of the United Nations was added at the third committee stage on the motion of the United States and Mexico. The paragraph on parental rights was, as we have seen, prompted by recollection of Nazi indoctrination tactics. It provides a bridge between the new right to education and the older family protection idea of Article 16.

Cassin saw the last three sections of the Declaration as the "pediment" of the portico, because they bring under one "roof" individuals, civil society, and the state, with all their respective rights and responsibilities. Like the Preamble and Articles 1 and 2, these three sections were intended to inform the document as a whole. They address the conditions that are necessary to the realization of the rights and freedoms enumerated in the Declaration.

Article 28. Everyone is entitled to a social and international order in which the rights and freedoms set forth in this Declaration can be fully realized.

Article 29. (1) Everyone has duties to the community in which alone the free and full development of his personality is possible.

(2) In the exercise of his rights and freedoms, everyone shall be subject only to such limitations as are determined by law solely for the purpose of securing due recognition and respect for the rights and freedoms of others and of meeting the just requirements of morality, public order and the general welfare in a democratic society.

(3) These rights and freedoms may in no case be exercised contrary to the purposes and principles of the United Nations.

Article 30. Nothing in this Declaration may be interpreted as implying for any State, group, or person any right to engage in any activity or perform any act aimed at the destruction of any of the rights and freedoms set forth herein.

Malik's Article 28 serves as a preamble to the pediment. Its affirmation of the need for a social and international order echoes the main Preamble's insistence on the rule of law and friendly relations among nations. Two essential features of such an order are then sketched out in Article 29, where the Declaration speaks of duties and limits. The reference to a democratic society, of course, harks back to Article 21's specification of the minimal elements of a democratic regime. A final limit on rights is the subject of the concluding article.

━━

Even a casual reading of the Universal Declaration reveals many gaps, ambiguities, and internal tensions. That was inevitable, given the need to speak in general terms and the uneasy relationship among freedom, equality, and social security. The open texture of the Declaration was not only a consequence of political compromise on controversial issues. It also reflected the framers' desire for a document of broad application that would endure through changing times. They had established a "common standard of achievement" that could be interpreted and implemented in a legitimate variety of ways. They were comfortable with the idea that there would always be different visions of freedom within one human family. At the same time, they were well aware that no principles were immune to manipulation: they had personally witnessed the work of the great propaganda machines of National Socialist and Marxist dictatorships. But they were hopeful that with improved means of communication, the "common understanding" called for by the Preamble would increase. As 1948 drew to a close, the Declaration's portico stood open to the future. It was an invitation to peaceful competition in making human rights come alive in diverse cultures.

The time had come, Eleanor Roosevelt told the General Assembly on December 9, "to rededicate ourselves to the unfinished task which lies before us. We can now move on with new courage and inspiration to the completion of an international covenant on human rights and to measures for the implementation of human rights." Even as she spoke, however, events unfolding at home and abroad would render that task impossible to complete in her lifetime.

*Charles Malik and Eleanor Roosevelt at the 1951 Geneva meeting
of the Human Rights Commission, where Malik was elected to succeed
Mrs. Roosevelt as chairman. Elliott Roosevelt sits by his mother.*

THE DEEP FREEZE

The Declaration in the Cold War Years

Publicly, Eleanor Roosevelt hailed the Declaration for giving an international, universal status to basic rights and freedoms. Privately, she knew the struggle was far from over, and not only because of Russian intransigence. Just before the final vote in the General Assembly on December 10, 1948, she predicted in a scribbled note to a friend, "We will have trouble at home for it can't be a U.S. document & get by with 58 nations & at home that is hard to understand."[1]

More trouble was brewing than she imagined. The first indication of a coming shift in attitude in the United States was a blast against the Universal Declaration from Frank E. Holman, the president of the American Bar Association, in January 1949. He derided it as a manifesto on "pink paper" whose adoption would "promote state socialism, if not communism, throughout the world."[2] The Human Rights Commission, he noted, had included only three members from "English-speaking countries."

On the other side of the Iron Curtain, the Declaration's initial reception was no warmer. Two days after its adoption, Russia's chief delegate Andrei Vishinsky predicted that the 1948 Paris session would go down in UN history as one in which the majority, led by the Anglo-American bloc, had ignored the sovereignty of member states and attempted to interfere in the domestic affairs of "certain countries" in direct contravention of the UN Charter.[3]

The General Assembly was becoming a stage for cold war polemics. No one relished the theater more than Carlos Romulo, elected president of the General Assembly in 1949. One celebrated exchange between Romulo and Vishinsky took place after Romulo had opposed a Soviet motion to abolish the Balkan Commission that had been formed to act as a UN watchdog after civil war had broken out in Greece in 1946.[4] Vishinsky lashed out with a personal attack that pressed all of Romulo's hot buttons at once: "[T]his small man who spreads noise wherever he goes, who represents an insignificant country like the Philippines, has attacked the Soviet Union's motives. He reminds me of the Russian proverb, 'His ambition is worth a ruble when his ammunition is only worth a cent.' " Romulo, never at a loss for words, replied: "I am not interested in [his] personal allusions to me, [but] that he should refer to my insignificant little country must be understood as his usual way of dealing with small countries in this council with arrogance. . . . I would like to remind Mr. Vishinsky that we the little Davids are here to fling our pebbles of truth between the eyes of the blustering Goliaths and make them behave. As for my ambition being worth a ruble when my ammunition is only worth a cent, may I also remind Mr. Vishinsky that at the present rate of exchange the cent is worth more than the ruble." A cartoon in the next morning's press showed little Romulo with a slingshot hitting a Russian Goliath right between the eyes.

The Declaration was soon implicated in these verbal cold war battles. The Soviets began to see some of their fears about the "non-binding" document come true on two occasions in early 1949. The first was the trial in February of Hungarian Cardinal Jøszef Mindszenty, arrested for his outspoken opposition to communism. The case, widely discussed in terms of human rights, received worldwide attention. The Declaration's ban on torture, the right to a fair trial, and the rights to freedom of religion and expression were all involved. Not long after that, the General Assembly adopted a resolution censuring the Soviet Union for its refusal to permit Soviet women married to non-Soviets to leave the country—citing Article 13 on freedom of movement and Article 16 on the right to marry. The wide publicity accorded to the plight of the "Russian wives" dramatized the importance of these rights in a way that everyone could understand. In return, Eastern-bloc delegates began citing the Declaration in their tirades against racial discrimination and economic injustice in the West.

When the Human Rights Commission, now meeting only on an annual basis, convened on May 9, 1949, to begin devising an acceptable structure for implementation, the Truman administration's strategy for containing Soviet expansionism appeared to be working. The Marshall Plan for the economic recovery of Western Europe was under way, and the North Atlantic Treaty Organization (NATO) for collective self-defense had been established in April. In May West Germany became a constitutional republic, and Stalin finally gave up the Berlin blockade, vindicating the airlift.

The United States was ready to proceed with the preparation of a Covenant, but Eleanor Roosevelt and her advisers were determined to oppose any document that could not pass muster in the Senate. Given the climate of suspicion in Washington, that meant working for a relatively weak instrument. And it meant disappointing Humphrey, Malik, Cassin, Mehta, and others who wanted a Covenant with real teeth.

A frustrated John Humphrey recorded in his diary that the cooperation among Roosevelt, Chang, and Malik—so effective and so essential the preceding fall—had broken down completely. Roosevelt and Chang (along with the representatives of Egypt, Iran, the United Kingdom, and the Soviet bloc) refused to support a procedure for individual petitions to any agency that might be created under the Covenant. Malik and Chang lapsed into their old rivalry.

> Mrs. Roosevelt's role will embarrass her biographer; for, while she is undoubtedly bound by her instructions, she will appear on the record as the chief opponent of the principle [of a right to petition]. Indeed it may be said that the role that she has played since we began to work on the Covenant fails to harmonize with her reputation.
>
> I had lunch with Malik. He, Cassin and Mrs. Mehta are now leading the fight. P. C. Chang's role, I regret to have to say, is quite negative. Incidentally, P. C. Chang and Malik hate each other.[5]

"Hate" was too strong a word. Humphrey saw the disputes between Chang and Malik in terms of a confrontation between Confucianism and Thomism, but the philosophical debates between these two thoroughly modern men were more complicated than that. So were their personal differences. In spite of everything, Chang's children recalled, their father always referred to Charles Malik as the "good" Malik, to distinguish him from "bad" Jacob Malik, a Soviet delegate to the UN.[6]

The Commission adjourned on June 20 without having made much progress. Later that summer, any hopes that the end of the Berlin blockade signaled a thaw in East-West relations were shattered when the Soviet Union successfully tested an atomic bomb. October brought the unsettling but not unexpected news that a victorious Mao Tse-tung had announced the founding of the People's Republic of China.

In the United States, the fears aroused by those events escalated when evidence of Soviet espionage surfaced in the early months of 1950: Alger Hiss, a high-level State Department employee, was convicted of perjury for having lied about passing secret documents to the Soviets; Klaus Fuchs, a scientist who had worked on the atom bomb project at Los Alamos, confessed to having spied for the Soviet Union; and the Rosenbergs were indicted for conspiracy to transmit atomic secrets to Russian agents. A previously obscure Republican senator, Joseph McCarthy, seized on those developments to gain nationwide attention with his sensational charges that large numbers of government employees were "card-carrying communists."

The resulting growth of isolationism and anticommunism complicated Roosevelt's task. When the Human Rights Commission held its next session on March 27, 1950, she felt compelled by the situation at home to argue for a Covenant that included only political and civil rights and that would not be self-executing.

The meeting did not go well. Mrs. Roosevelt was herself uncomfortable with the tension between her role as chairman and as representative of a nation whose position antagonized many members. In a rueful "My Day" column, she confessed that she had started things "all wrong" one day by making "a speech on our amendment at the opening of the session without letting anybody else speak first and the result was that I hurt everybody's feelings and made them all feel injured for the rest of the morning. I apologized profusely because I knew only too well how stupid I had been. But one can never undo stupid things of that kind once they are done, nor can one change the way people feel about them."[7]

Roosevelt's advocacy of a relatively weak Covenant was particularly resented by John Humphrey, who felt that she was obstructing the Commission's progress. He aired his views on April 13, through a speech given by his close associate in the Secretariat, Henri Laugier. Laugier told a group of observers from nongovernmental organizations that the Covenant should provide a right of petition to individuals and groups and that it should include social and economic rights. He concluded that it was better to have no covenant than a weak covenant: "Just as bad money drives out good, an ineffective pact will deprive the Declaration of the immense moral authority it presently possesses. In my opinion, that would be a disastrous development."[8]

The next day Mrs. Roosevelt announced that there would be a closed meeting. When observers had left the room, she brought up the matter of the speech. "Mrs. Roosevelt was furious," Humphrey recalled. "After the adjournment, her eyes flashing, she scolded Laugier in the presence of a number of people." He had, she said, "compromised the future of the covenant." Partisans of a strong Covenant, including Malik and the Danish representative Max Sorenson, came to Laugier's defense. The incident threatened to cause a deep rift within the Commission.

By the end of the week, however, the chairman was taking steps to repair strained relationships. Humphrey recorded:

> The fuss soon died down; and, contrary to what might have been expected—for they knew very well that the ideas expressed in the speech came from me—it apparently did not harm my relations with either the American delegation or with Mrs. Roosevelt. I had lunch with her tête-à-tête and an opportunity for a frank talk at the end of the week. . . . She asked me for my uninhibited opinion about the work of the commission, and I told her what I thought. She then said that her government was now ready to have the commission recommend [an optional provision giving a right of petition to certain NGOs], but she warned me that this did not necessarily mean that the United States would itself accept it. No one could have been more friendly. . . .
>
> There was an element of comedy in the affair, which gave it a wider currency than it might otherwise have had. For, while Laugier's trial took place in a closed meeting, the conference officers forgot to turn off the loudspeakers in the pressroom so that everyone in [the building] knew what had happened.

When the Commission adjourned in May, Roosevelt told her side of the story in "My Day."[9] "I held a press conference yesterday, since we had finished the first Covenant on Human Rights. The press at Lake Success will undoubtedly write stories reflecting the questions they asked me as the United States delegate. They do listen now and then to the actual work of the committees, and so they know the atmosphere that prevails there. For that reason I anticipate they will reflect the fact that a number of members of the Commission are unhappy over the work which has been done in the last eight weeks. Monsieur Laugier, head of the Social Division of the United Nations, and Dr. John Humphrey, director of the Human Rights Division, will be included among this particular group.

"The two major gripes against the document," she continued, "are first, that the implementation is unsatisfactory, because only a state can complain against a state, and secondly, it has left out the newer social and economic rights." Some members of the Commission "think that if the first Covenant does not cover as many rights and freedoms as the Declaration, then it will hurt the Declaration to have a first Covenant," while other members "for one reason or another, have no desire ever to see a Covenant written." Still another group "want a Covenant ultimately but only when it reaches the perfection they desire."

Roosevelt herself was too pragmatic to let the best defeat the good. Her preference was for an incremental approach: "Personally, I feel that it is as well for the first covenant to cover only a limited number of these rights. Wide ratification is needed to make any right legally effective, and this has to be achieved step by step."

When Soviet-backed North Korean troops invaded South Korea on June 25, the chances for U.S. acceptance of even a watered-down convention dwindled. Once again, American soldiers were sent to fight in a foreign land, this time as part of a U.S.-led United Nations force aiding South Korea. Many people feared that a third world war was just around the corner. The internationalist spirit that had arisen in the United States during World War II was overcome by a furious wave of anticommunism.

By the time of the next Human Rights Commission meeting, in April and May of the following year, conservative Republican Senator John Bricker was calling for the United States to cease participating in the preparation of any human rights treaties. Bricker would soon follow up with an unsuccessful campaign to curtail the U.S. government's treaty-making power by constitutional amendment.

The poor outlook for ratification must have contributed to Eleanor Roosevelt's decision to step down from her chairmanship of the Human

Rights Commission in April 1951. The growing resentment of small nations against the United States had been a factor, too. "I have never seen such bitterness as I have in Committee #3 this year on the race problem and on the 'haves' against the 'have nots,' and small nations against big nations," she had written to a friend after a turbulent meeting of the General Assembly the previous December.[10] That hostility toward big nations, she reported to President Truman, had impaired her own effectiveness: "The mere fact that we spoke for something would be enough to make them suspicious." She told the president that it might be better for the United States to be represented by a black woman "or some other person chosen because he or she could not be accused of siding with the white race against the colored races of the world." Announcing her decision in "My Day," she said simply that "as representative of the United States, one of the great powers, I did not feel I should continue to hold the chairmanship of this important commission."

⁄⁄⁄

At the April-May 1951 meeting of the Human Rights Commission, held in Geneva, Charles Malik was elected chairman. John Humphrey was relieved. As much as he admired Eleanor Roosevelt, he had come to believe that, with the deepening cold war, she no longer exerted much influence on her country's State Department. "Everyone who really knows anything about our work," he wrote in his diary, "will welcome the change; for while Mrs. R's prestige with the multitude was undoubtedly an asset, . . . as spokesman for the State Department, she had also become one of the most reactionary forces."[11]

Humphrey's judgment was harsh and naive. Eleanor Roosevelt was a practical politician as well as a visionary statesperson. Her support of a watered-down "first" Covenant was probably the only feasible position for an American who still hoped for a document that might pass the U.S. Senate. Such a treaty would at least be a step in the right direction, to be followed by others when conditions improved. If not for Roosevelt's insistence, it is likely the State Department would have given up on the Covenant altogether.

She soldiered on at the Geneva meeting, writing in "My Day" that "if there is going to be an article written, one might as well get the best phrasing one possibly can and not give up."[12] But she acknowledged sadly that "there are a number of people who agree with a few of our own lawyers in the United States in feeling that no covenant can be written at this time."

Accompanied for part of the time by her son Elliott and relieved of her duties as chairman, Eleanor Roosevelt enjoyed Geneva as never before. In "My Day" she wrote not only of politics, but of the sight of Mont Blanc shrouded in clouds, the swans and ducks on Lake Leman, the narrow streets of the old city, the statue of Jean-Jacques Rousseau with its "fine and interesting head," and the public gardens "laid out in little squares of yellow and purple flowers." On May Day, she reported, René Cassin observed a local custom by presenting the women with fragrant bunches of lilies of the valley.

She even delighted in the Palace of the Nations as though noticing it for the first time: "I am impressed every day by the lovely views from different places. For instance, we walk up a flight of steps to the level of our present meeting room and, as we look up, the most beautiful blue sky is framed in the white archway at the top of the stairs. A lovelier sight can hardly be imagined, and as you reach the top, you get a vista through another archway in the wing on the other side and of the trees beyond it."

Within the meeting room, however, one of the Covenant's strongest supporters was defecting. "The attitude of the United Kingdom on the covenant," Eleanor Roosevelt told her "My Day" readers, "is very interesting. It was Britain's delegation, under the leadership of Lord Dukeston, that originally insisted a covenant should be part of the charter on human rights. . . . Now, however, the British delegate says she will abstain from voting because she feels everything is so badly phrased."

We now know, from a 1951 Foreign Office memo, that the United Kingdom had lost interest in the Covenant. Its strategy was now "to prolong the international discussions, to raise legal and practical difficulties, and to delay the conclusion of the Covenant for as long as possible."[13] John Humphrey had guessed as much after dining with Marguerite Bowie, who had replaced Geoffrey Wilson as the United Kingdom's representative on the Human Rights Commission. Bowie told Humphrey that she had instructions on every detail and that her voting was "closely watched by the Foreign Office."[14] Historian Brian Simpson surmises that the United Kingdom's disillusionment with the UN human rights program was "in part a product of the Cold War, in part a product of the beleaguered condition of the U.K. in the period during which the colonial empire was being dismantled, in part a genuine disgust at the hypocrisy exhibited by numerous members of the UN, and in part a dislike of the use of the notion of human rights in political warfare."[15]

The United Kingdom had in any event decided to participate in a human rights system at the European level, based on the 1950 European Convention for the Protection of Human Rights and Fundamental Freedoms. That regional convention was the first major project of the Council of Europe, an association formed in 1949 by the countries of Western Europe to promote European unity. Since the European Convention was based in large part on a proposal that the Foreign Office had submitted to the Human Rights Commission, and since Britain had played a key role in its negotiation, the British found the European document congenial.[16] They also appreciated the fact that the parties were not obliged to extend its protection to their dependent territories, unless they expressly agreed to do so. Like the proposal submitted by the United Kingdom to the UN, the European Convention contained no social and economic rights. It did, however, provide for a tribunal where private citizens could present complaints against their own governments.

As the 1951 meeting drew to a close, Eleanor Roosevelt resigned herself to the fact that the Commission would not be able to finish its agenda. Her thoughts turned homeward: "I wonder if the lilacs are out as yet and if their fragrance scents all the walks around our cottage buildings."[17] An encounter with a friendly Scottish terrier "made me homesick for Fala and Tama and I hope that they will not have completely forgotten us when we get home at the end of almost six weeks."

In a column written on her last day in Geneva, after a meeting with the UN high commissioner for refugees, she brooded on the problem that had first claimed her attention on committee three. "Whenever I talk to these people who are responsible for those in the world who suffer because of past wars, I say a little prayer in my heart that we have seen the sad results of war for the last time, and that somehow the comradeship which can be built up among the members of the Human Rights Commission may extend to the peoples of the 60 nations that meet in the United Nations."[18]

Comradeship had worn thin on the Commission, however, and the spring 1951 meeting ended in a stalemate.

The UN General Assembly took up the problem of the logjam on the Covenant at its fall 1951 session and adopted the solution toward which

Roosevelt had been leaning. Two separate Covenants would be devised to implement the Declaration—one would cover political and civil liberties, the other economic, social, and cultural rights. To signal that the two categories of rights should be treated equally, the General Assembly approved Roosevelt's recommendation that the two instruments should be presented for signature and ratification at the same time.

In practical terms the move made sense, but separating the political/civil liberties from the social/economic rights had a heavy cost: it undercut the Declaration's message that one set of values could not long endure without the other. It suggested a retreat from the proposition that a better standard of living cannot be accomplished without larger freedom, and that freedom is threatened by dehumanizing living conditions.

≡

Mrs. Roosevelt remained an active American delegate after she resigned her chairmanship of the Human Rights Commission. A memoir by Elliott Roosevelt provides a glimpse of his mother's busy life in her last years at the UN. Then in her late sixties, she continued to keep a schedule that would have left many a younger person breathless—rising at seven, writing her newspaper column, attending turbulent Commission meetings, entertaining guests most evenings at dinner, and often working until midnight. At the end of each long day, wrote Elliott, his mother would put on her old blue robe, and "by the bed with its uncompromising hard mattress, she knelt to say her prayers." Her nightly prayer, according to her son, was this:

Our Father, who has set a restlessness in our hearts and made us all seekers after that which we can never fully find, forbid us to be satisfied with what we make of life. Draw us from base content and set our eyes on far-off goals. Keep us at tasks too hard for us that we may be driven to Thee for strength. Deliver us from fretfulness and self-pitying; make us sure of the good we cannot see and of the hidden good in the world. Open our eyes to simple beauty all around us and our hearts to the loveliness men hide from us because we do not try to understand them. Save us from ourselves and show us a vision of a world made new.[19]

There was something profoundly moving about the tall, plain woman with stern principles, a wise heart, and a radiant smile. When Katharine Hepburn had difficulty getting into the role of Rose Sayer in *The African*

Queen (1951), the director, John Huston, could think of no better suggestion than, "Play her like Eleanor Roosevelt."[20]

In the General Assembly, where the Soviet Union was now regularly accusing the United States of human rights violations, she responded by sticking to the line that she had laid down in the beginning. In 1952 she summed up that position for the last time:

> I can only say that I wish it were possible for all of us to be allowed to go to the Soviet Union, for example, to see for ourselves the actual conditions which exist there. It would be very helpful if even some impartial observers were allowed to report to us on the actual conditions existing there.
>
> Now let me turn to the charge made by some of the delegates . . . that the United States is disregarding the interests of the Negroes in our country. Unfortunately there are instances of American Negroes being victims of unreasoning racial prejudice in my country. However, we do not condone these acts in the United States. We do everything possible to overcome and eliminate such discrimination and racial prejudice as may still exist. . . . Recently the President of the United States issued an executive order to insure protection against racial discrimination in employment under Government contracts.[21]

She herself was still doing "everything possible" to overcome racial prejudice as a writer, speaker, and consultant to groups like the National Association for the Advancement of Colored People, on whose board she had long served. She frequently used her column to teach about the injustice of racial discrimination. In 1952, for example, she wrote of a Phoenix, Arizona, cemetery's insistence that a black Korean War veteran be buried in a segregated plot.

> Pfc. Reed fought in Korea for all of the free world, for its freedom and protection from aggression. The bullet that killed him might just as well have killed a white boy, and neither the colored nor the white boy would have died only for his own race. Somehow it saddens one greatly, as one works for freedom and human rights throughout the world, to have these rights flouted in our own United States.[22]

It infuriated her that some of the organizations with which she had been associated, and some of her friends, like the African American educator Mary McLeod Bethune, had been accused of Communist leanings. She despised McCarthyism and said so in her column:

> I know the danger of Communism. I know it perhaps better than many other American citizens because for nearly five months of every year for the last six years, I have sat in meetings with the Communist representatives of the USSR.
>
> I despise the control they insist on holding over men's minds. And that is why I despise what Senator McCarthy has done, for he would use the same methods of fear to control all thought that is not according to his own pattern—in our free country![23]

The day after Dwight Eisenhower was elected president in November 1952, Mrs. Roosevelt wrote to the State Department that she would tender her resignation from the Human Rights Commission—even though her appointment was for a five-year term—so that the incoming president "may feel free to appoint a Republican woman."[24] When her friend financier Bernard Baruch heard of this, he asked her to hold off until he could talk to Eisenhower. Her reply to Baruch is revealing of the unique relationship she had enjoyed with the White House and the State Department in the Truman administration:

> I want you to think over the problem in the following way. I have been able, because the President has always been willing to see me, to discuss with him at the end of every meeting or of any mission which I undertook, everything that had occurred. The State Department, which always received my report first, was glad to have me do this because they felt that frequently reports sent from the State Department go to secretaries and never reach the President. Therefore I was able to get to the President what I thought the non-government organizations and the women of this country generally felt on a great many subjects, as well as the routine report of what had occurred and my opinion of what other nations felt.
>
> This would be impossible with General Eisenhower, since I hardly know him and since I do not belong to the party that will be in power.

Not surprisingly, the Republican president-elect chose to dispense with the services of a person so firmly identified with the liberal wing of the Democratic Party. On December 30 Eisenhower sent Mrs. Roosevelt a note thanking her for her services and accepting her resignation. She answered by return mail, thanking him for his "extremely kind letter" and telling him that he would receive her formal resignation when the State Department thought it proper to present it, adding, "This would naturally have to wait until you become President."

Shortly after Eisenhower's inauguration in January 1953, the new secretary of state, John Foster Dulles, announced a major shift in policy: the United States would no longer participate actively in the Human Rights Commission's work on a binding Convention and would not become a party to any such Covenant.[25] Later that year Dulles told a meeting of the American Bar Association that those who had voiced concerns that treaties might be used to impose "socialistic conceptions" upon the United States had "performed a genuine service in bringing the situation to the attention of the American public."[26] With U.S. troops in Korea, the Soviet Union in possession of "the Bomb," and McCarthyism aggravating a climate of fear, the country was in no mood to think internationally.

Eleanor Roosevelt lost no time in finding another way to support the United Nations. Clark Eichelberger, then director of the American Association for the United Nations, recalled that one day not long after Eisenhower took office, Eleanor Roosevelt walked into the association's New York headquarters and asked, "Do you think you could use me as an educational volunteer?"[27] She proposed to help build chapters of the association, to speak around the country on behalf of the UN, and to spend two days a week in the office. Eichelberger, so astonished that he "practically fell on the floor," readily accepted the offer. From then on the former First Lady devoted much of her time to unofficial efforts on behalf of the United Nations.

She also traveled widely in her later years, often accompanied by the Gurewitsches and Maureen Corr, who succeeded Malvina Thompson as her personal secretary. In his volume of photographs and reminiscences from "the eighteen years I knew and loved her," David Gurewitsch recalled Eleanor Roosevelt's enthusiasm for seeing new places and her "eagerness to learn," especially about education, social services, and medical care, in India, Israel, Greece, Yugoslavia, Hong Kong, Indonesia, the Soviet Union, and other countries she visited.[28]

When Eleanor Roosevelt died in 1962, at the age of seventy-eight, she was eulogized for the work she had done on behalf of human rights at home and abroad. She herself had always considered her membership on the American UN delegation as the most important position of her life and her role in framing the Universal Declaration her most important contribution toward a better world. Historians later endorsed that belief.

Though she participated little in the actual drafting of the Declaration, it is hard to imagine how it could have been brought to completion without her. Her contributions were as important in their way as Malik's and Chang's diplomacy or Humphrey's and Cassin's drafting. An analogy from American history might be George Washington's chairmanship of the Constitutional Convention: the Constitution was framed by others, but Washington's presence is commonly held to have been decisive for its acceptance, owing to the great respect in which he was held. As chairman of the Human Rights Commission, Eleanor Roosevelt provided the leadership that kept the project moving along, the political influence that held the State Department on board, and the personal attentions that made each member of the Commission feel respected. She had shaped as well as wielded the influence of the country that had emerged from the war as the most powerful in the world.[29] She had helped in countless ways to improve conditions for cross-cultural cooperation and had personally modeled the spirit of the Declaration's vision of "a world made new."

Seeking to explain her immense prestige, E. J. Kahn had written in the year the Declaration was adopted, "[I]n an era conspicuous for the self-interest of both nations and individuals, she has become more and more widely recognized as a person of towering unselfishness."[30] Kahn went on to quote an unnamed source "with impressive overseas connections":

> Mrs. Roosevelt never cares if there's nothing in it for herself. She has absolutely no pride of station and no personal ambition. What's more, many Americans who have neither the time, the energy, the contacts, nor the ability that she has look upon her efforts to improve the lives of her fellow-men as the kind of thing they would like to do themselves if only they were capable of it and could get around to it. To them—and I suspect there are an awful lot of them—she is the personification of the American conscience.

After Mrs. Roosevelt's departure, work on the Covenants proceeded with painful slowness. From the point of view of the UN Secretariat, Charles

Malik "was in many respects a better chairman than Mrs. Roosevelt."[31] For one thing, he was and could be more flexible. He did not come with a train of advisers, and he did not have detailed instructions from his government. Yet the old tug-of-war between partisans of the social and economic rights and those who gave pride of place to traditional political and civil liberties worsened under Malik's tenure. The Eisenhower administration took a dim view of economic and social rights and invoked the principle of national sovereignty to oppose binding Covenants, including the 1948 Genocide Convention, which had emerged with a favorable report from a Senate subcommittee in 1950 but was still awaiting ratification. The United States did not ratify that widely accepted treaty until 1988, when the Reagan State Department realized its value in the propaganda war against communism.

In September 1952, a little over a year after he had assumed the chair of the Commission, Malik admitted in the *U.N. Weekly Bulletin,* "Those of us who have followed closely this enterprise ever since San Francisco now realize that we have all along underestimated the complexity and difficulty of this issue."[32] "Power politics," he wrote, was "entering into and vitiating everything." He and his colleagues now understood "that the nobility and importance of our task is matched only by its inherent difficulty and by the long time we must in all fairness allow for its unfolding." To his diary he had confided the previous January that, having seen the UN at its birth, he was "sad to see it weakening into a debating society."[33]

There had been, Malik wrote, a "quiet revolution" in the Human Rights Commission since the adoption of the Declaration, a revolution reflecting the hardening of the division between "two more or less solid blocs"— one Soviet-led and composed of the Ukraine, Poland, Yugoslavia, Chile, Uruguay, Pakistan, and Egypt; the other U.S.-led and composed of the United Kingdom, France, Australia, Belgium, Sweden, Greece, and Nationalist China. Malik described his own country and India as unaligned but voting "for the most part" with the Soviet bloc.

That division between what was then called "East" and "West," together with the increasing numbers of new nations from the "South," had produced a shift of emphasis where human rights were concerned. "The whole atmosphere of human rights in the United Nations," Malik wrote, was now charged with two themes: "the host of questions subsumed under the rubric of 'self-determination of peoples' and the antithesis between the developed and the less developed." The economic, social, and cultural rights, he noted, "have come into their own, and indeed with a vengeance."

Dividing the Covenant work in two, whatever its merits, did not speed up the drafting process. "Now that we have reached this crucial stage," Malik wrote in frustration, "people are losing heart."[34] He was as disappointed by the lack of leadership from the United States and Europe as he was by the (intransigence) of the Soviet bloc. "Certain powerful countries which by reason of humane and Christian traditions are by nature called to lead in this field exhibit yet a halting style . . . they fail to speak with conviction and authority."[35]

With the UN "police action" raging in Korea and the brooding menace of atomic war, Malik lamented, "The more we are removed in time from the original moral indignation evoked by the Second World War, the more questions of war and peace cast their pall on our work. Certainly the sense of urgency and drive that characterized the preparation of the Declaration back in 1947 and 1948 are absent."[36] It was impossible to brush aside the thought, he added, "that the proclamation of the Declaration in 1948 was really something of a miracle, so that if it were not proclaimed then, possibly we would still be working on it now."

The dedicated John Humphrey began to think of leaving the UN; chiefly, he said, because of "the dark view I had of the future of the covenants."[37] To Humphrey's dismay, Swedish diplomat Dag Hammarskjöld, who became secretary-general in 1953, did not accord a high priority to the UN's human rights program. Humphrey's diary for that period portrays a constant struggle within the UN bureaucracy over the status of the Human Rights Division. In one conversation Hammarskjöld instructed Humphrey: "There is a flying speed below which an airplane will not remain in the air. I want you to keep the program at that speed and no greater."[38] His wish to slow down the human rights program, he told the shocked director, was dictated by concern for larger issues. Humphrey, though torn by misgivings, remained at his post, struggling to keep the program alive.

The somber mood that had come over Hammarskjöld and many other intellectuals in those tense cold war years was captured by Albert Camus in his speech accepting the 1957 Nobel Prize for literature. Describing the world as one where "second-rate powers can destroy everything . . . but are unable to win anyone over," he said: "Probably every generation sees itself as charged with remaking the world. Mine, however, knows that it will not remake the world. But its task is perhaps even greater, for it consists in keeping the world from destroying itself."[39]

René Cassin complained vigorously in the 1950s about another growing threat to the international human rights project: the expansion and bureaucratization of the UN had been attended by what he considered to be the "scandalous politicization" of UN agencies.[40] The Paris-based UNESCO office, especially, attracted his disapproving attention. Though Cassin remained on the Human Rights Commission, he had too many responsibilities at home to be as active as he had been in the first years. In addition to his duties as head of the Conseil d'État, he was president of France's prestigious National School of Administration, from which a large proportion of that country's leaders have emerged.

Like the men in the British Foreign Office, moreover, Cassin was drawn to the idea of a regional European human rights system. The 1950 European Convention on Human Rights, which came into force in 1953, established a Commission on Human Rights, the world's first supranational tribunal where individuals could present complaints against their own governments.[41] It also created a Court of Human Rights with jurisdiction over cases concerning the interpretation and application of the Convention. In 1958 Cassin was named one of its first judges, even though France had not yet ratified the Convention.

The relationship between Cassin and de Gaulle, never an easy one, came to an end in 1967 over the still-festering Palestine question, when de Gaulle, then president of the Fifth Republic, placed an embargo on the delivery of arms to the Middle East, including fifty Mirage jets for which Israel had already paid. In a press conference called to explain his action, the president touched off a firestorm of protest by referring to the Jews as "an elite people, self-confident and dominating" (*"peuple d'élite, sûr de lui-même et dominateur"*).[42] That was too much for Cassin. Nor was he mollified when de Gaulle reacted to Jewish indignation with an air of lofty surprise, saying that he personally considered those qualities to be admirable. In November 1967 Cassin signed an open letter of protest against the leader he had served for so long in war and peace. The following year Cassin's efforts on behalf of human rights were crowned with the Nobel Peace Prize.

Though Cassin and de Gaulle were united during the war years by intense patriotism, each loved a different France. De Gaulle's was the France of Joan of Arc, a fatherland to be protected from external dangers, a nation whose greatness lay in the "Frenchness" of its ancient culture and traditions. He looked askance at the multinational staff of the European Common Market and referred contemptuously to international civil servants as *"des gens sans patrie."* De Gaulle was buried, at his request, in the little cemetery of his native village, Colombey-les-Deux-Églises. Cassin, as he had hoped, lies in the Pantheon in Paris with the Enlightenment figures he so admired.

Cassin's France was the home of a revolution that had proclaimed liberty, equality, and fraternity and given full civil rights to its Jewish citizens. He thought of France as the motherland not only of the French, but of all men and women who love justice and freedom. Cassin held to this notion so passionately that he concluded his acceptance speech of the Nobel Peace Prize in 1968 with, "I adore my country with a heart that transcends its borders; the more I am French, the more I feel a part of humanity."[43]

Charles Malik was at the height of his prestige during the 1950s. Though his name, like Cassin's, is little remembered today, the personable Lebanese diplomat was a familiar figure on the little gray TV screens of those days. With his insider's knowledge of the UN, his fluent English, and his schoolteacher's eagerness to talk about ideas, he was much sought after by journalists.

But the philosopher-turned-statesman would soon be brought down by the crosscurrents of Middle East politics. His strenuous advocacy of the internationalization of Jerusalem antagonized fellow Arabs and Israelis alike. Meanwhile his political base in Lebanon was eroding. The combination of Palestinian immigration and Christian exodus upset the delicate balance among the many ethnic and religious groups in Lebanon. Tragically, the country Malik had hoped would be a model of multicultural harmony became a symbol of civil strife.

Toward the end of 1956 Malik was named Lebanon's foreign minister, the number two man in the beleaguered government of President Camille Chamoun. Faced with civil war and the threat of Syrian annexation, the Chamoun administration made the fateful decision in 1958 to ask for

American intervention. When that strategy backfired, the government fell, and from that time onward Arab nationalists regarded Malik with hostility and contempt.

With his political career at an end, Malik returned at last to his first love, philosophy and teaching. But times had changed, and the students at the American University of Beirut in those troubled years were no longer so receptive to Malik and his passion for ideas. Yet he never considered exile, even when Beirut was in flames after successive Israeli and Syrian bombardments in 1982.

Howard Schomer visited his old boss in Beirut on two occasions in the 1980s. After his own stint at the UN, Schomer, a United Church of Christ minister, had gone on to teach at and eventually become president of the Chicago Theological Seminary; during the 1960s, as a friend of Martin Luther King's and a teacher of Jesse Jackson's, he was active in the American civil rights movement and in the campaign to discourage American investment in South Africa. Schomer was impressed that the elderly Malik "would not abandon his home in the hills above Beirut even as artillery shells skimmed over his roof, or give up his daily walks in the hills. He deplored the exodus of Lebanese Christians to safety in other lands, which he believed threatened the very survival of the Christian church in the Bible land where it had sustained itself unbrokenly since the time of Jesus."[44]

In 1987, when Charles Malik died at the age of eighty-one, the wire services reported, "None of Lebanon's Moslem or pro-Syrian politicians or militia leaders mourned his passing."[45]

From 1948 onward, P. C. Chang was the target of attacks by the Soviet bloc seeking to seat Mao Tse-tung's government in the UN (efforts that succeeded only much later, in 1971, when the United States under the Nixon administration dropped its opposition).[46] When Malik lunched with him in the fall of 1949, he found Chang especially bitter against the United States, complaining of its "dollar policy—all business and materialism without moral principles."[47] Chang resigned from the UN in 1952 because of his worsening heart condition, and he died in 1957. John Humphrey, on hearing the news, wrote in his diary:

> P. C. Chang is dead. Of all the delegates who came into the Council, he was the one with whom I felt most in spiritual and intellectual com-

munion. And the one I liked the best. . . . He was a scholar and, in a way, an artist although he performed his diplomatic functions well in spite of these superior gifts. What a giant he seems in contrast with the time-servers.[48]

Humphrey himself retired from the Secretariat in April of 1966 after having served with distinction for twenty years as the first director of the UN's Human Rights Division. At sixty-one, having witnessed and partic-ipated in historic events on the international stage, Humphrey returned to teaching in the law faculty at McGill University in Montreal. He remained active in the cause of human rights, helped to establish the Canadian branch of Amnesty International, championed the cause of Korean com-fort women, wrote his memoirs, and lived to the ripe old age of eighty-nine.

More than once, Humphrey had expressed the belief that "every indi-vidual can make some contribution to the development of the [human] race, and that he lives on as it were in that contribution."[49] The boy from New Brunswick, by his own lights, had acquitted himself honorably. Ac-cording to his friend and literary executor, John Hobbins, "Prior to 1952, Humphrey worked for love of his job and a belief in what the UN was doing. After this, he appears to have stayed on from a sense of duty to pro-tect the programme and the division from an unfriendly world."[50]

〆

Carlos Romulo became president of the University of the Philippines in 1962 and later served as foreign secretary in the government of President Ferdinand Marcos. His defense of that corrupt regime tarnished his repu-tation as a champion of human rights. Romulo left the Marcos govern-ment after the murder of Benigno Aquino in 1983. Shortly before his own death in 1985, he broke a long silence to condemn the Marcos govern-ment in an interview with Richard C. Holbrooke. "Everything I have worked for in U.S.-Philippine relations for over forty years is ruined," the dying general said.[51]

By the time the two human rights Covenants were finally completed in 1966, all the major participants in the framing of the Declaration had left the UN, except Hernán Santa Cruz. A close friend since boyhood of Chilean President Salvador Allende, Santa Cruz resigned from his post at the time of the 1973 military coup that led to Allende's death and brought General Augusto Pinochet to power. During the early years of the Pinochet regime, Santa Cruz remained in Europe working for various international organizations, but in 1980 he retired to Santiago, where he died in 1999, at the age of ninety-two.

✐

René Cassin took the occasion of his 1968 Nobel acceptance speech to rejoice that the two Covenants were open for signature and ratification but to deplore the length of time it had taken to reach that stage. He blamed mainly the "desire of certain powers to delay even modest measures of implementation out of concern for their national sovereignty."[52] There is no doubt that he meant to contrast the Western European states—most of which had by then accepted the 1950 European Convention on Human Rights—with the United States and the Soviet Union, both of which had avoided binding human rights commitments. But Cassin was also taking a shot at France, whose government had signed, but still not ratified, the European Convention. It was not until 1974 that France finally entered the European human rights system.

As for the two UN Covenants, ten years would pass between their completion and the time when they received a sufficient number of ratifications to go into effect. It was then 1976—the year of René Cassin's death—a full twenty-eight years after the adoption of the Universal Declaration. The United States did not ratify the Covenant on Civil and Political Rights until 1992, and then only with a brace of reservations to ensure it would have little or no domestic effect. As of 2000, the United States had signed, but still not ratified, the Covenant on Economic, Social and Cultural Rights.

While the Covenants were stalled for decades during the cold war years, the Declaration was slowly making an impact in the world. Though many human rights supporters had had doubts about the effectiveness of a nonbinding "standard," the Soviets had always understood that ideas are as real as tanks. After the furor over the Mindszenty case, the Eastern-bloc delegates began trying to harness the moral power of the Declaration for their own purposes. A bemused John Humphrey noted in June 1949 that Pavlov, of all people, had based one of his arguments on the Declaration, saying, "We've all adopted it"![53] Humphrey commented, "[I]f one were to judge by their frequent references to it, . . . an uninitiated person might well think that the Soviets had voted for the Declaration." Three years later Mrs. Roosevelt, replying to Soviet-bloc attacks on the U.S. attitude toward the Covenant, could not resist commenting on the tactical reversal that had taken place:

> I am interested that these five countries [Byelorussia, Czechoslovakia, Poland, the Ukraine, and the USSR] place so much stress on the unity of the provisions of the Universal Declaration in our debates here. In 1948 those five countries did not vote for the Declaration. At that time they were critical of it. Now they cite it for their own purposes. They seem to praise the Declaration one time and minimize its importance another time, so that I must question the sincerity of their reliance on the Declaration at this point.[54]

All through the cold war, the United States and the USSR traded charges of human rights violations while overlooking their own failures and those of their client states.[55] The Soviet Union used the Declaration's antidiscrimination articles and its social and economic provisions to berate the United States and its friends, while the Western bloc badgered the Communist countries for failing to protect free expression and free elections. A wedge was driven through the heart of the Declaration, severing its firm link between freedom and solidarity. Thus began the now prevalent pick-and-choose approach to interpreting its thirty integrated articles.

That problem worsened as newly independent countries entered the United Nations. With its emphasis on political and civil rights and its affirmation that government should be based on the will of the people, the Declaration had helped to legitimate struggles against colonial oppression. In 1963 the founders of the Organization of African Unity (OAU)—among them Jomo Kenyatta, Kwame Nkrumah, and Julius Nyerere—expressly affirmed their adherence to the Declaration in the Preamble to the OAU Charter.[56] But many leaders of new nations showed little interest in according political liberties to their own citizens and proved as resistant to outside meddling as the colonial powers had been.

At the behest of several new nations in the General Assembly, strongly supported by Hernán Santa Cruz, the Human Rights Commission added "the right of peoples to self-determination" to its drafts of the two

Covenants. But as Malik wrote in 1952, the debate on the meaning of that right was "genuinely and objectively complex."[57] Who was entitled to claim the right—an individual, a group, a nation? What constitutes a "people"? What action may legitimately be taken to achieve this right? How does it relate to the rights in the Universal Declaration? Or to the responsibility of the individual to obey and respect national law? The 1966 Covenants announced the right but did not provide guidance on those questions.

To Carlos Romulo and others from developing nations at the UN's founding conference, the right of peoples to self-determination had simply meant the right to be free of colonial rule. But the leading Soviet international law text defined it in such a way as to put Communist regimes beyond constitutional control: "Self determination consists of a people or a nation throwing off the imperialist control of the bourgeois class. . . . [A]ny subsequent attempt to induce a change of the social system or government in that state is an infringement of state sovereignty."[58]

To the rulers of some newly independent nations, eager to consolidate their control and quell dissent, self-determination became a Third World version of the old national sovereignty claim. It provided an excuse for immunity from international scrutiny of their treatment of their own citizens and minority groups. Ethnic minorities in some countries came to see the concept as including the principle of protection of minorities that had been omitted from the Universal Declaration—and as justifying secession.

The first international conference of African and Asian nations at Bandung, Indonesia, in 1955 signaled trouble ahead. Though the final conference communiqué supported the Universal Declaration as a "common standard of achievement for all peoples and all nations," China's Premier Chou En-lai had initially balked on the ground that "the People's Republic of China was not a member of the United Nations and therefore had no opportunity to participate in the formulation of such United Nations statements or policies."[59] Anti-Western sentiment, moreover, ran high at the gathering.

African American novelist Richard Wright, who went to Bandung as a freelance reporter, was especially struck by the "race-conscious and stinging" words of Carlos Romulo, whom he described as "a man who knew and loved America, who had the American outlook and attitude of pragmatism; but he had suffered under colonialism and he had sympathy for those who were not free." Wright quoted from Romulo's speech at length:

> I have said that besides the issues of colonialism and political freedom, all of us here are concerned with the matter of racial equality. This is a touchstone, I think, for most of us assembled here and the people we represent. The systems and the manner of it have varied, but there has not been and there is not a Western colonial regime which has not imposed, to a greater or lesser degree, on the people it ruled the doctrine of their own racial inferiority. We have known, and some of us still know, the searing experience of being demeaned in our own lands, of being systematically relegated to subject status not only politically and economically and militarily—but racially as well. Here was a stigma that could be applied to rich and poor alike, to prince and slave, boss-man and workingman, landlord and peasant, scholar and ignoramus. To bolster his rule, to justify his own power to himself, the Western white man assumed that his superiority lay in his very genes, in the color of his skin. This made the lowest drunken sot superior in colonial society to the highest product of culture and scholarship and industry among subject people. . . . For many it has made the goal of regaining a status of simple manhood the be-all and end-all of a lifetime of devoted struggle and sacrifice.[60]

Before long, a potent mixture of resentment and political expediency would fuel a Third World critique of the whole Declaration as "Western," a charge that went far beyond Saudi Arabia's objection to parts of the marriage and religion provisions.

The United States remained steadfastly aloof to the Covenants for many years after they were opened for signature in 1966. America's reluctance to ratify UN treaties readily accepted by nearly every other country in the world reflected not only a widespread conviction that its own system for protecting rights was second to none, but a distrust of international institutions where enemies and critics of the United States had become a majority.

In the event, the two UN Covenants—and others that followed, banning torture and discrimination—proved less important to the cause of human rights than the principles announced in the Declaration. For, as one astute analyst has pointed out, "[The rhetoric of the human rights movement] rarely depends on careful arguments about legality, and both the content and sources of international human rights law are much too diffuse for illegality to be the criterion of opprobrium it is in domestic legal systems. It is the *moral* quality of the acts in question, not their illegality, that actually triggers the international community's opprobrium. The successful characterization of an act as 'illegal' can of course change perceptions about the moral worth of the act, but it is moral worth, and not legality, that counts."[61]

One world leader who was early to recognize the Declaration's importance as a moral statement was Angelo Roncalli, who became Pope John XXIII ten years after he had given "encouragements" to René Cassin in Paris in the fall of 1948. Finding its principles compatible with Catholic social teaching, he adopted (to the surprise of many) its dignitarian language of rights in his 1963 encyclical *Pacem in Terris*. This new mode of speaking about freedom and social justice enabled him and his successors to break new ground in interfaith relations, by addressing themselves not only to members of their own faith, but to "all men and women of good will." René Cassin often expressed his pleasure at these developments, noting the many echoes of the Declaration in the documents of the Second Vatican Council, which he called "the very image of universality."[62]

Martin Luther King, too, warmly embraced the Declaration's vision of "better standards of life in larger freedom" when he accepted the Nobel Peace Prize in 1964. "I have the audacity to believe," he said, "that peoples everywhere can have three meals a day for their bodies, education and culture for their minds, and dignity, equality and freedom for their spirits."[63]

The cold war, the indifference of the superpowers, and the turbulent transition to a postcolonial world hindered but did not halt the progress of the Universal Declaration and the ideas it embodied. The rights embraced in most postwar constitutions are broadly similar to those in the Universal Declaration and, in many cases, are accompanied by an effective system of judicial review.[64] At the regional level, the European Court of Human Rights at Strasbourg provided a supranational forum for individuals claiming that their governments had violated their political or civil rights. The European Court in turn served as a model for the Inter-American Court of

Human Rights based in Costa Rica. All in all, as the members of the first Human Rights Commission had hoped, the Declaration's principles were flowing into the capillaries of the world's legal systems.

Quite independently of legal enforceability, those principles were helping human rights organizations to articulate their aims, to spotlight abuses, and to mobilize grassroots support. The 1960s and 1970s saw the rise of numerous highly effective organizations whose programs were rooted explicitly in parts of the Universal Declaration. One of the largest, Amnesty International, was founded in 1961 to aid "prisoners of conscience"—persons jailed on account of their beliefs or origins, who had not advocated or used violence. The group received the Nobel Peace Prize in 1977 for its work in protecting prisoners from torture and flagrantly unfair procedures. Today, with over a million members and with chapters in nearly every country, Amnesty pursues an expanded agenda of opposing "grave violations of the rights of every person to hold and express his or her convictions and to be free from discrimination and of the right of every person to physical and mental integrity."[65] In recent years it has added opposition to the death penalty to its main concerns.

Human Rights Watch, the other giant of the international human rights movement, grew out of the "Helsinki Watch" groups that were formed to monitor compliance with the human rights provisions of the 1975 Helsinki Accords. As part of the process of détente, the signers of those agreements—every European nation except Albania, as well as Canada and the United States—had gathered to discuss the improvement of East-West relations. In the final act that emerged from the Helsinki conference, the nations pledged, among other things, "to act in conformity with the purposes and principles of the Charter of the United Nations and with the Universal Declaration of Human Rights" and acknowledged the right of all persons "to know and act upon their rights."

It was a historic occasion, for it marked the first time that the Soviet Union had signed such a document. Though the accords did not have the status of a treaty, their nonbinding human rights provisions played a significant role in galvanizing dissidents and freedom movements in the Soviet Union, Czechoslovakia, Hungary, and Poland. Following the fall of the Eastern European Communist regimes, Human Rights Watch devoted itself to "stand[ing] with victims and activists to prevent discrimination, to uphold political freedom, to protect people from inhumane conduct in wartime, and to bring offenders to justice."

Over the years, Amnesty International, Human Rights Watch, and numerous other groups with specialized agendas became a major presence—advocating, lobbying, and monitoring in every part of the world. As these movements gathered momentum, it was only to be expected that attacks on the Declaration's universality would increase. And so they did, with surprising force.

Eleanor Roosevelt surveys a job well done.

CHAPTER 12

UNIVERSALITY
UNDER SIEGE

In 1998, a few days before the fiftieth anniversary of the Universal Declaration of Human Rights, Chinese activist Xu Wenli, who had spent twelve years in prison for his part in the 1978 "democracy wall" movement, was jailed for trying to register a new political party. The Beijing government issued its standard response to the charge that such treatment of dissidents violates human rights: Rights are relative to local conditions and many so-called human rights are merely parochial Western notions inapplicable to Chinese circumstances.

Protesting her father's arrest in a *Boston Globe* article, Xu Wenli's daughter scornfully dismissed the idea of blanket cultural exemptions from universal rights. One of the most influential framers of the Universal Declaration, she pointed out, was P. C. Chang—who "believed that rights are for everyone, not just westerners."[1] And his credo lives on: "When the Chinese people have spoken—P. C. Chang in 1948, Wei Jinsheng, Xu Wenli and other members of the democracy wall movement in 1978, Tiananmen worker and student demonstrators in 1989, and Xu Wenli again this year—they have claimed their right to all of the universally acknowledged human liberties, not to a list impoverished by some supposed peculiarity of culture."

The problem of what universality might mean in a multicultural world haunted the United Nations human rights project from the beginning. In

June 1947, when word of a proposed human rights declaration reached the American Anthropological Association, that group's executive board sent a letter to the Human Rights Commission warning that the document could not be "a statement of rights conceived only in terms of the values prevalent in the countries of Western Europe and America."[2] The challenge would be "to formulate a statement of human rights that will do more than just phrase respect for the individual as an individual. It must also take into full account the individual as member of the social group of which he is part, whose sanctioned modes of life shape his behavior, and with whose fate his own is thus inextricably bound." Earlier that year some of the world's best-known philosophers had been asked to ponder the question, "How is an agreement conceivable among men who come from the four corners of the earth and who belong not only to different cultures and civilizations, but to different spiritual families and antagonistic schools of thought?"[3]

No one has yet improved on the answer of the UNESCO philosophers: Where basic human values are concerned, cultural diversity has been exaggerated. The group found, after consulting with Confucian, Hindu, Muslim, and European thinkers, that a core of fundamental principles was widely shared in countries that had not yet adopted rights instruments and in cultures that had not embraced the language of rights. Their survey persuaded them that basic human rights rest on "common convictions," even though those convictions "are stated in terms of different philosophic principles and on the background of divergent political and economic systems."[4] The philosophers concluded that even people who seem to be far apart in theory can agree that certain things are so terrible in practice that no one will publicly approve them and that certain things are so good in practice that no one will publicly oppose them.[5]

The Human Rights Commission heeded the anthropologists' advice, and its experience seemed, on the whole, to bear out the philosophers' conclusion. In 1948, when Saudi Arabia made the isolated claim that freedom to marry and to change one's religion were Western ideas ill suited for universal application, no other country objected on cultural or religious grounds to those or any other parts of the Declaration. Nor did any country use those grounds to oppose the idea of a universal standard of human rights. The most philosophical of the framers, Charles Malik, believed that, over time, the Declaration's principles would "either bring to light an implicit agreement already operative, perhaps dimly and unconsciously, in the systems and ways of life of the various states, or consciously and creatively advance further and higher the area of agreement."[6]

Though the UNESCO philosophers were confident that such an implicit agreement existed, they left the task of proving it for another day. What needed to be investigated was precisely how, and to what extent, various cultural, philosophical, and religious traditions have affirmed the universality of certain basic values. That long-postponed work, pioneered by third committee member Zafrulla Khan's 1967 book on Islam and human rights, is now well under way in many parts of the world.[7]

The exploration of the different bases for human rights will be amply justified even if it does no more than improve mutual understanding. As Eleanor Roosevelt once said of the United Nations, "We've found ourselves in a situation where we must know about all the other peoples of the world. We must know about the way they live, what they are like, what their beliefs are, what their aspirations are. . . . To me, the fact that there is contact, a bridge on which we can meet and talk, has value."[8] One need not be motivated by any love affair with the United Nations to recognize the importance of having such a "bridge" or starting point for cross-cultural discourse.

The stakes are high. To accept the claim that meaningful cross-cultural discussions of freedom and dignity are impossible is to give up on the hope that the political fate of humanity can be affected by reason and choice.[9] It is to accept that human affairs are inexorably determined by force and accident. It is to give the last word to the Athenians at Melos and all their successors throughout the ages.

⟋⟋⟋

The hopeful view of the UNESCO philosophers was challenged when a host of new nations appeared on the international stage in the 1950s. With sixteen new members joining the United Nations in 1955 alone and with many Latin American countries retreating from their pro-U.S. positions, the balance of power in the General Assembly had shifted. Small or relatively weak nations found strength in numbers and in support from the Soviet Union, but often little common ground. The Bandung gathering of African and Asian nations achieved unity mainly through shared resentment of the dominance of a few rich and powerful countries in world affairs, prompting Richard Wright to comment: "And what had these nations in common? Nothing, it seemed to me, but what their past relationship to the Western world had made them feel. This meeting of the rejected was in itself a kind of judgment upon that Western world!"[10]

Over the years that mood was expressed in characterizations of the Declaration as an instrument of neocolonialism and in attacks on its universality in the name of cultural integrity, self-determination of peoples, or national sovereignty. In some cases the motivations are transparently self-serving. When leaders of authoritarian governments claim that the Declaration is aimed at imposing "foreign" values, their real concern is often domestic: the pressure for freedom building among their own citizens. That might have been the case, for example, when the Iranian representative at a ceremony commemorating the Declaration's fiftieth anniversary in 1998 charged that the document embodies a "Judeo-Christian" understanding of rights, unacceptable to Muslims.[11] Or on the occasions when Singapore's Lee Kuan Yew attempted to justify the suppression of human rights in the name of economic development or national security.

Defenders of universal rights often lash back with the charge that such criticisms ring false from the lips of some of the world's worst rights violators. But that response is obviously inadequate. Even an allegation made hypocritically can be correct, and many challenges to the Declaration's universality are made by individuals who are genuinely concerned about ideological imperialism. At a Harvard University symposium on the fiftieth anniversary of the Universal Declaration in 1998, for example, University of Buffalo law professor Makau Mutua described the Declaration as an arrogant attempt to universalize a particular set of ideas and to impose them upon three-quarters of the world's population, most of whom were not represented at its creation. Kenya-born Mutua said, "Muslims, Hindus, Africans, non-Judeo-Christians, feminists, critical theorists, and other scholars of an inquiring bent of mind have exposed the Declaration's bias and exclusivity."[12]

These accusations of cultural relativism and cultural imperialism need to be taken seriously. *Is* the Declaration a "Western" document in some meaningful sense, despite its aspiration to be universal? *Are* all rights relative to time and place? *Is* universality a cover for cultural imperialism? Let us examine the charges on their merits.

Those who label the Declaration "Western" base their claim mainly on two facts: 1) many peoples living in non-Western nations or under colonial rule, especially those in sub-Saharan Africa, were not represented in the United Nations in 1948; and 2) most of the Declaration's rights first appeared in the European and North or South American documents on which John Humphrey based the original draft. Those statements are accurate, but do they destroy the universality of the Declaration?

As far as participation by developing countries in the framing of the Declaration is concerned, we have seen that it was by no means negligible.[13] It is true that much of the world's population was not represented in the UN in 1948: large parts of Africa and some Asian countries remained under colonial rule; and the defeated Axis powers—Japan, Germany, Italy, and their allies—were excluded as well. But Chang, Malik, Romulo, Mehta, and Santa Cruz were among the most influential, active, and independent members of the Human Rights Commission. And the members of the third committee, who discussed every line of the draft over two months in the fall of 1948, represented a wide variety of cultures.

On the third committee, besides Europeans and North Americans, there were six members from Asia—giants such as China, India, and Pakistan, plus Burma, the Philippines, and Siam. Islamic culture was predominant in nine nations—Afghanistan, Egypt, Iran, Iraq, Pakistan, Saudi Arabia, Syria, Turkey, Yemen—and strong in India and Lebanon. Three countries had large Buddhist populations—Burma, China, and Siam. Only four were from the African continent—Ethiopia and Liberia, plus two that would not count as representative of black Africa, Egypt and South Africa. In addition, there was the numerous and outspoken Latin American contingent. Six of the European members belonged to the Communist bloc.[14] Charles Malik's chairmanship of the third committee assured that each country was given ample opportunity to participate, an opportunity seized enthusiastically by most representatives.

Before the whole two-year process from drafting and deliberation to adoption reached its end, literally hundreds of individuals from diverse backgrounds had participated. Thus Malik could fairly say, "The genesis of each article, and each part of each article, was a dynamic process in which many minds, interests, backgrounds, legal systems and ideological persuasions played their respective determining roles."[15]

Proponents of the cultural-imperialism critique sometimes say that the educational backgrounds or professional experiences of men like Chang and Malik "westernized" them, but their performance in the Human Rights Commission suggests something rather different. Not only did each contribute significant insights from his own culture, but each possessed an exceptional ability to understand other cultures and to "translate" concepts from one frame of reference to another. Those skills, indispensable for effective cross-cultural collaboration, were key to the successful adoption of the Declaration without a single dissenting vote.

Over nearly two years, between the first Human Rights Commission meeting and the Declaration's adoption, there was remarkably little disagreement regarding its basic substance, despite intense wrangling over some specifics. At every stage, even the Communist bloc and Saudi Arabia voted in favor of most of the articles when they were taken up one by one.[16] The "traditional" political and civil rights—the ones now most often labeled "Western"—were the least controversial of all.

The biggest battles, as P. C. Chang told the General Assembly just before the final vote on the Declaration, were occasioned by purely political preoccupations.[17] They occurred, as we have seen, mainly over the Soviet bloc's efforts to protect its national sovereignty or to establish exceptions from certain rights (for instance, by denying them to "fascist elements"). On December 10, 1948, Brazil's Belarmino de Athayde summed up sentiments that had been expressed by many other third committee members when he told the General Assembly that the Declaration did not reflect the particular point of view of any one people or group of peoples or any particular political or philosophical system.[18] The fact that it was the product of cooperation among so many nations, he said, gave it great moral authority.

Not every country in the world had its say, but many did, and their response supported the UNESCO philosophers' conclusion that a few basic practical concepts of human rights are so widely shared that they "may be viewed as implicit in man's nature as a member of society."[19]

But what of the fact that the initial elaboration of these concepts as "rights" was a European phenomenon? Does the circumstance that several key principles in the Declaration were first described as "rights" in early modern Europe endow them with a genetic taint that prevents them from being "universal"? No one would say so if the concepts in question were scientific or mathematical. Even in the murkier realm of human affairs, shouldn't the question be whether the idea is a good one rather than who had the idea first? Whether the idea is conducive to human flourishing rather than where it was born?

It is true that the Declaration's provisions were derived from provisions of the world's existing and proposed constitutions and rights instruments—that is, mostly from countries with well-developed legal traditions. But the label "Western" obscures the fact that the Declaration's acceptance in non-Western settings was facilitated by the very features that made it seem "foreign" to a large part of the West: Britain and the United States.

The Declaration, as we have seen, was far more influenced by the modern dignitarian rights tradition of continental Europe and Latin America than by the more individualistic documents of Anglo-American lineage. The fact is that the rights dialect that prevails in the Anglo-American orbit would have found little resonance in Asia or Africa. It implicitly confers its highest priority on individual freedom and typically formulates rights without explicit mention of their limits or their relation to other rights or to responsibilities. The predominant image of the rights bearer, heavily influenced by Hobbes, Locke, and John Stuart Mill, is that of a self-determining, self-sufficient individual.

Dignitarian rights instruments, with their emphasis on the family and their greater attention to duties, are more compatible with Asian and African traditions. In these documents, rights bearers tend to be envisioned within families and communities; rights are formulated so as to make clear their limits and their relation to one another as well as to the responsibilities that belong to citizens and the state. As comparative political theorist Donald Kommers puts it: "[O]ne vision is partial to the city perceived as a private realm in which the individual is alone, isolated, and in competition with his fellows, while the other vision is partial to the city perceived as a public realm where individual and community are bound together in reciprocity."[20]

In the spirit of the latter vision, the Declaration's "Everyone" is an individual who is constituted, in important ways, by and through relationships with others. "Everyone" is envisioned as uniquely valuable in himself (there are three separate references to the free development of one's personality), but "Everyone" is expected to act toward others "in a spirit of brotherhood." "Everyone" is depicted as situated in a variety of specifically named, real-life relationships of mutual dependency: families, communities, religious groups, workplaces, associations, societies, cultures, nations, and an emerging international order. Though its main body is devoted to basic individual freedoms, the Declaration begins with an exhortation to act in "a spirit of brotherhood" and ends with community, order, and society.

Whatever else may be said of him or her, the Declaration's "Everyone" is not a lone bearer of rights. As the German Constitutional Court put it in a much-cited decision: "The image of man in the Basic Law is not that of an isolated, sovereign individual. The Basic Law resolves the tension between individual and society by relating and binding the individual to society, but without detracting from the intrinsic value of the person."[21] That departure from classical individualism while rejecting collectivism is the hallmark of dignitarian rights instruments such as the Declaration.[22] They are permeated by something very like P. C. Chang's "two-man mindedness."

In the years since its adoption, the Declaration's aspiration to universality has been reinforced by endorsements from most of the nations that were not present at its creation.[23] Specific references to the Declaration were made in the immediate post-independence constitutions of Algeria, Burundi, Cameroon, Chad, Congo, Dahomey, Equatorial Guinea, Gabon, Guinea, Ivory Coast, Madagascar, Mali, Mauritania, Niger, Rwanda, Senegal, Somalia, Togo, and Upper Volta (now Burkina Faso). Typical of those in francophone West Africa is the preamble to the 1963 Constitution of Senegal: "The People of Senegal solemnly proclaim their independence and their adherence to fundamental rights as they are defined in the Declaration of the Rights of Man and of the Citizen of 1789 and in the Universal Declaration of 10 December 1948."

The Soviet Union's abstention in 1948 was finally nullified when it endorsed the Helsinki Accords in 1975. All in all, it has been estimated that the Declaration has inspired or served as a model for the rights provisions of some ninety constitutions. The great majority of nations have also signed the two 1966 Covenants based on the Declaration: 144 for the Covenant on Civil and Political Rights and 142 for the Covenant on Economic, Social and Cultural Rights as of May 15, 2000. And in 1993, responding to the UN's call for renewed attention to human rights in the aftermath of the cold war, representatives of 171 countries at the Vienna Conference on Human Rights affirmed by consensus their "commitment to the purposes and principles contained in the Charter of the United Nations and the Universal Declaration of Human Rights." It would be foolish to dismiss this overwhelming display of support of the principles of the Declaration as a vestige of colonialism. The chief obstacle to practicing those principles is not their "Western" character, but a feature of the human condition that appears, alas, to be universal: the gap that often exists between what we say we believe is right and what we actually do.

It would be unwise, however, to minimize the danger of human rights imperialism. Today governments and interest groups increasingly deploy the language of human rights in the service of their own political, economic, or military ends. One of the twentieth century's most distinguished diplomats, George F. Kennan, expressed his misgivings about the United States' statements and demands concerning human rights in a 1993 memoir. He sensed in them, he said, "an implied assumption of superior understanding and superior virtue."

> I sense it in the anxious inquiries as to whether the "human rights record" of this or that government is found, upon lofty inquiry, to be adequate or inadequate from our standpoint. I sense it in our inclination to rate other governments, independently of their remaining practices, outstandingly on the basis of our judgment of their performance in this one particular field.[24]

And while it is hard to stick the label "Western" on the Declaration itself, that description can fairly be applied to the membership and finances of the most influential human rights organizations. The UN and the governments of major powers are surrounded by—and their agencies are often symbiotically intertwined with—a host of nongovernmental organizations. Some are humanitarian groups, others special interest lobbies, and many a little of both. As William Korey explains in his history of human rights NGOs, much of the mistrust of human rights activism in developing countries stems from the belief that these groups have ulterior motives.[25] The extent of these dangers will not be known until someone makes a comprehensive study of the financing, agendas, and influence of these organizations. But to the extent that human rights become the instrument of this or that nation or interest group bent on universalizing its own agenda, the charge of cultural imperialism must be taken seriously.

If relativism and imperialism were the only choices, the prospect for the Declaration's vision of human rights would be bleak indeed. Fortunately that is not the case. Much confusion has been created in current debates by two assumptions that would have been foreign to the framers of the Declaration. Today both critics and supporters of universal rights tend to take for granted that the Declaration mandates a single approved model of human rights for the entire world. Both also tend to assume that the only alternative would be to accept that all rights are relative to the circumstances of time and place.

Nothing could be further from the views of the principal framers. They never envisioned that the document's "common standard of achievement" would or should produce completely uniform practices.[26] In his speech to the General Assembly urging adoption of the Declaration, P. C. Chang had in fact deplored the efforts of colonial powers to impose on other peoples a standardized way of thinking and a single way of life. That sort of uniformity could be achieved, he said, only by force or at the expense of truth. It could never last.[27]

The Declaration's architects expected that its fertile principles could be brought to life in a legitimate variety of ways. Their idea was that each local tradition would be enriched as it put the Declaration's principles into practice and that all countries would benefit from the resulting accumulation of experiences. That is evident from the leeways they afforded in the text for different modes of imagining, weighting, and implementing various rights (except the tightly drawn rights not to be tortured, enslaved, or otherwise subjected to aggression). As Jacques Maritain put it, many different kinds of music could be played on the document's thirty strings.[28] In keeping with that spirit, the 1993 Vienna Declaration provides that, in protecting human rights, "the significance of national and regional particularities and various historical, cultural and religious backgrounds must be borne in mind." Kofi Annan, shortly after he became the UN's secretary-general in 1997, made a point of insisting that "no single model of human rights, Western or other, represents a blueprint for all states."[29]

Chang, Cassin, Malik, and Roosevelt were not homogenizers, but they were universalists in the sense that they believed that human nature was everywhere the same and that the processes of experiencing, understanding, and judging were capable of leading everyone to certain basic truths. "It seems to me that there is the chance that we were given our intelligence and our gifts as a part of God's plan, and it might well be that each and every one of us should develop our faculties to the best of our ability, that we should seek information from others," Eleanor Roosevelt mused in "My Day" after returning from a 1951 conference of religious leaders from Eastern and Western faiths. "I think I believe that the Lord looks upon His children with compassion and allows them to approach Him in many ways."[30]

The Declaration's framers did not imagine in 1948 that they had discovered the whole truth about human beings and human rights. They never claimed that the document they had produced under difficult circumstances represented the last word. Indeed, one speaker after another on December 9, 1948, had acknowledged that the Declaration was not perfect. The dominant metaphor was that of an important milestone on a long and difficult journey. They were content to have advanced the quest and confident that experiences gained in implementing the Declaration's principles would lead to deeper understanding in the future.

Eleanor Roosevelt summed up their attitude well in her speech to the General Assembly on December 9, 1948. She began with a quotation from Gladstone Murray, a Canadian journalist and public intellectual: "The central fact is that man is fundamentally a moral being; that the light we have is imperfect does not matter so long as we are always trying to improve it . . . we are equal in sharing the moral freedom that distinguishes us as men."[31] The Declaration, she said, "is based on the spiritual fact that man must have freedom in which to develop his full stature and through common effort to raise the level of human dignity."

If the door is left open to different ways of balancing and enforcing the Declaration's principles, friends of human rights must wonder nervously whether this will not play into the hands of international actors, who, like China's rulers, maintain that cultural and economic disparities among nations require all human rights to be understood as relative. Does pluralism not give comfort to leaders who have argued that temporary suspension of civil liberties is necessary in order to build democratic systems in the wake of repressive regimes? Or to liberal democratic governments that, while paying lip service to universality, often turn a blind eye when their allies or trading partners commit the same abuses that they condemn in an enemy or rival?

The Declaration's vulnerability to political manipulation is heightened by the popularity of philosophies that deny the existence of any moral truths. One hopes the trend is a passing one, for to accept that faith is surely to invite the coming of a very dark age. It is one thing to acknowledge that the human mind can glimpse truth only partially, quite another to deny its existence altogether. As Hannah Arendt argues in *The Origins of Totalitarianism,* "The ideal subject of totalitarian rule is not the convinced Nazi or the convinced Communist, but people for whom the distinction between fact and fiction (i.e., the reality of experience) and the distinction between true and false (i.e., the standards of thought) no longer exist."[32]

The framers were not oblivious of such dangers. All they could do was to state the truths they believed to be self-evident and suggest the outer bounds of legitimate pluralism in the document itself. The structure they fashioned is flexible enough to allow for differences in emphasis and means of implementation, but not so malleable as to permit any basic human right to be completely eclipsed or unnecessarily subordinated for the sake of other rights.

At the 1998 Harvard symposium mentioned at the beginning of this chapter, a Chinese dissident, Xiao Quiang, departed from his prepared remarks in order to respond to the charge that the Declaration was an arrogant attempt to impose "Judeo-Christian" values on non-Western peoples. Xiao said he had often heard that argument in China—and Burma, and North Korea, and Indonesia. He agreed that human rights was a Western idea insofar as its origin was concerned. Communism, he noted, was a Western idea, too. But had Professor Mutua considered what a luxury it was to be able to voice his critical opinions on that subject freely? he asked. Turning to Mutua, he said, "If you were to voice dissent from the prevailing view in China, you would end up in jail, and there you would soon be asking for your rights, without worrying about whether they were 'American' or 'Chinese.' "[33]

There is little doubt about how the principal framers of the Universal Declaration would have responded to the charge of "Western-ness." What was crucial for them—indeed, what made universal human rights possible—was the *similarity* among all human beings. Their starting point was the simple fact of the common humanity shared by every man, woman, and child on earth, a fact that, for them, put linguistic, racial, religious, and other differences into their proper perspective. A strong emphasis on racial and cultural difference was, after all, one of the worst evils of colonialism and Nazism.

Cassin, Chang, Humphrey, Malik, and Roosevelt would have agreed with the eloquent statement made by a representative of Human Rights

Watch/Asia shortly before the 1993 Vienna Human Rights Conference. Speaking in Jakarta to an audience that included many skeptics, Daniel S. Lev said:

> Values, traditions, customs, and habits naturally vary, as do languages and religions, but do they differ on the fundamental questions with which we are concerned? Whatever else may separate them, human beings belong to a single biological species, the simplest and most fundamental commonality before which the significance of human differences quickly fades. . . . The argument of cultural specificity cannot over-ride the reality that we all share the most basic attributes in common. We are all capable, in exactly the same ways, of feeling pain, hunger, and a hundred kinds of deprivation. Consequently, people nowhere routinely concede that those with enough power to do so ought to be able at will to kill, torture, imprison, and generally abuse others. There may be no choice in the matter, given realities of power, but submission is different from moral approval.
>
> The great religious traditions . . . take for granted the principle of common humanity. Islam, Buddhism, Catholicism, Protestantism, Judaism, Hinduism, Taoism, and most of their variants share a recognition of the human condition. Their explanations of it and their solutions for it may differ, but not their concern. The idea of universal human rights shares the recognition of one common humanity, and provides a minimum solution to deal with its miseries.[34]

THE DECLARATION
TODAY

The Universal Declaration charted a bold new course for human rights by presenting a vision of freedom as linked to social security, balanced by responsibilities, grounded in respect for equal human dignity, and guarded by the rule of law. That vision was meant to protect liberty from degenerating into license and to repel the excesses of individualism and collectivism alike. By affirming that all its rights belong to everyone, everywhere, it aimed to put an end to the idea that a nation's treatment of its own citizens or subjects was immune from outside scrutiny.

When the Declaration was adopted, friends of human rights were of different minds about its prospects. Many regarded it as a milestone in the history of freedom, but to others it seemed to be just a collection of pious phrases—meaningless without courts, policemen, and armies to back them up. The latter view was common among men impatient for action and progress, including the most famous international law scholar of the day, Hersch Lauterpacht, who commented disparagingly that "the Declaration is not in itself an achievement of magnitude."[1] It possessed, he said, "no legal force and, probably only inconsiderable moral authority."

Eleanor Roosevelt saw the matter differently. Her confidence was due in part to her lively sense of the Declaration of Independence as a bright thread running through American history. That document, too, had proclaimed certain truths as self-evident and declared certain rights to be unalienable. It too was nonbinding. Just before the Human Rights Commission held its last drafting session, the State Department explained the U.S. view of the Declaration's nature and purpose by referring to what Abraham Lincoln had said about the assertion of human equality in the Declaration of Independence:

> They [the drafters] did not mean to assert the obvious untruth, that all were then actually enjoying that equality, nor yet, that they were about to confer it immediately upon them. In fact they had no power to confer such a boon. They meant simply to declare the *right* so that the *enforcement* of it might follow as fast as circumstances should permit.
>
> They meant to set up a standard maxim for free society which should be familiar to all: constantly looked to, constantly labored for, and thereby constantly spreading and deepening its influence and augmenting the happiness and value of life to all people, of all colors, everywhere.[2]

In the April 1948 *Foreign Affairs* Eleanor Roosevelt wrote in a similar vein of her own hopes for the Declaration then nearing completion: "In the first place, we have put into words some inherent rights. Beyond that, we have found that the conditions of our contemporary world require the enumeration of certain protections which the individual must have if he is to acquire a sense of security and dignity in his own person. The effect of this is frankly educational. Indeed, I like to think that the Declaration will help forward very largely the education of the people of the world."[3]

Was her confidence justified? After fifty years the answer is a qualified yes. The Declaration's moral authority has made itself felt in a variety of ways. The most impressive advances in human rights—the fall of apartheid in South Africa and the collapse of the Eastern European totalitarian regimes—owe more to the moral beacon of the Declaration than to the many covenants and treaties that are now in force. Its nonbinding principles, carried far and wide by activists and modern communications, have vaulted over the political and legal barriers that impede efforts to establish international enforcement mechanisms. Most, though not all, flagrant and repeated instances of rights abuse now are brought to light, and most governments now go to great lengths to avoid being blacklisted as notorious violators. Extreme suffering and deprivation—whether due to human or natural causes—often, though not often enough, elicit practical responses.

By 1986 Charles Malik, who had been one of the staunchest supporters of human rights covenants, had come around to Roosevelt's view, admitting, "Whenever the question of human rights has arisen throughout the world, the appeal has been far more to the Declaration than to the covenants."[4] He now appreciated, he said, that "[i]n the long run, the morally disturbing or judging is far more important than the legally binding."

The Declaration's principles, moreover, have increasingly acquired legal force, mainly through their incorporation into national legal systems. It would be hard to overestimate the importance of that development. Though the Declaration is rightly hailed for establishing that nations are accountable to others for the way they treat their own people, the fact is that international institutions can never provide first-line protection for victims of rights violations. When protection at the national level is absent or breaks down, there are severe limitations to what international enforcement mechanisms can accomplish. The greatest success story—that of the European human rights system established by the 1950 European Convention on Human Rights—serves only to underline the point. The effectiveness of that system has been due largely to the willingness of the states involved to comply promptly and fully with the judgments of the European Court of Human Rights, adapting their laws to its rulings. In the Inter-American human rights system, where many of the cases that come before the regional court in Costa Rica have involved disappearances, torture, and deaths, securing compliance has been far more difficult. Unlike in Europe, a number of states-parties to the Inter-American Convention have not yet submitted themselves to the jurisdiction of the court in Costa Rica.

The difficulty with international legal remedies is that they work best where their legitimacy is widely acknowledged. They are apt to be least effective in the situations where the worst violations occur. It can be expected, therefore, that the strength of the European human rights system will be tested as it assimilates its new Eastern European members.

The most intractable problems arise where rogue nations are themselves the rights violators and in the increasing number of cases where anarchy prevails owing to civil war or other conflicts between groups. The responses of the community of nations to the most appalling rights violations of the past half century have ranged from inaction, to diplomatic initiatives and censure, to economic incentives and sanctions, to arms embargoes, to military intervention, and, in the post–cold war years, to international criminal prosecutions.

Though the framers of the Declaration knew that military intervention was sometimes necessary, and some backed the establishment of a permanent international criminal court, those subjects figured very little in their deliberations about implementation of the Declaration. This was due in part to their understanding of the division of labor among the Human Rights Commission, the International Law Commission, the Nuremberg prosecutors, and the role of the Security Council. But it also reflected a certain philosophy—the conviction that culture is prior to law. Criminal prosecutions, they knew, have little effect on the basic causes of the conduct they aim to punish and deter. The same is true of military intervention, which often triggers fresh cycles of resentment and retaliation.

One of the most basic assumptions of the founders of the UN and the framers of the Declaration was that the root causes of atrocities and armed conflict are frequently to be found in poverty and discrimination. That is why Franklin Roosevelt included the "freedom from want" among his four freedoms, and that is why Harry Truman took the occasion of the signing of the UN Charter to warn, "Experience has shown how deeply the seeds of war are planted by economic rivalry and social injustice." Those ideas found expression in the Declaration's insistence on the link between freedom and social security and on the relation of both to peace. That aspect of the Declaration, unfortunately, is commonly ignored today—just at a time when the poorest people and countries, a quarter of the world's population, are being increasingly marginalized in the global economic order. A pressing challenge for the future is to reunite the sundered halves of the Declaration—its commitment to individual liberty and its acknowledgment of a link between freedom and economic opportunity.

Like the American Declaration of Independence, the Universal Declaration was radically ahead of its time. After fifty years, its transformative potential has still barely begun to be realized. The further progress of its principles will be complicated, however, by globalization and the upsurge of regional and ethnic conflict. In a surprising development that none of the Declaration's framers could have anticipated, national sovereignty—

which loomed so large in 1948—has begun to lose a great part of its meaning, challenged from without by economic forces that know no borders and from within by movements for regional and local self-determination. The world, and with it the human rights project, seems to have entered a new phase of upheaval.

The Declaration's ability to weather the turbulence ahead has been compromised by the practice of reading its integrated articles as a string of essentially separate guarantees. Nations and interest groups continue to use selected provisions as weapons or shields, wrenching them out of context and ignoring the rest. Even persons and governments that are well disposed toward human rights often tend to think of rights violations only or mainly in terms of the most violent abuses—violations of five or six articles out of thirty. Forgetfulness, neglect, and opportunism have thus obscured the Declaration's message that rights have conditions—that everyone's rights are importantly dependent on respect for the rights of others, on the rule of law, and on a healthy civil society.

The principal framers, though they differed on many points, were as one in their belief in the priority of culture. René Cassin, though a strong backer of international criminal law, wrote, "In the eyes of the Declaration's authors, effective respect for human rights depends primarily and above all on the mentalities of individuals and social groups."[5] Malik, who labored long and hard on the Covenants, agreed. "Men, cultures and nations must first mature inwardly," he wrote, "before there can be effective international machinery to adjudicate complaints about the violation of human rights."[6] Chang, citing the Chinese proverb "Laws alone are not sufficient to bring about results by themselves," said the Declaration's main goal was "to build up better human beings, and not merely to punish those who violate human rights."[7]

Eleanor Roosevelt was of the same mind. In 1940, with war on the horizon, she had written a pamphlet to emphasize that democracy rested on a moral basis. "Court decisions, and laws and government administration," she said then, "are only the results of the way people progress inwardly."[8] She returned to the point in one of her last speeches at the UN, emphasizing the importance of the small settings where people first learn of their rights and responsibilities:

Where, after all, do universal human rights begin? In small places, close to home—so close and so small that they cannot be seen on any maps of the world. Yet they *are* the world of the individual person; the neighborhood he lives in; the school or college he attends; the factory, farm or office where he works.[9]

Those convictions of the framers undergird one of the most remarkable features of the Declaration: its attention to the "small places" where people first learn about their rights and how to exercise them responsibly—families, schools, workplaces, and religious and other associations. These little seedbeds of character and competence, together with the rule of law, political freedoms, social security, and international cooperation, are all part of the Declaration's dynamic ecology of freedom.

The hopes and the fears of the men and women who framed the Declaration were grounded in their understanding of human nature. The events of their times had shown them human beings at their best and worst—with their potential for good and evil, reason and impulse, trust and betrayal, creativity and destruction, selfishness and cooperation. They had also seen governments at their best and worst—capable of atrocities at home and abroad, but also of restoring their former enemies to a dignified place in the community of nations. The framers took encouragement from the fact that human beings are capable not only of violating human rights, but also of imagining that there are rights to violate, of articulating those rights in declarations and constitutions, of orienting their conduct toward the norms they have recognized, and of feeling the need to make excuses when their conduct falls short.

There is a sculpture by Arnaldo Pomodoro on the plaza outside the UN building in New York that captures the spirit of Eleanor Roosevelt and her colleagues. A gift from the government of Italy, it consists of an enormous sphere of burnished bronze, suggesting a globe. The sphere is pleasing to behold, even though it startles with its imperfection. There are deep, jagged cracks in its golden-hued surface, cracks too large ever to be repaired. Perhaps it's cracked because it's defective (like the broken world), one thinks. Or maybe (like an egg) it has to break in order for something else to emerge. Perhaps both. Sure enough, when one peers into the gashes on its surface, there is another brightly shining sphere coming along inside. But that one is already cracked, too!

Whatever is going on inside those spheres, it does not seem to be all chance and accident. There is a tremendous sense of motion, of dynamism, of potency, of emergent probabilities. And so it has been with the human rights project. Yes, the enterprise is flawed. Yes, dreadful violations of human dignity still occur. But thanks in great measure to those who framed the Universal Declaration, growing numbers of women and men have been inspired to do something about them.

The journey of human rights thus far has been marked by impressive advances and heartbreaking setbacks. Force and happenstance have played their roles in its uneven progress. What is most encouraging, however, is the proof that men and women of goodwill can make a difference. The imaginations, actions, decisions, sacrifices, and personal examples of countless individuals have helped to bolster the chances of reason and conscience against power and interest.

Today's friends of human rights are in the process of building on the legacy of the Declaration's framers. Fifty years hence, others will form opinions regarding the present generation's stewardship. People not yet born will pass judgment one day on whether we enhanced or squandered the inheritance handed down to us by Eleanor Roosevelt, Charles Malik, John Humphrey, Peng-chun Chang, René Cassin, and other large-souled men and women who strove to bring a standard of right from the ashes of terrible wrongs. How we measure up will depend in part on today's leaders, especially those who chart the course of the world's one remaining superpower. But what will be decisive is whether or not sufficient numbers of men and women in "small places, close to home" can imagine, and then begin to live, the reality of freedom, solidarity, and peace.

NOTES

PREFACE

1. Thucydides, *The Peloponnesian War* (New York: Modern Library, 1951), 331.
2. In an essay celebrating the Declaration's fiftieth anniversary, Louis Henkin described it as "the authoritative articulation of the international human rights standard: the symbol, the representation, the scriptures." Henkin, "Human Rights: Ideology and Aspiration, Reality and Prospect," in Samantha Power and Graham Allison, eds., *Realizing Human Rights: Moving from Inspiration to Impact* (New York: St. Martin's Press, 2000), 3, 12.
3. As described in a leading text, "It is the parent document, the initial burst of enthusiasm and idealism, terser, more general and grander than the treaties, in some sense the constitution of the entire movement—the single most invoked human rights instrument." Henry Steiner and Philip Alston, *International Human Rights in Context* (Oxford: Clarendon Press, 1996), 120.
4. Convention on the Prevention and Punishment of the Crime of Genocide, *United Nations Treaty Series* 78 (December 9, 1948), 277, Article I. Genocide was defined as any of a series of enumerated acts "committed with intent to destroy, in whole or in part, a national, ethnical, racial, or religious group, as such."
5. Universal Declaration of Human Rights, Preamble.
6. Eleanor Roosevelt, "Making Human Rights Come Alive," in *What I Hope to Leave Behind: The Essential Essays of Eleanor Roosevelt,* Allida Black, ed. (Brooklyn: Carlson, 1995), 559. See also Mrs. Roosevelt's advice to "know the Declaration" in her interview with Howard Langer in *Human Rights: A*

Documentary on the United Nations Declaration of Human Rights (Folkways Records, 1958).

7. Eleanor Roosevelt, "The U.N. and the Welfare of the World," *National Parent-Teacher* 47 (1953), 14.

CHAPTER I: THE LONGING FOR FREEDOM

1. Kenneth Thompson, *Ethics and International Relations* (New Brunswick, N.J.: Transaction Books, 1985), 17.

2. Remarks on signing the United Nations Relief and Rehabilitation Administration Act, November 9, 1943, *The Public Papers and Addresses of Franklin D. Roosevelt, 1943* (New York: Random House, 1950), 503.

3. Radio Address of December 24, 1943, quoted in Townsend Hoopes and Douglas Brinkley, *FDR and the Creation of the U.N.* (New Haven: Yale University Press, 1997), 108.

4. Edward R. Stettinius, Jr., *Roosevelt and the Russians* (New York: Doubleday, 1949), 321.

5. Quoted in Doris Kearns Goodwin, *No Ordinary Time: Franklin and Eleanor Roosevelt: The Home Front in World War II* (New York: Simon & Schuster, 1994), 596.

6. Milovan Djilas, *Conversations with Stalin,* M. Petrovich, trans. (New York: Harcourt Brace & World, 1962), 73.

7. George F. Kennan, *Memoirs 1925–1950* (Boston: Little, Brown, 1967), 216–17.

8. Anthony Eden, *The Reckoning* (Boston: Houghton Mifflin, 1965), 370.

9. Quoted in A. W. Brian Simpson, *Human Rights and the End of Empire: Britain and the Genesis of the European Convention* (London: Oxford University Press, forthcoming), chapter 5.

10. See, generally, *The Oxford History of the British Empire,* William R. Louis, ed. (London: Oxford University Press, 1998–99).

11. See, generally, William H. McNeill, *America, Britain, and Russia: Their Cooperation and Conflict, 1941–1946* (London: Oxford University Press, 1953).

12. Dumbarton Oaks Proposals for a General International Organization, ch. 9A, s. 1, in *United Nations Conference for International Organization: Documents,* vol. 3 (New York: UNIO, 1945), 18: "[T]he Organization should facilitate solutions of international economic, social, and other humanitarian problems and promote respect for human rights and fundamental freedoms. Responsibility for the discharge of this function should be vested in the General Assembly and, under the authority of the General Assembly, in an Economic and Social Council."

13. Stettinius diary entry for September 27, 1944, excerpted in *Foreign Relations of the United States: Diplomatic Papers, 1944,* vol. 1 (Washington, D.C.: U.S. Government Printing Office, 1966), 842.

14. Eleanor Roosevelt, *This I Remember* (New York: Harper, 1949), 339–40.

15. Winston Churchill, *Triumph and Tragedy* (Boston: Houghton Mifflin, 1953), 345.

16. McNeill, *America, Britain, and Russia,* 528–29.

17. Stettinius, *Roosevelt and the Russians,* 301.

18. James MacGregor Burns, *Roosevelt: The Soldier of Freedom* (New York: Harcourt Brace Jovanovich, 1970), 573.

19. Stettinius, *Roosevelt and the Russians,* 301.

20. Roosevelt, *This I Remember,* 340–41.

21. Diane S. Clemens, *Yalta* (New York: Oxford University Press, 1970), 129–30.

22. Id. at 241.

23. Telford Taylor, *The Anatomy of the Nuremberg Trials* (New York: Alfred A. Knopf, 1992), 28–33.

24. All countries that had declared, or would declare, war on Germany and Japan by March 1, 1945, were invited. Those who attended were Argentina, Australia, Belgium, Bolivia, Brazil, Byelorussia, Canada, Chile, China, Colombia, Costa Rica, Cuba, Czechoslovakia, Denmark, Dominican Republic, Ecuador, Egypt, El Salvador, Ethiopia, France, Greece, Guatemala, Haiti, Honduras, India, Iran, Iraq, Lebanon, Liberia, Luxembourg, Mexico, Netherlands, New Zealand, Nicaragua, Norway, Panama, Paraguay, Peru, Philippine Commonwealth, Saudi Arabia, South Africa, Syria, Turkey, Ukraine, Union of Soviet Socialist Republics, United Kingdom, United States, Uruguay, Venezuela, and Yugoslavia. (At Yalta the USSR had asked for and received U.S. support for admitting two of its component republics, Byelorussia and the Ukraine; the United States, in turn, had convinced several Latin American countries to drop their opposition to the two seats by agreeing to vote for the admission of Argentina, which, after four years of pro-Axis neutrality, had entered the war on the side of the Allies in March 1945.)

25. *The Public Papers and Addresses of Franklin D. Roosevelt, 1938–1950,* vol. 9 (Washington, D.C., 1969), 672.

26. Richard C. Holbrooke, "Romulo: The Problem Is Marcos," *New York Times,* January 24, 1986, A27.

27. Carlos P. Romulo, "I'm Glad I'm a Little Guy," *Reader's Digest,* August 1953, 111–13.

28. Carlos Romulo and Beth Day Romulo, *Forty Years: A Third World Soldier at the UN* (New York: Greenwood Press, 1986), 2.

29. Id. at 9–10.

30. *The Diaries of Sir Alexander Cadogan 1938–45,* David Dilks, ed. (New York: Putnam, 1972), 746.

31. Romulo and Romulo, *Forty Years,* 41.

32. Carlos Romulo, "Human Rights as a Condition of Peace in the Far East," *Annals of the Academy of Political and Social Science* (January 1946), 8.

33. For details, see Paul G. Lauren, "First Principles of Racial Equality: The History and Politics and Diplomacy of Human Rights Provisions in the United Nations Charter," 5 *Human Rights Quarterly* 1 (1983).

34. Hoopes and Brinkley, *FDR and the Creation of the U.N.,* 187.
35. H. V. Evatt, "Economic Rights in the United Nations Charter," *Annals of the Academy of Political and Social Science* (January 1946), 4, 5.
36. Malik Diary, no. 2102, "Reflections on the Conference."
37. Charles Malik, speech of April 28, 1945, in *The Challenge of Human Rights: Charles Malik and the Universal Declaration,* Habib C. Malik, ed. (Oxford: Centre for Lebanese Studies, 2000), 14–15.
38. Johannes Morsink, *The Universal Declaration of Human Rights: Origins, Drafting, and Intent* (Philadelphia: University of Pennsylvania Press, 1999), 2, 130.
39. For a comprehensive treatment of the role of NGOs in relation to the UDHR, see William Korey, *NGOs and the Universal Declaration of Human Rights: "A Curious Grapevine"* (New York: St. Martin's Press, 1998).
40. Vera Micheles Dean, "The San Francisco Conference," *Foreign Policy Reports* (July 15, 1945), 110, 111.
41. *Documents on Polish-Soviet Relations 1939–45,* vol. II (London: Heinemann, 1967), 536–41.
42. M. Glen Johnson, "The Contributions of Eleanor and Franklin Roosevelt to the Development of International Protection for Human Rights," 9 *Human Rights Quarterly* 26 (1987).
43. Taylor, *Anatomy of the Nuremberg Trials,* 32.
44. *Cadogan Diaries,* 738.
45. Taylor, *Anatomy of the Nuremberg Trials,* 39.
46. The meeting is recounted in O. Frederick Nolde, *Free and Equal: Human Rights in Ecumenical Perspective* (Geneva: World Council of Churches, 1968), 22–24. See also Johnson, "Contributions," 26, and Korey, *NGOs and the Universal Declaration,* 38.
47. Johnson, "Contributions," 26.
48. UN Charter, Article 2(7).
49. UN Charter, Preamble and Articles 1, 13, 55, 62, 68, 76.
50. UN Charter, Article 68.
51. Harry Truman, *Truman Speaks,* Cyril Clemens, ed. (New York: Kraus Reprint, 1969), 56.
52. Goodwin, *No Ordinary Time,* 619.
53. UN Charter, Article 2(7).
54. Malik Diary, no. 2102, "Reflections on the Conference."

CHAPTER 2: MADAM CHAIRMAN

1. Eleanor Roosevelt, *On My Own* (New York: Harper, 1958), 39.
2. Alfred Steinberg, *Mrs. R.: The Life of Eleanor Roosevelt* (New York: Putnam, 1958), 320.
3. Blanche Wiesen Cook, *Eleanor Roosevelt, Volume 2, 1933–38* (New York: Viking, 1999), 7, 74.

4. Quoted by Cook, *Eleanor Roosevelt,* at 37.
5. David McCullough, *Truman* (New York: Simon & Schuster, 1992), 355.
6. Roosevelt, *On My Own,* 39.
7. Roosevelt, *On My Own,* 2; Joseph Lash, *Eleanor: The Years Alone* (New York: W. W. Norton, 1972), 297.
8. Quoted by Cook, *Eleanor Roosevelt,* 114–15.
9. Eleanor Roosevelt, *What I Hope to Leave Behind,* Allida M. Black, ed. (New York: Carlson, 1995), 35.
10. Quoted in Steinberg, *Mrs. R.,* 320.
11. *Mother and Daughter: The Letters of Eleanor and Anna Roosevelt,* Bernard Asbell, ed. (New York: Coward, McCann, and Geoghegan, 1982), 202.
12. Irene Sandifer, *Mrs. Roosevelt as We Knew Her* (Silver Spring, Md.: Mrs. Durward Sandifer, 1975), 22.
13. *Mother and Daughter,* 203.
14. Ibid., 204.
15. Lash, *Eleanor: The Years Alone,* 21–22.
16. Harry S. Truman, *Memoirs: Year of Decisions, Vol. I* (Garden City, N.Y.: Doubleday, 1955), 5.
17. Eleanor Roosevelt, "My Day," April 17, 1945 (courtesy of the Roosevelt Library, Hyde Park, New York).
18. Eleanor Roosevelt, *This I Remember* (Harper, 1949), 348–49.
19. Id. at 349.
20. James F. Byrnes, *All in One Lifetime* (New York: Harper, 1958), 377.
21. Sandifer, *Mrs. Roosevelt,* 2.
22. Roosevelt, *On My Own,* 44.
23. Ibid., 41–42.
24. "George VI Bids UNO Lay the Foundation for Warless World," *New York Times,* January 10, 1946, A1, 10.
25. *Mother and Daughter,* 208.
26. Roosevelt, *On My Own,* 47.
27. Ibid.
28. *Mother and Daughter,* 209–10.
29. Id. at 207.
30. Roosevelt, *On My Own,* 49.
31. Ibid., 51.
32. Ibid., 53.
33. McCullough, *Truman,* 486, 490–91.
34. Ibid., 486–92.
35. Those present, besides Roosevelt, were Dusan Brkish (Yugoslavia), René Cassin (France), C. L. Hsia (China), Nikolai Kriukov, replaced in midmeeting by Alexander Borisov (Soviet Union), and K. C. Neogi (India). Absent: Paul Berg (Norway), Fernand Dehousse (Belgium), and Victor Raul Haya de la Torre (Peru).
36. *Yearbook of Human Rights for 1947* (New York: United Nations, 1949), 454.

37. Eleanor Roosevelt, "The Promise of Human Rights," *Foreign Affairs* (April 1948), 470, 473.

38. *Yearbook of Human Rights for 1947,* 421–22.

39. Byelorussia and the Ukraine, though part of the Soviet Union, had been given separate membership in the UN pursuant to an arrangement made at Yalta and ratified at San Francisco.

40. John P. Humphrey, *Human Rights and the United Nations: A Great Adventure* (Dobbs Ferry, N.Y.: Transnational Publishing, 1984), 18.

41. *U.N. Weekly Bulletin,* August 12, 1946, 14.

42. Humphrey, *Human Rights,* 23.

43. Id. at 4–5.

44. "A New Loyalty," in *Peng Chun Chang 1892–1957: Biography and Collected Works,* Ruth H. C. and Sze-Chuh Cheng, eds. (privately printed, 1995), 150.

45. *Report of Valentin Tepliakov,* March 2, 1947 (Moscow: Russian Center for Documents on Modern History, Department for UN Matters), index 2a, folder 7a, 1–17.

CHAPTER 3: A ROCKY START

1. Australia, Belgium, Chile, China, Egypt, France, India, Iran, Lebanon, Panama, Philippines, the Soviet Union, the United Kingdom, the United States, Uruguay, and Yugoslavia.

2. See her pamphlet, *Civil Liberties* (Bombay: Aundh Publishing Trust, 1945).

3. Eleanor Roosevelt, "Why I Do Not Choose to Run," in *What I Hope to Leave Behind,* Allida M. Black, ed. (New York: Carlson, 1995), 35.

4. Eleanor Roosevelt, *My Day: The Post-War Years, 1945–1952,* David Emblidge, ed. (New York: Pharos, 1990), 87–88.

5. "William Roy Hodgson," in *United States Handbook No. 2, Human Rights Commission, Third Session* (Eleanor Roosevelt Papers, Box 4595, Roosevelt Library, Hyde Park, New York).

6. Human Rights Commission, First Session, Summary Records (E/CN.4/SR.2, p. 4; SR.9, p. 3; SR.15, pp. 2–3; SR.16, p. 2).

7. Ibid.; (E/CN.4/SR.7, pp. 3–4; SR.15, p. 5). For the full U.S. position, see *Department of State Bulletin,* February 16, 1947, 277.

8. Ibid.; (E/CN.4/SR.7, p. 4).

9. Ibid.

10. *The More Important Speeches and Interventions of Charles Malik, Taken from the Verbatim Records of the First Session of the Human Rights Commission,* 11–12 (Papers of Charles Habib Malik, Library of Congress, Manuscript Division).

11. Human Rights Commission, First Session, Summary Records (E/CN.4/SR.8, p. 4).

12. "Vladislav S. Ribnikar," in *United States Handbook No. 2, Human Rights*

Commission, Third Session (Eleanor Roosevelt Papers, Box 4595, Roosevelt Library, Hyde Park, New York).

13. Human Rights Commission, First Session, Summary Records (E/CN.4/SR.8, p. 4).

14. Verbatim Record, in *The More Important Speeches and Interventions of Charles Malik,* 35–37; Human Rights Commission, First Session, Summary Records (E/CN.4/SR.9, p. 3).

15. Verbatim Record, in "Four Basic Principles," in *The Challenge of Human Rights: Charles Malik and the Universal Declaration,* Habib C. Malik, ed. (Oxford: Centre for Lebanese Studies, 2000), 27.

16. Verbatim Record, in *The More Important Speeches and Interventions of Charles Malik,* 37–38; Human Rights Commission, First Session, Summary Records (E/CN.4/SR 14, p. 4).

17. Verbatim Record, in *The More Important Speeches and Interventions of Charles Malik,* 38.

18. Id. at 38–39.

19. Id. at 39–40.

20. Id. at 42–43.

21. Id. at 44.

22. Id. at 46.

23. Ibid.

24. The cartoon, reprinted here, is from Alois Derso and Emery Kelen, *United Nations Sketchbook: A Cartoon History of the United Nations* (New York: Funk & Wagnalls, 1950).

25. Verbatim Record, in *The More Important Speeches and Interventions of Charles Malik,* 44.

26. Roosevelt, *My Day,* 17.

27. See Joseph Lash, *Eleanor: The Years Alone* (New York: W. W. Norton, 1972), 62–63.

28. Verbatim Record, in *The More Important Speeches and Interventions of Charles Malik,* 47.

29. John P. Humphrey, *Human Rights and the United Nations: A Great Adventure* (Dobbs Ferry, N.Y.: Transnational Publishing, 1984), 17, 23–24, 37.

30. Ibid. On Humphrey's social democratic political views, see A. J. Hobbins, "Mentor and Protégé: Percy Corbett's Relationship with John Humphrey," 1999 *Canadian Yearbook of International Law,* 3.

31. Hernán Santa Cruz, *Cooperar o Perecer: El dilema de la comunidad mundial* (Buenos Aires: Grupo Editor Latinoamericano, 1984), 120.

32. Quoted in A. W. Brian Simpson, *Human Rights and the End of Empire: Britain and the Genesis of the European Convention* (London: Oxford University Press, forthcoming), chapter 7.

33. Quoted in Margaret Bruce, "Personal Notes on an Important Anniversary," *U.N. Chronicle,* December 1, 1998.

34. Lash, *Eleanor: The Years Alone,* 62–63.
35. Human Rights Commission, First Session, Summary Records (E/CN.4/SR.12, p. 5).
36. Ibid.; (E/CN.4/SR.10, pp. 3–4).
37. Ibid.; (E/CN.4/SR.2, p. 3, and SR.13, p. 8).
38. V. Tepliakov, *Report on the Work of the Human Rights Commission,* March 2, 1947 (Moscow: Russian Center for Documents on Modern History, Department for UN Matters), index 2a, folder 7a, 1–17.
39. Eleanor Roosevelt, *On My Own* (New York: Harper, 1958), 77.
40. Humphrey, *Human Rights,* 29.
41. A. J. Hobbins, "René Cassin and the Daughter of Time: The First Draft of the Universal Declaration of Human Rights," 2 *Fontanus* 7 (Montreal: McGill University Library Publications, 1989), 22.
42. John P. Humphrey, unpublished letter of February 21, 1947 (McGill University Achives, reprinted with permission of Humphrey's literary executor, A. J. Hobbins, associate director of libraries, McGill University).
43. John P. Humphrey, *No Distant Millennium: The International Law of Human Rights* (Paris: UNESCO, 1989), 149.
44. Pauline Maier, *American Scripture: Making the Declaration of Independence* (New York: Alfred A. Knopf, 1997), 98–99.
45. John P. Humphrey, *The Inter-American System, a Canadian View* (Toronto: Macmillan, 1942).
46. A. J. Hobbins, " 'Dear Rufus . . .': A Law Student's Life at McGill in the Roaring Twenties from the Letters of John P. Humphrey," 44 *McGill Law Journal* 753, 775 (1999).
47. René Cassin, *La Pensée et l'Action* (Boulogne-sur-Seine: F. Lalou, 1972), 105, 106.
48. According to Cassin biographer Marc Agi: *"On se rappelle que René Cassin n'avait pas une très bonne connaissance de la langue anglaise."* Marc Agi, *René Cassin 1887–1976* (Mesnil-sur-l'Estrée: Perrin, 1998), 211 n. 3.
49. Agi, *René Cassin 1887–1976,* 211.
50. Human Rights Commission, First Session, Summary Records (E/CN.4/SR.12, p. 2).
51. Cassin, *La Pensée et l'Action,* 107.
52. Eleanor Roosevelt, "The Promise of Human Rights," in *Courage in a Dangerous World: The Political Writings of Eleanor Roosevelt,* Allida M. Black, ed. (New York: Columbia University Press, 1999), 158.
53. *U.N. Weekly Bulletin,* June 17, 1947, 639.
54. Hobbins, "René Cassin and the Daughter of Time," 22; *U.N. Weekly Bulletin,* June 17, 1947, 639.
55. "The Universal Declaration of Human Rights," speech delivered by Charles Malik at the American University of Beirut, January 5, 1949 (Malik Papers, Library of Congress, Manuscript Collection), 7.

56. David McCullough, *Truman* (New York: Simon & Schuster, 1992), 541, 546–48.
57. The countries are listed in chapter 8 at n. 31.
58. Human Rights Commission, First Session, Summary Records (E/CN.4/SR.4, p. 9).

CHAPTER 4: EVERY CONCEIVABLE RIGHT

1. Gérard Israël, *René Cassin* (Paris: Desclée de Brouwer, 1990), 178.
2. Marc Agi, *René Cassin 1887–1976* (Mesnil-sur-l'Estrée: Perrin, 1998), 209; Joseph Lash, *Eleanor: The Years Alone* (New York: W. W. Norton, 1972), 110.
3. The following account is based on Lash, *Eleanor: The Years Alone,* 94–99.
4. Verbatim Record of the June 9, 1947, Drafting Committee Meeting (Charles Malik Papers, Library of Congress, Manuscript Collection).
5. H. G. Wells, *The Rights of Man, or What Are We Fighting For?* (Middlesex: Penguin, 1940), 14–17, 78–84.
6. John P. Humphrey, *Human Rights and the United Nations: A Great Adventure* (Dobbs Ferry, N.Y.: Transnational Publishers, 1984), 31–32. See also *U.N. Weekly Bulletin,* June 17, 1947, 639.
7. American Declaration of the Rights and Duties of Man, in *Basic Documents on Human Rights,* Ian Brownlie, ed. (Oxford: Clarendon Press, 1994), 489.
8. "Statement of Essential Human Rights," in American Law Institute, *Seventy-Fifth Anniversary 1923–1998* (Philadelphia: American Law Institute, 1998), 269.
9. Verbatim Record of June 9, 1947, Drafting Committee Meeting (Charles Malik Papers, Library of Congress, Manuscript Division).
10. Ibid. See also E/CN.4/AC.1/3/Add. 1.
11. "International Bill of Rights to Be Drafted," *U.N. Weekly Bulletin,* June 17, 1947, 639.
12. Verbatim Record of June 9, 1947, Drafting Committee Meeting (Charles Malik Papers, Library of Congress, Manuscript Division).
13. A. W. Brian Simpson, *Human Rights and the End of Empire: Britain and the Genesis of the European Convention* (Oxford: Oxford University Press, forthcoming), chapter 8.
14. Ibid.
15. Verbatim Record, June 12, 1947, Drafting Committee Meeting (Charles Malik Papers, Library of Congress, Manuscript Division).
16. Ibid.
17. Human Rights Commission, Drafting Committee, First Session (E/CN.4/AC.1/SR.6, p. 2).
18. Ibid.; (E/CN.4/21 pp. 3–4).
19. Agi, *René Cassin 1887–1976,* 22.
20. René Cassin, *La Pensée et l'Action* (Boulogne-sur-Seine: F. Lalou, 1972), 23.

21. Israël, *René Cassin,* 19, 21.

22. Agi, *René Cassin 1887–1976,* 55.

23. René Cassin, *Les Hommes Partis de Rien* (Paris: Plon, 1975), 75, 79.

24. Agi, *René Cassin 1887–1976,* 140–42.

25. Charles de Gaulle, *The Complete War Memoirs of Charles de Gaulle* (New York: Simon & Schuster, 1964): "Professor Cassin was my assistant—and what a valuable one!—with regard to all those agreements and other documents of which, starting from nothing, our international and external structure was established" (99).

26. This description, from the Report of the Drafting Committee (E/CN.4/21, p. 4), fits the French-language draft, dated June 16, 1947, reprinted in Agi, *René Cassin,* at 359–65. The working group made a few minor revisions in Cassin's initial redraft before forwarding it to the full drafting committee. This slightly revised "Cassin draft" (E/CN.4/AC.1/W.1 and W.2/Rev. 2) is set forth as appendix 2.

27. Comparison of the drafts in appendices 1 and 2 bears out Johannes Morsink's conclusion that "over three-quarters of the Cassin draft was taken from Humphrey's first draft." Morsink, *The Universal Declaration of Human Rights: Origins, Drafting, and Intent* (Philadelphia: University of Pennsylvania Press, 1999), 8.

28. Humphrey, *Human Rights,* 44.

29. Ibid., 31.

30. Verbatim Record, June 17, 1947, Drafting Committee Meeting (Charles Malik Papers, Library of Congress, Manuscript Division).

31. Simpson, *Human Rights,* chapter 8.

32. Humphrey, in fact, expressly disclaimed authorship. Humphrey, *Human Rights,* 43.

33. Cassin, "Historique de la Déclaration Universelle," reprinted in *La Pensée et l'Action,* 108: "[J]e fus chargé par mes collègues de rédiger, sous ma seule responsabilité, un premier avant-projet."

34. Clinton Rossiter, "Introduction," to Alexander Hamilton, James Madison, John Jay, *The Federalist Papers* (New York: Mentor, 1961), x–xi.

35. Marc Agi's 1998 biography, *René Cassin 1887–1976,* is misleadingly subtitled *Père de la Déclaration Universelle des droits de l'homme.* In the text, Agi concedes that Cassin was not the "sole father" of the Declaration and correctly notes that the Declaration is a "collective work." Agi claims too much for the man he justly admires, however, when he says that "in comparison with what other persons brought to the project in their individual capacity, [Cassin] was its principal animating spirit" (229–30). Similar claims are made by Geoffrey Best, "Whatever Happened to Human Rights?" 16 *Review of International Studies* (1991) 3.

36. Humphrey, *Human Rights,* 42–43. Some writers have stated, incorrectly, that Cassin was rapporteur of the Human Rights Commission, a mistake apparently

based on the fact that he was made rapporteur of the small working group on the Declaration at the Commission's Geneva meeting. Israël, *René Cassin*, 186–87. Disregarding Humphrey's role, Israël mentions only that Cassin was "greatly aided" by the "documentation" that the Secretariat assembled.

37. Humphrey, *Human Rights*, 43. For an overall appreciation of John Humphrey and his distinguished legal career, see R. St. J. MacDonald, "Leadership in Law: John P. Humphrey and the Development of the International Law of Human Rights," 29 *Canadian Yearbook of International Law* 3 (1991); and the many highly informative articles, cited herein, by A. J. Hobbins, editor of the Humphrey papers and diaries.

38. My examination of the records confirms Humphrey's account of the process in all material respects. Other scholars have previously come to the same conclusion. See the careful examination of the evidence and the detailed chronology in Hobbins, "René Cassin." Johannes Morsink's research finds that Humphrey's draft was "both the first and the most basic draft of the Universal Declaration." Morsink, *Universal Declaration*, 6.

39. Verbatim Record, June 17, 1947, Drafting Committee Meeting (Charles Malik Papers, Library of Congress, Manuscript Division).

40. Human Rights Commission, Drafting Committee, First Session (E/CN.4/AC.1/SR.3, p. 5).

41. Ibid.; (E/CN.4/AC.1/SR.2, p. 2).

42. Ibid.; (E/CN.4/AC.1/SR.5, 7).

43. Verbatim Record, June 17, 1947, Drafting Committee Meeting (Charles Malik Papers, Library of Congress, Manuscript Division).

44. Human Rights Commission, Drafting Committee, First Session (E/CN.4/AC.1/SR.8, p. 2).

45. Human Rights Commission, Drafting Committee Meeting, First Session, Verbatim Record, June 20, 1947 (Charles Malik Papers, Library of Congress, Manuscript Division).

46. Cassin, *La Pensée et l'Action*, 108.

47. Verbatim Record, June 17, 1947, Drafting Committee Meeting (Charles Malik Papers, Library of Congress, Manuscript Division).

48. Human Rights Commission, Drafting Committee (E.CN.4/AC.1/SR.13, pp. 19–20).

49. Verbatim Record, June 23, 1947, Drafting Committee Meeting (Charles Malik Papers, Library of Congress, Manuscript Division).

50. Ibid.

51. *Report of the Soviet Representative on the Drafting Committee of the U.N. Commission on Human Rights,* July 1, 1947 (Moscow: Russian Center for Documents on Modern History, Department for UN Matters), index 2a, folder 7a, 18–26.

52. James P. Hendrick, Memorandum of July 3, 1947 (Eleanor Roosevelt Papers, Box 4587, Roosevelt Library, Hyde Park, New York).

53. Verbatim Record, June 9, 1947, Drafting Committee Meeting (Charles Malik Papers, Library of Congress, Manuscript Division).

CHAPTER 5: A PHILOSOPHICAL INVESTIGATION

1. The committee's report, the questionnaire, and several of the responses are collected with an introduction by Jacques Maritain in *Human Rights: Comments and Interpretations* (London: Wingate, 1949).
2. Id. at 186.
3. S. V. Puntambekar, "The Hindu Concept of Human Rights," in *Human Rights,* 193, 195.
4. Humayun Kabir, "Human Rights: The Islamic Tradition and the Problems of the World Today," in *Human Rights,* 191.
5. Shirin Abbas Sinnar, "Culture and Human Rights: A Historical Inquiry into the Context of the Universal Declaration of Human Rights 1945–50" (Harvard University, Department of History Honors Thesis, 1998), 90.
6. Quoted in Sinnar, "Culture and Human Rights," 91.
7. Puntambekar, "The Hindu Concept," in *Human Rights,* 196.
8. Mohandas Gandhi, "Letter Addressed to the Director-General of UNESCO," in *Human Rights,* 18.
9. Chung-Shu Lo, "Human Rights in the Chinese Tradition," in *Human Rights,* 186, 187.
10. Id. at 187.
11. The article later evolved into the Declaration's more cryptic Article 29 (1): "Everyone has duties to the community in which alone the free and full development of his personality is possible."
12. Salvador de Madariaga, "Rights of Man or Human Relations?" in *Human Rights,* 47. See also Pierre Teilhard de Chardin, "Some Reflections on the Rights of Man," id. at 105, 106.
13. Benedetto Croce, "The Rights of Man and the Present Historical Situation," in *Human Rights,* 93, 94.
14. Aldous Huxley, "The Rights of Man and the Facts of the Human Situation," in *Human Rights,* 199, 201–2.
15. Maritain, "Introduction," in *Human Rights,* 10.
16. Id. at 268–71.
17. Ibid.
18. Id. at 259.
19. Maritain, "Introduction," in *Human Rights,* 9.
20. Id. at 10 (reiterating a point he had made in an address given to the Second General Conference of UNESCO in 1947).
21. See Michael Novak's analysis of Maritain's thought on human rights in "The Gospels, Natural Law, and the American Founding," in *Festschrift for Ralph McInerny* (forthcoming). See also Ralph McInerny, "Natural Law and Human Rights," 36 *American Journal of Jurisprudence* 1 (1991).

22. Richard P. McKeon, "Philosophic Bases," in *Human Rights*, 35.

23. "Memorandum and Questionnaire Circulated by UNESCO on the Theoretical Bases of the Rights of Man," in *Human Rights*, 255.

24. Richard P. McKeon, *Freedom and History and Other Essays* (Chicago: University of Chicago Press, 1968), 40.

25. Maritain, in *Human Rights*, 10.

CHAPTER 6: LATE NIGHTS IN GENEVA

1. Eleanor Roosevelt, *My Day: The Post-War Years, 1945–1952*, David Emblidge, ed. (New York: Pharos, 1990), 118.

2. Joseph Lash, *Eleanor: The Years Alone* (New York: W. W. Norton, 1972), 182.

3. A. David Gurewitsch, *Eleanor Roosevelt: Her Day* (New York: Interchange Foundation, 1973), 30–31.

4. Lash, *Eleanor: The Years Alone*, 38.

5. Durward Sandifer interview quoted in A. W. Brian Simpson, *Human Rights and the End of Empire: Britain and the Genesis of the European Human Rights Convention* (London: Oxford University Press, forthcoming).

6. Lash, *Eleanor: The Years Alone*, 66–67.

7. Id., 29.

8. Eleanor Roosevelt, *On My Own* (New York: Harper, 1958), 80.

9. John P. Humphrey, *Human Rights and the United Nations: A Great Adventure* (Dobbs Ferry, N.Y.: Transnational Publishers, 1984), 48.

10. Roosevelt, *On My Own*, 81–82.

11. Human Rights Commission, Second Session (E/CN.4/SR.26, p. 11).

12. Ibid.; (E/CN.4/SR.28, p. 10).

13. Ibid.; (E/CN.4/SR.25, p. 10).

14. Eleanor Roosevelt, "My Day," December 8, 1947 (Roosevelt Library, Hyde Park, New York).

15. Alexander Bogomolov, *Report on the Human Rights Commission Session*, December 31, 1947 (Moscow: Russian Center for Documents on Modern History), Fund of Secretariat of A. Vishinsky, drawer 21-b, folder 48, file 37, 55.

16. Human Rights Commission, Second Session (E/CN.4/SR.28, pp. 11–12).

17. Roosevelt, "The Promise of Human Rights," *Foreign Affairs* (April 1948), 470, 473.

18. Bogomolov, *Report*, p. 60.

19. Ibid.

20. Simpson, *Human Rights*.

21. James P. Hendrick, Memorandum of July 3, 1947, Meeting (Eleanor Roosevelt Papers, Box 4587, Roosevelt Library, Hyde Park, New York).

22. Roosevelt, "My Day," December 18, 1947.

23. *Mother and Daughter: The Letters of Eleanor and Anna Roosevelt*, Bernard Asbell, ed. (New York: Coward, McCann, and Geoghegan, 1982), 233.

24. Letter from Eleanor Roosevelt to David Gurewitsch, quoted in Lash, *Eleanor: The Years Alone,* 183.
25. Human Rights Commission, Second Session (E/CN.4/SR.34, p. 5).
26. Shirin Abbas Sinnar, "Culture and Human Rights: A Historical Inquiry into the Context of the Universal Declaration of Human Rights 1945–50" (Harvard University, Department of History Honors Thesis, 1998), 101.
27. Human Rights Commission, Second Session (E/CN.4/SR.34, p. 4).
28. Blanche Wiesen Cook, *Eleanor Roosevelt, Volume 2, 1933–38* (New York: Viking, 1999), 75.
29. Roosevelt, "My Day," January 28, 1946.
30. Eleanor Roosevelt, "Women in Politics," in Allida M. Black, *Courage in a Dangerous World: The Political Writings of Eleanor Roosevelt* (New York: Columbia University Press, 1999), 69.
31. Id. at 66–67.
32. Statement by Mrs. Eleanor Roosevelt on the Draft Convention on the Political Rights of Women, *Department of State Bulletin,* December 12, 1951, 181.
33. Eleanor Roosevelt, "My Day," February 16, 1962, in Black, *Courage in a Dangerous World,* at 299.
34. For the Chilean and Lebanese proposals, see appendix 3 ("Alternative texts for Article 7"). For the USSR's statement on capital punishment, see Human Rights Commission, Drafting Committee (E/CN.4/AC.1/SR.2, p. 11).
35. Human Rights Commission, Second Session (E/CN.4/AC.2/SR.6, pp. 1–9).
36. Ibid.; (E/CN.4/SR.37, pp. 11–12).
37. Bogomolov, *Report,* 58.
38. Human Rights Commission, Second Session (E.CN.4/SR.41, pp. 9–11).
39. Report of the Human Rights Commission, Second Session (E/600, p. 35).
40. Human Rights Commission, Second Session (E/CN.4/SR.38, p. 8).
41. Ibid.; (E/CN.4/SR.38, p. 10). Bogomolov's report to Molotov describes this speech as delivered "according to our prior arrangement," *Report,* 66.
42. Human Rights Commission, Second Session (E/CN.4/SR.38, p. 14).
43. Bogomolov, *Report,* 58–59.
44. Report of the Human Rights Commission, Second Session (E/600, p. 20).
45. Bogomolov, *Report,* 63.
46. Roosevelt, "My Day," December 16, 1947.
47. Letter from Roosevelt to David Gurewitsch, December 18, 1947, quoted in Lash, *Eleanor: The Years Alone,* 72.

CHAPTER 7: IN THE EYE OF THE HURRICANE

1. *Mother and Daughter: The Letters of Eleanor and Anna Roosevelt,* Bernard Asbell, ed. (New York: Coward, McCann and Geoghegan, 1982), 238.
2. Eleanor Roosevelt, *On My Own* (New York: Harper, 1958), 63.
3. Joseph Lash, *Eleanor: The Years Alone* (New York: W. W. Norton, 1972), 69.

4. Quoted in Alfred Steinberg, *Mrs. R.: The Life of Eleanor Roosevelt* (New York: Putnam, 1958), 326.

5. David McCullough, *Truman* (New York: Simon & Schuster, 1992), 534.

6. "British Decision on Palestine," *U.N. Weekly Bulletin,* October 7, 1947, 443; "Five Countries in Opening of Palestine Debate," *U.N. Weekly Bulletin,* October 14, 1947, 479.

7. Carlos Romulo and Beth Day Romulo, *Forty Years: A Third World Soldier at the UN* (New York: Greenwood Press, 1986), 67.

8. General Assembly, Official Records, November 26, 1947, 1314–15.

9. Abba Eban, *Personal Witness* (New York: Putnam, 1992), 122.

10. New York Congressman Sol Bloom was chairman of the House of Representatives Foreign Affairs Committee.

11. Romulo and Romulo, *Forty Years,* 68. According to Joseph Lash, while the U.S. State Department was assuring Arab representatives that the United States would not pressure other UN members in joining it to vote for partition, one of President Truman's assistants had issued instructions to "twist arms if necessary." Lash, *Eleanor: The Years Alone,* 123.

12. Eban, *Personal Witness,* 122–23.

13. Tamara Harven, *Eleanor Roosevelt: An American Conscience* (Chicago: Quadrangle Books, 1968), 228.

14. Lash, *Eleanor: The Years Alone,* 122.

15. Letter from Eleanor Roosevelt to Harry Truman, March 22, 1948, quoted in Lash, *Eleanor: The Years Alone,* 130.

16. McCullough, *Truman,* 603–4.

17. Letter from Eleanor Roosevelt to David Gurewitsch, April 17, 1948, quoted in Lash, *Eleanor: The Years Alone,* 183.

18. Ibid.

19. "Opening Statement to Be Made by Mrs. Roosevelt at Human Rights Drafting Committee Session," Eleanor Roosevelt Papers, Box 4588 (Roosevelt Library, Hyde Park, New York).

20. Eleanor Roosevelt, *My Day: The Post-War Years, 1945–1952,* David Emblidge, ed. (New York: Pharos, 1990), 137–38.

21. Eban, *Personal Witness,* 118, 210.

22. John P. Humphrey, *Human Rights and the United Nations: A Great Adventure* (Dobbs Ferry, N.Y.: Transnational Publishers, 1984), 56.

23. Human Rights Commission, Drafting Committee (E/CN.4/AC.1/SR.21, p. 4); Roosevelt, *On My Own,* 63.

24. Human Rights Commission, Drafting Committee (E/CN.4/AC.1/SR.21, p. 4).

25. Politburo Directives, approved April 24, 1948 (Moscow: Russian Foreign Policy Archive), Fund of A. Vishinsky, index 21-b, folder 48, file 37, 90–92, 146–47.

26. Human Rights Commission, Third Session (E/CN.4/SR.46, pp. 4–14.)

27. Malik Diary, May 25, 1948.

28. Human Rights Commission, Third Session (E/CN.4/SR.50, p. 9).

29. James Madison, *Federalist No. 55.*
30. Malik Diary, May 31, 1948.
31. John Humphrey, Letter of May 31, 1948 (courtesy of Humphrey's literary executor, A. J. Hobbins).
32. Human Rights Commission, Third Session (E/CN.4/SR.49, p. 12; SR.61, p. 7; SR.63. pp. 2–10).
33. Basic Law of the Federal Republic of Germany, Articles 21 (2) and 18.
34. René Cassin, *La Pensée et l'Action* (Boulogne-sur-Seine: F. Lalou, 1972), 110.
35. Ibid. See also Marc Agi, *René Cassin 1887–1976* (Mesnil-sur-l'Estrée: Perrin, 1998), 230.
36. Roosevelt, *My Day,* 144–45.
37. Humphrey, *Human Rights,* 4.
38. Ibid.
39. Roosevelt, *On My Own,* 62–65.
40. Human Rights Commission, Third Session (E/CN.4/SR.64, pp. 5–6).
41. Cassin, *La Pensée et l'Action,* 111.
42. Human Rights Commission, Third Session (E/CN.4/120 and 127); see also (E/CN.4/SR.67, pp. 2, 4, 5).
43. Human Rights Commission, Third Session (E/CN.4/SR.72, pp. 7–10).
44. Malik Diary, June 14, 1948.
45. Human Rights Commission, Third Session (E/CN.4/132).
46. Ibid. (E/CN.4/SR. 73, p. 7).
47. Ibid. (E/CN.4/SR. 73, p. 5).
48. Ibid. (E/CN.4/SR.77, pp. 28–29).
49. Howard Schomer, "Present at the Creation of the Universal Declaration of Human Rights" (United Church of Christ: United Church Board for World Ministries and the Office for Church in Society), 6.
50. Eleanor Roosevelt, "My Day," June 22, 1948 (Roosevelt Library, Hyde Park, New York).
51. E.g., Human Rights Commission, Third Session (E/CN.4/SR.77, pp. 5–13). See also "Further Progress Toward Universal Declaration," *U.N. Weekly Bulletin,* June 15, 1948, 487.

CHAPTER 8: AUTUMN IN PARIS

1. *Mother and Daughter: The Letters of Eleanor and Anna Roosevelt,* Bernard Asbell, ed. (New York: Coward, McCann and Geogeghan, 1982), 241–42.
2. Charles Malik, "1948—The Drafting of the Universal Declaration of Human Rights," *U.N. Bulletin of Human Rights* (1986), 91.
3. Letter from Charles Malik to Alfred North Whitehead, June 27, 1945 (Malik Papers, Library of Congress, Manuscript Division).
4. E. J. Kahn, "Talk of the Town," *The New Yorker,* December 9, 1950, 32.
5. Howard Schomer, "In Homage to My Icons and Mentors," *Berkeley Outlook Club,* February 20, 1992, 19–20.

6. Kahn, "Talk of the Town," 33.
7. Charles Malik, *Fourteen Months in Germany* (c. 1937; unpublished manuscript in the Malik Papers, Library of Congress, Manuscript Division).
8. Schomer, "Homage," 20.
9. Malik Diaries, August 20, 1944.
10. Kahn, "Talk of the Town," 33.
11. Malik Diaries, September 18, 1946.
12. Quoted in *Current Biography 1948,* Anna Rothe, ed. (New York: H. W. Wilson, 1949), 411.
13. Alois Derso and Emery Kelen, *United Nations Sketchbook* (New York: Funk & Wagnalls, 1950), 9.
14. John P. Humphrey, *Human Rights and the United Nations: A Great Adventure* (Dobbs Ferry, N.Y.: Transnational Publishers, 1984), 56.
15. John P. Humphrey, *On the Edge of Greatness: The Diaries of John Humphrey, First Director of the United Nations Division of Human Rights,* vol. I, A. J. Hobbins, ed. (Montreal: McGill University Libraries, 1994), 24–25, 31.
16. René Cassin, *La Pensée et l'Action* (Boulogne-sur-Seine: F. Lalou, 1972), 112.
17. *CIA Cold War Records: The CIA Under Harry Truman,* Michael Warner, ed. (Washington, D.C.: Central Intelligence Agency, 1994), xx.
18. Eleanor Roosevelt, *My Day: The Post-War Years, 1945–1952,* David Emblidge, ed. (New York: Pharos, 1990), 141.
19. Id., 157–58.
20. Humphrey, *Human Rights,* 66.
21. Cassin, *La Pensée et l'Action,* 152.
22. Ruth H. C. and Sze-Chuh Cheng, eds., *Peng Chun Chang 1892–1957: Biography and Collected Works* (privately printed, 1995), 33, 177.
23. Peng-chun Chang, "Text of Two Lectures," reprinted in *Peng Chun Chang,* 143.
24. Charles Malik, "Introduction," O. Frederick Nolde, *Free and Equal: Human Rights in Ecumenical Perspective* (Geneva: World Council of Churches, 1968), 7–9.
25. Irene Sandifer, *Mrs. Roosevelt as We Knew Her* (Silver Spring, Md.: Mrs. Durward V. Sandifer, 1975), 69–70.
26. Humphrey, *On the Edge of Greatness,* 49.
27. Humphrey, *Human Rights,* 60.
28. George Marshall, "No Compromise on Essential Freedoms," *State Department Bulletin* 19 (October 3, 1948), 432–35.
29. Humphrey, *On the Edge of Greatness,* 49.
30. Charles Malik, *Address to General Assembly,* September 27, 1948, in *The Challenge of Human Rights: Charles Malik and the Universal Declaration,* Habib C. Malik, ed. (Oxford: Centre for Lebanese Studies, 2000), 113, 116.
31. The fifty-eight member states were Afghanistan, Argentina, Australia, Belgium, Bolivia, Brazil, Burma, Byelorussia, Canada, Chile, China, Colombia, Costa Rica, Cuba, Czechoslovakia, Denmark, Dominican Republic, Ecuador,

Egypt, El Salvador, Ethiopia, France, Greece, Guatemala, Haiti, Honduras, Iceland, India, Iran, Iraq, Lebanon, Liberia, Luxembourg, Mexico, Netherlands, New Zealand, Nicaragua, Norway, Pakistan, Panama, Paraguay, Peru, Philippines, Poland, Saudi Arabia, Siam, Sweden, Syria, Turkey, Ukraine, Union of South Africa, USSR, United Kingdom, United States, Uruguay, Venezuela, Yemen, Yugoslavia.

32. Eleanor Roosevelt, "Making Human Rights Come Alive," in *What I Hope to Leave Behind: The Essential Essays of Eleanor Roosevelt,* Allida Black, ed. (Brooklyn, N.Y.: Carlson, 1995), 559, 560.

33. Hernán Santa Cruz, *Cooperar o Perecer: El dilema de la comunidad mundial,* vol. 1 (Buenos Aires: Grupo Editor Latinoamericano, 1984), 184–85.

34. Humphrey, *On the Edge of Greatness,* 49–50.

35. Eleanor Roosevelt, *On My Own* (New York: Harper, 1958), 84; *My Day,* 149–50; Sandifer, *Mrs. Roosevelt,* 67.

36. Eleanor Roosevelt, "The Struggle for Human Rights," *Department of State Bulletin,* October 10, 1948, 457, 458–59.

37. Sandifer, *Mrs. Roosevelt,* 68.

38. Jason Berger, *A New Deal for the World: Eleanor Roosevelt and American Foreign Policy* (New York: Columbia University Press, 1981), 73.

39. Humphrey, *On the Edge of Greatness,* 50.

40. Humphrey, *Human Rights,* 61.

41. Third Committee, Eighty-ninth Meeting, September 30, 1948, SR., 32–33.

42. *Mother and Daughter,* 242.

43. Humphrey, *Human Rights,* 66; Humphrey, *On the Edge of Greatness,* 52.

44. Third Committee, Ninety-first Meeting, October 2, 1948, SR., 49–51.

45. Third Committee, Ninety-fifth Meeting, October 6, 1948, SR., 87.

46. Third Committee, Ninetieth Meeting, October 1, 1948, SR., 39.

47. Roosevelt, *My Day,* 151.

48. Third Committee, Ninety-first Meeting, October 2, 1948, SR., 49.

49. Third Committee, Ninety-second Meeting, October 2, 1948, SR., 57–59. See also *Memorandum from Molotov to Pavlov,* November 11, 1948 (Moscow: Russian Center for Documents on Modern History), Fund of Secretariat of A. Vishinsky, index 21b, folder 48, file 37, 308–310.

50. Roosevelt, *On My Own,* 83.

51. Humphrey, *On the Edge of Greatness,* 55–56.

52. Third Committee, Ninety-first Meeting, October 2, 1948, SR., 49.

CHAPTER 9: THE NATIONS HAVE THEIR SAY

1. Eleanor Roosevelt, *On My Own* (New York: Harper, 1958), 85.

2. Joseph Lash, *Eleanor: The Years Alone* (New York: W. W. Norton, 1972), 78.

3. John P. Humphrey, *Human Rights & the United Nations: A Great Adventure* (Dobbs Ferry, N.Y.: Transnational Publishers, 1984), 71.

4. John P. Humphrey, *On the Edge of Greatness: The Diaries of John Humphrey,* vol. 2, A. J. Hobbins, ed. (Montreal: McGill University Libraries, 1996), 53.
5. Irene Sandifer, *Mrs. Roosevelt as We Knew Her* (Silver Spring, Md.: Mrs. Durward Sandifer, 1975), 73.
6. Third Committee, Ninety-fifth Meeting, October 6, 1948, 91–92.
7. Humphrey, *Human Rights,* 67. See also Humphrey, *On the Edge of Greatness,* 54–55.
8. Third Committee, Ninety-sixth Meeting, October 7, 1948, 96.
9. Third Committee, Ninety-eighth Meeting, October 9, 1948, 110.
10. Third Committee, Ninety-sixth Meeting, October 7, 1948, 98; Ninety-eighth Meeting, October 9, 1948, 114.
11. Eleanor Roosevelt, "Making Human Rights Come Alive," in *What I Hope to Leave Behind: The Essential Essays of Eleanor Roosevelt,* Allida Black, ed. (Brooklyn: Carlson, 1995), 559.
12. Third Committee, Ninety-seventh Meeting, October 8, 1948, 107, and One Hundredth Meeting, October 12, 1948, 127.
13. The following is based on *Peng Chun Chang 1892–1957: Biography and Collected Works,* Ruth H. C. and Sze-Chuh Cheng, eds. (a 1995 memorial volume privately printed by the Chang family).
14. Third Committee, Ninety-eighth Meeting, October 9, 1948, 110.
15. Third Committee, Ninety-ninth Meeting, October 11, 1948, 122.
16. Third Committee, Ninety-sixth Meeting, October 7, 1948, 100.
17. Third Committee, Ninety-sixth Meeting, October 7, 1948, 99.
18. Sandifer, *Mrs. Roosevelt,* 70–71.
19. Third Committee, 101st Meeting, October 13, 1948, 136.
20. Quoted in Sandifer, *Mrs. Roosevelt,* 71.
21. Third Committee, 101st Meeting, October 13, 1948, 146.
22. Id. at 150.
23. Third Committee, 104th Meeting, October 16, 1948, 163.
24. Third Committee, 105th Meeting, October 18, 1948, 177.
25. John P. Humphrey, Letter of October 14, 1948 (Montreal: McGill University Archives; reprinted with permission of Humphrey's literary executor, A. J. Hobbins).
26. Quoted in Sandifer, *Mrs. Roosevelt,* 76.
27. Third Committee, 108th Meeting, October 20, 1948, 200.
28. Sandifer, *Mrs. Roosevelt,* 77; *Mother and Daughter: The Letters of Eleanor and Anna Roosevelt,* Bernard Asbell, ed. (New York: Coward, McCann and Geoghegan, 1982), 247.
29. Charles Malik, "The Drafting of the Universal Declaration of Human Rights," *U.N. Bulletin of Human Rights,* 1986, 91, 97.
30. Third Committee, 108th Meeting, October 20, 1948, 199–200.
31. Malik, "The Drafting of the Universal Declaration," 97.
32. Sandifer, *Mrs. Roosevelt,* 74.

33. Eleanor Roosevelt, *This I Remember* (New York: Harper, 1949), 341–42.
34. Third Committee, 125th Meeting, November 8, 1948, 370, 374.
35. Third Committee, 183rd Meeting, December 10, 1948, 912.
36. Third Committee, 183rd Meeting, December 10, 1948, 913.
37. Humphrey, *On the Edge of Greatness,* 39.
38. Id. at 80, 87–88.
39. Jean-Louis Crémieux-Brilhac, *La France Libre* (Paris: Gallimard, 1996), 183.
40. See Gérard Israël, *René Cassin* (Paris: Desclée de Brouwer, 1990), 134, 137, 142; Marc Agi, *René Cassin 1887–1976* (Mesnil-sur-l'Estrée: Perrin, 1998), 153–54.
41. Third Committee, 137th Meeting, November 15, 1948, 498.
42. Third Committee, 139th Meeting, November 16, 1948.
43. Johannes Morsink, *The Universal Declaration of Human Rights: Origins, Drafting and Intent* (Philadelphia: University of Pennsylvania Press, 1999), 90.
44. Third Committee, 157th Meeting, November 25, 1948, 679, 689.
45. Third Committee, 158th Meeting, November 26, 1948, 690.
46. Sandifer, *Mrs. Roosevelt,* 79.
47. Humphrey, *On the Edge of Greatness,* 87.
48. Eleanor Roosevelt, *My Day: The Post-War Years 1945–1952,* David Emblidge, ed. (New York: Pharos, 1990), 152–53.
49. Malik, "The Drafting of the Universal Declaration," 91, 93.
50. René Cassin, *La Pensée et l'Action* (Boulogne-sur-Seine: F. Lalou, 1972), 114.
51. Humphrey, *On the Edge of Greatness,* 88.
52. Archival research by William A. Schabas suggests that "provincial jurisdiction was little more than a pretext for federal politicians who wanted to avoid international human rights commitments": "Canada and the Adoption of the Universal Declaration of Human Rights," 43 *McGill Law Journal* 403 (1998). See also A. J. Hobbins, "Eleanor Roosevelt, John Humphrey and Canadian Opposition to the Universal Declaration of Human Rights," 53 *International Journal,* 325 (1998).
53. Humphrey, *Human Rights,* 72.
54. Id. at 71.
55. Id. at 63.
56. Durward Sandifer interview quoted in Lash, *Eleanor: The Years Alone,* 78.
57. Letter from Roosevelt to Maude Gray, December 9, 1948, quoted in Lash, *Eleanor: The Years Alone,* 79.
58. *The New York Times,* December 10, 1948. For a history of the Genocide Convention, see Samantha Power, *The Quiet Americans: U.S. Responses to Genocide Since the Holocaust* (New York: Random House, forthcoming).
59. Charles Malik, December 9, 1948, speech to the General Assembly, in *The Challenge of Human Rights: Charles Malik and the Universal Declaration,* Habib C. Malik, ed. (Oxford: Centre for Lebanese Studies, 2000), 117.

60. Hernán Santa Cruz, *Cooperar o Perecer: El dilema de la comunidad mundial,* vol. 1 (Buenos Aires: Grupo Editor Latinoamericano, 1984), 195–96.

61. Plenary Meetings of the General Assembly, 180th plenary meeting, December 9, 1948, 867.

62. "Statement by Mrs. Franklin D. Roosevelt," *Department of State Bulletin,* December 19, 1948, 751–52.

63. Santa Cruz, *Cooperar o Perecer,* 196.

64. Plenary Meetings of the General Assembly, 183rd Plenary Meeting, December 10, 1948, 925.

65. Id. at 890.

66. Id. at 922.

67. Santa Cruz, *Cooperar o Perecer,* 194.

68. Humphrey, *Human Rights,* 71; Humphrey, *On the Edge of Greatness,* 90.

69. Roosevelt, "Making Human Rights Come Alive," 565–66, 573.

70. Plenary Meetings of the General Assembly, 183rd Plenary Meeting, December 10, 1948, 934

71. Quoted in Alfred Steinberg, *Mrs. R.: The Life of Eleanor Roosevelt* (New York: Putnam, 1958), 335.

72. Malik Diary, December 1948, no. 2635. These words appear in a 1947 prose-poem, "Aus der Erfahrung des Denkens": "The world's darkening never reaches to the light of Being / We are too late for the gods and too early for Being / Being's poem, just begun, is man." Martin Heidegger, *Poetry, Language, and Thought,* Albert Hofstadter, trans. (New York: Harper & Row, 1975), 4. Malik, however, must have had some other source, since Heidegger did not publish that poem until 1954.

73. Cassin, *La Pensée et l'Action,* 117.

CHAPTER 10: THE DECLARATION OF INTERDEPENDENCE

1. Marc Agi, *René Cassin: Fantassin des Droits de l'Homme* (Paris: Plon, 1979), 317.

2. Most of the constitutions and treaties of the latter half of the twentieth century belong to the dignitarian family. One of the most influential of these documents is the German Basic Law of 1949, which begins with the statement in Article 1, "The dignity of man shall be inviolable. To respect and protect it shall be the duty of all state authority."

3. Third Committee, Summary Records (A/C.3/257,383).

4. Gérard Israël, *René Cassin* (Paris: Desclée de Brouwer, 1990), 197.

5. In his State of the Union Speech of January 6, 1941, Roosevelt actually spoke of "freedom of every person to worship God in his own way," rather than "freedom of belief." *The Public Papers and Addresses of Franklin D. Roosevelt: 1938–1950,* vol. 9 (Washington, D.C., 1969), 672.

6. See note to Article 25 in appendix 3.

7. "Statement by Mrs. Franklin D. Roosevelt," *Department of State Bulletin*, December 19, 1948, 751.

8. UN Document E/CN.4/L.610.

9. See the comprehensive survey by Hurst Hannum, "The Status of the Universal Declaration in National Law," 25 *Georgia Journal of International and Comparative Law* 287 (1995–96).

10. See Jack Goldsmith, "International Human Rights Law and the United States Double Standard," 1 *The Green Bag* 365, 366, 371 (1998); J. Patrick Kelly, "The Twilight of Customary International Law," 40 *Virginia Journal of International Law* 449 (2000).

11. See John N. Hazard, "The Soviet Union and a World Bill of Rights," 47 *Columbia Law Review* 1095 (1947).

12. Telford Taylor, *The Anatomy of the Nuremberg Trials* (New York: Alfred A. Knopf, 1992), 635.

13. Politburo Directives to the Soviet Representative on the Human Rights Commission Drafting Committee, April 24, 1948 (Moscow: Russian Center for Documents on Modern History).

14. E.g., Preamble to the French Constitution of 1946: "The nation ensures to the individual and the family the conditions necessary to their development"; Article 6, German Basic Law (1949): "Marriage and family shall enjoy the special protection of the state."

15. *Loving v. Virginia,* 388 U.S. 1, 12 (1967).

16. Hazard, "Soviet Union," 1097.

17. Peng-chun Chang, "World Significance of Economically 'Low Pressure' Areas," Speech at the Second Session of the Economic and Social Council, June 4, 1946, reprinted in *Peng Chun Chang 1892–1957: Biography and Collected Works,* Ruth H. C. and Sze-Chuh Cheng, eds. (privately printed, 1995), 151.

18. See Mary Ann Glendon, "Rights in Twentieth Century Constitutions," 59 *University of Chicago Law Review* 519 (1992).

19. Charles Malik, "Introduction," in O. Frederick Nolde, *Free and Equal: Human Rights in Ecumenical Perspective* (Geneva: World Council of Churches, 1968), 70.

20. Franklin Delano Roosevelt, State of the Union Message (January 11, 1944), in *1944–45: The Public Papers and Addresses of Franklin D. Roosevelt* (1950), 32.

21. Eleanor Roosevelt, *The Moral Basis of Democracy* (New York: Howell, Soskin & Co., 1940), 49–50.

CHAPTER 11: THE DEEP FREEZE

1. Joseph Lash, *Eleanor: The Years Alone* (New York: W. W. Norton, 1972), 79.

2. Frank E. Holman, "Human Rights on Pink Paper," *American Affairs* (January 1949), 18, 24.

3. UN General Assembly, Summary Record of 187th Plenary Meeting, December 12, 1948, 1050.

4. "M. Vychinski se fait rappeler à l'ordre par le président de la commission politique," *Le Monde,* November 4, 1948, p. 2; "Le général Romulo répond aux insultes de M. Vychinski," *Le Monde,* November 6, 1948, p. 12; Pio Andrade, Jr., *The Fooling of America: The Untold Story of Carlos P. Romulo* (privately published, Pio Andrade, Jr.), 79; Carlos P. Romulo and Beth Day Romulo, *Forty Years: A Third World Soldier at the U.N.* (New York: Greenwood Press, 1986), 77–78.

5. John P. Humphrey, *On the Edge of Greatness: The Diaries of John Humphrey,* vol. 2, A. J. Hobbins, ed. (Montreal: McGill University Libraries, 1996), 174.

6. Yuan-Feng Chang, "Thoughts on My Beloved Father," in *Peng Chun Chang 1892–1957: Biography and Collected Works,* Ruth H. C. and Sze-Chuh Cheng, eds. (privately printed, 1995), 176, 179.

7. Eleanor Roosevelt, *My Day: The Post-War Years, 1945–1952,* David Emblidge, ed. (New York: Pharos, 1990), 204.

8. This account of the incident is based on John P. Humphrey, *Human Rights and the United Nations: A Great Adventure* (Dobbs Ferry, N.Y.: Transnational Publishers, 1984), 106.

9. Eleanor Roosevelt, "My Day," May 20 and May 26, 1950 (Roosevelt Library, Box 3153).

10. Lash, *Eleanor: The Years Alone,* 194, 195.

11. Humphrey, *On the Edge of Greatness,* 193.

12. Roosevelt, "My Day," May 11, 1951 (Roosevelt Library, Box 3153).

13. Memorandum by Foreign Secretary Herbert Morrison, quoted in Anthony Lester, "Fundamental Rights: The United Kingdom Isolated?" *Public Law* (Spring 1984), 55.

14. Humphrey, *On the Edge of Greatness,* 210–11.

15. Letter to the author from A. W. Brian Simpson, February 15, 1998.

16. For a critical view of the Anglo-Saxon influence on the European Convention by a leading continental comparatist, Marie-Thérèse Meulders-Klein, "Internationalisation des droits de l'homme et évolution du droit de la famille," *Annales de Droit de Louvain* (1996), 1–37.

17. Roosevelt, "My Day," May 7, 1951 (Roosevelt Library, Box 3153).

18. Roosevelt, "My Day," May 21, 1951 (Roosevelt Library, Box 3153).

19. Elliott Roosevelt and James Brough, *Mother R.* (New York: G. P. Putnam's Sons, 1977), 151–52.

20. Quoted in *Eleanor Roosevelt: An American Journey,* J. Flemion and C. O'Connor, eds. (San Diego: San Diego State University Press, 1987), 253.

21. Eleanor Roosevelt, "Reply to Attacks on U.S. Attitude Toward Human Rights Covenant," *Department of State Bulletin,* January 14, 1952, 59–60.

22. Roosevelt, *My Day,* 256.

23. Id. at 271.

24. This account of the resignation is based on Lash, *Eleanor: The Years Alone,* 215–18.
25. Humphrey, *Human Rights,* 178. See also *Department of State Bulletin,* April 20, 1953, 592.
26. John Foster Dulles, "U.S. Constitution and U.N. Charter: An Appraisal," *Department of State Bulletin,* September 7, 1953, 1, 3.
27. Lash, *Eleanor: The Years Alone,* 220.
28. David Gurewitsch, *Eleanor Roosevelt: Her Day* (New York: Interchange, 1973), 31, 92.
29. For an account of her subtle but influential role, see Lash, *Eleanor: The Years Alone,* 56–81.
30. E. J. Kahn, Jr., "Profiles: The Years Alone—1," *The New Yorker,* June 12, 1948, 30.
31. Humphrey, *Human Rights,* 85, 141.
32. Charles Malik, "Human Rights in the United Nations," *United Nations Weekly Bulletin* 13, 1 (September 1, 1952).
33. Malik Diary, no. 3123 (between January 8 and 28, 1951).
34. Malik, "Human Rights," 1.
35. Malik, "The Challenge of Human Rights," *Behind the Headlines* (December 1949), 1.
36. Malik, "Human Rights," 1.
37. Humphrey, *Human Rights,* 165–66.
38. Quoted in Hobbins, "Human Rights," 163–65.
39. Albert Camus, *Discours de Suède* (Paris: Gallimard, 1958), 17.
40. Gérard Israël, *René Cassin* (Paris: Desclée de Brouwer, 1990), 234.
41. In 1998 the Commission was replaced by a single European Court of Human Rights. See generally the magisterial history by A. W. Brian Simpson, *Human Rights and the End of Empire: Britain and the Genesis of the European Convention* (Oxford University Press, forthcoming), chapter 10.
42. Marc Agi, *René Cassin 1887–1976* (Mesnil-sur-l'Estrée: Perrin, 1998), 296–97.
43. René Cassin, *La Pensée et l'Action* (Boulogne-sur-Seine: F. Lalou, 1972), 175.
44. Howard Schomer, "In Homage to My Icons and Mentors," *Outlook Club of Berkeley,* February 20, 1992, 23.
45. "Lebanon's Christians Mourn Veteran Diplomat Charles Malik," *Reuters Library Reports,* December 29, 1987.
46. Humphrey, *Human Rights,* 105.
47. Malik Diary, October 15, 1949.
48. Humphrey, *On the Edge of Greatness,* 232–33.
49. See Hobbins, "Human Rights," 153; and John Humphrey's Letter of September 30, 1928, to his sister, Ruth, in A. J. Hobbins, " 'Dear Rufus . . .': A Law Student's Life at McGill in the Roaring Twenties, from the Letters of John P. Humphrey," 44 *McGill Law Journal* 753, 775 (1999).

50. A. J. Hobbins, "René Cassin and the Daughter of Time: The First Draft of the Universal Declaration of Human Rights," *Fontanus* 2, 10 (1989).
51. Richard C. Holbrooke, "Romulo: 'The Problem Is Marcos,' " *New York Times,* January 24, 1986, A27.
52. Cassin, *La Pensée et l'Action,* 170–71.
53. Humphrey, *On the Edge of Greatness,* 175.
54. Roosevelt, "Reply to Attacks," 59–60.
55. Even the administration of President Jimmy Carter, friendly in principle to human rights, was selective in criticizing human rights violators. Arthur M. Schlesinger, Jr., *The Cycles of American History* (Boston: Houghton Mifflin, 1986), 99.
56. A. B. Assensoh, *African Political Leadership: Jomo Kenyatta, Kwame Nkrumah and Julius K. Nyerere* (Malbar, Fla.: Krieger, 1998), 3, 160.
57. Malik, "Human Rights," 5.
58. Quoted in Jacob Sundberg, "Human Rights as Comparative Constitutional Law," 20 *Akron Law Review* 1, 6 (1987).
59. Carlos P. Romulo, *The Meaning of Bandung* (Chapel Hill, N.C.: University of North Carolina Press, 1956), 14.
60. Richard Wright, *The Color Curtain: A Report on the Bandung Conference* (Cleveland: World Publishing, 1956), 151–52.
61. Jack Goldsmith, "International Human Rights Law and the United States Double Standard," *The Green Bag* (summer 1998), 365, 372 (emphasis added).
62. Cassin, "Vatican II et la Protection de la Personne," reprinted in *La Pensée et l'Action,* 151–55.
63. Martin Luther King, Jr., "Nobel Prize Acceptance Speech (1964)," in *A Testament of Hope* (New York: HarperCollins, 1991), 224, 226.
64. Hurst Hannum, "The Status of the Universal Declaration of Human Rights in National and International Law," *Georgia Journal of International and Comparative Law* 289, 1 and 2 (1995).
65. Statute of Amnesty International, as amended in 1997.

CHAPTER 12: UNIVERSALITY UNDER SIEGE

1. Xu Jin and Greg Carr, "A Loving Father Jailed in China for Loving Democracy," *Boston Globe,* December 9, 1998.
2. American Anthropological Association, "Statement on Human Rights," 49 *American Anthropologist* 539 (1947).
3. Jacques Maritain, *Man and the State* (Chicago: University of Chicago Press, 1966), 77–79.
4. UNESCO Committee on the Theoretical Bases of Human Rights, "Final Report," in *Human Rights: Comments and Interpretations* (London and New York: Wingate, 1949), 258–59.
5. For an illuminating discussion of this point, see Michael Novak, "Human Dignity, Human Rights," *First Things* (November 1999), 39.

6. Charles Malik, "The Basic Issues of the International Bill of Rights," Speech delivered to Conference of American Educators, Lake Success, New York, February 26, 1948 (Malik Papers, Library of Congress, Manuscript Division).

7. See Muhammad Zafrulla Khan, *Islam and Human Rights* (Tilford: Islam International Publications, 1967). The literature is vast and growing. See, for instance, Paul G. Lauren, *The Evolution of International Human Rights: Visions Seen* (Philadelphia: University of Pennsylvania Press, 1998); *Human Rights in Judaism,* Milton R. Konvitz, ed. (New York: Norton, 1972); Giorgio Filibeck, *Human Rights in the Teaching of the Church: From John XXIII to John Paul II* (Vatican City: Libreria Editrice Vaticana, 1994); Abdullahi An-Naim, "Religious Minorities Under Islamic Law and the Limits of Cultural Relativism," 9 *Human Rights Quarterly* 1 and 3 (1987); Kwame Anthony Appiah, "Human Rights and Cosmopolitan Liberalism," in *Human Rights at Harvard Faculty Symposium 1997* (Cambridge: Human Rights Program, 1999), 10; Amartya Sen, "Our Culture, Their Culture," *The New Republic,* April 1, 1996, 27; Joseph Chan, "A Confucian Perspective on Human Rights for Contemporary China," in *The East Asian Challenge for Human Rights,* Joanne Bauer and Daniel Bell, eds. (Cambridge: Cambridge University Press, 1999), 212; Tu Weiming, "Joining East and West: A Confucian Perspective on Human Rights," *Harvard International Review* (Summer 1998), 44, 46.

8. Eleanor Roosevelt, "The U.N. and the Welfare of the World," 47 *National Parent-Teacher* 14 (1953).

9. Cf. *Federalist No. 1* (Hamilton): "It has been frequently remarked that it seems to have been reserved to the people of this country, by their conduct and example, to decide the important question, whether societies of men are really capable or not of establishing good government from reflection and choice, or whether they are forever destined to depend for their political destinies on accident and force."

10. Richard Wright, *The Color Curtain: A Report on the Bandung Conference* (Cleveland: World Publishing, 1956), 12.

11. UN Summary Record, E/CN.4/1998/SR.2, p. 9.

12. Mutua's speech was given at the Human Rights Policy Conference, sponsored by the Belfer Center of the Kennedy School of Government, Harvard University, on November 4, 1998. See also Makau Mutua, "The Ideology of Human Rights," 36 *Virginia Journal of International Law* 589 (1996), charging that because "non-Western views were largely unrepresented" in the framing of the Universal Declaration, "it was presumptuous and shamelessly ethnocentric for the UDHR to refer to itself as the 'common standard of achievement for all peoples and all nations' " (605).

13. See also the discussions by Philip Alston, "The Universal Declaration at 35: Western and Passé or Alive and Universal," 30 *International Commission of Jurists Review* 60, 61 (1983); and Johannes Morsink, *The Universal Declaration of Human Rights: Origins, Drafting, and Intent* (Philadelphia: University

of Pennsylvania, 1999), especially the concise summary of the drafting process in pp. 1–12.

14. Philippe de la Chappelle, *La Déclaration universelle des droits de l'homme et le Catholicisme* (Paris: Librairie Générale de Droit et de Jurisprudence, 1967), 44.

15. Malik, "Introduction," 12.

16. John P. Humphrey, *Human Rights and the United Nations: A Great Adventure* (Dobbs Ferry, N.Y.: Transnational Publishers, 1984), 74.

17. Summary Records, UN General Assembly, 182nd Plenary Session, 895.

18. Summary Records, UN General Assembly, 181st Plenary Session, 878.

19. Richard P. McKeon, "The Philosophic Bases and Material Circumstances of the Rights of Man," in *Human Rights: Comments and Interpretations* (London: Wingate, 1949), 45.

20. Donald Kommers, "German Constitutionalism: A Prologomenon," 40 *Emory Law Journal* 867 (1991).

21. The Investment Aid Case, 4 *Bundesverfassungsgericht Entscheidungen* 7 (1954).

22. See generally Mary Ann Glendon, *Rights Talk: The Impoverishment of Political Discourse* (New York: Free Press, 1991); Marie-Thérèse Meulders-Klein, *La Personne, la Famille et le Droit 1968–1998: Trois décennies de mutations en occident* (Brussels: Bruylant, 1999).

23. Most of the information in this and the following paragraph is drawn from Hurst Hannum, "The Status of the Universal Declaration of Human Rights in National and International Law," 25 *Georgia Journal of International and Comparative Law* 287, 313 (1995–96).

24. George F. Kennan, *Around the Cragged Hill: A Personal and Political Philosophy* (New York: Norton, 1993), 72.

25. William Korey, *NGOs and the Universal Declaration of Human Rights* (New York: St. Martin's Press, 1998), 476.

26. Jacques Maritain, "Introduction," in *Human Rights: Comments and Interpretations,* UNESCO, ed. (New York: Wingate, 1949), 16.

27. Summary Records, UN General Assembly, 182nd Plenary Session, 895.

28. Maritain, "Introduction," 16.

29. "As Guide to Future, History Must Be Seen Through Moral Prism," M2 Presswire, October 16, 1997.

30. Eleanor Roosevelt, *My Day: The Post-War Years, 1945–1952,* David Emblidge, ed. (New York: Pharos, 1990), 247.

31. "Statement by Mrs. Franklin D. Roosevelt," *State Department Bulletin,* December 19, 1948, 751, 752.

32. Hannah Arendt, *The Origins of Totalitarianism,* 2d ed. (New York: Meridian Books, 1958), 474.

33. Remarks delivered at the Human Rights Policy Conference, sponsored by the Belfer Center of the Kennedy School of Government, Harvard University, on November 4, 1998.

34. Daniel S. Lev, "Confronting Human Rights" (unpublished speech delivered May 11, 1993, at a symposium sponsored by the *Jakarta Post,* courtesy of the author).

EPILOGUE: THE DECLARATION TODAY

1. Hersch Lauterpacht, *International Law and Human Rights* (New York: Praeger, 1950), 425.
2. Human Rights Commission, April 13, 1948, E/CN.4/82, p. 8. The quoted language is from the last Lincoln-Douglas debate, *The Collected Works of Abraham Lincoln,* vol. III, Roy P. Basler, ed. (New Brunswick, N.J.: Rutgers University Press, 1953), 301.
3. Eleanor Roosevelt, "The Promise of Human Rights," *Foreign Affairs* (April 1948), 470.
4. Charles Malik, "1948—The Drafting of the Universal Declaration of Human Rights," *U.N. Bulletin of Human Rights* (1986), 97.
5. René Cassin, *La Pensée et l'Action* (Boulogne-sur-Seine: F. Lalou, 1972), 155.
6. Charles Malik, "Introduction," in O. Frederick Nolde, *Free and Equal: Human Rights in Ecumenical Perspective* (Geneva: World Council of Churches, 1968), 12.
7. Human Rights Commission, Drafting Committee, Second Session (E/CN.4/AC.1/SR.11, p. 10).
8. Eleanor Roosevelt, *The Moral Basis of Democracy* (New York: Howell, Soskin & Co., 1940), 8.
9. Eleanor Roosevelt, Remarks at the United Nations, March 27, 1953, quoted in Joseph Lash, *Eleanor: The Years Alone* (New York: W. W. Norton, 1972), 81.

THE "HUMPHREY DRAFT"

A Draft Outline of an International Bill of Human Rights (Prepared by the Division of Human Rights of the Secretariat)

The Preamble shall refer to the four freedoms and to the provisions of the Charter relating to human rights and shall enunciate the following principles:

1. That there can be no peace unless human rights and freedoms are respected;
2. That man does not have rights only; he owes duties to the society of which he forms part;
3. That man is a citizen both of his State and of the world;
4. That there can be no human freedom or dignity unless war and the threat of war are abolished.

ART. 1. Everyone owes a duty of loyalty to his State and to the [international society] United Nations. He must accept his just share of such common sacrifices as may contribute to the common good.

ART. 2. In the exercise of his rights every one is limited by the rights of others and by the just requirements of the State and of the United Nations.

ART. 3. Everyone has the right to life. This right can be denied only to persons who have been convicted under general law of some crime to which the death penalty is attached.

ART. 4. No one shall be subjected to torture, or to any unusual punishment or indignity.

ART. 5. Everyone has the right to personal liberty.

ART. 6. No one shall be deprived of his personal liberty save by a judgement of a court of law, in conformity with the law and after a fair public trial at which he has had an opportunity for a full hearing, or pending his trial which must take place within a reasonable time after his arrest. Detention by purely executive order shall be unlawful except in time of national emergency.

ART. 7. Every one shall be protected against arbitrary and unauthorized arrest. He shall have the right to immediate judicial determination of the legality of any detention to which he may be subject.

ART. 8. Slavery and compulsory labour are inconsistent with the dignity of man and therefore prohibited by this Bill of Rights. But a man may be required to perform his just share of any public service that is equally incumbent upon all, and his right to a livelihood is conditioned by his duty to work. Involuntary servitude may also be imposed as part of a punishment pronounced by a court of law.

ART. 9. Subject to any general law adopted in the interest of national welfare or security, there shall be liberty of movement and free choice of residence within the borders of each State.

ART. 10. The right of emigration and expatriation shall not be denied.

ART. 11. No one shall be subjected to arbitrary searches or seizures, or to unreasonable interference with his person, home, family relations, reputation, privacy, activities, or personal property. The secrecy of correspondence shall be respected.

ART. 12. Every one has the right to a legal personality. No one shall be restricted in the exercise of his civil rights except for reasons based on age or mental condition or as a punishment for a criminal offense.

ART. 13. Every one has the right to contract marriage in accordance with the laws of the State.

ART. 14. There shall be freedom of conscience and belief and of private and public religious worship.

ART. 15. Every one has the right to form, to hold, to receive and to impart opinions.

ART. 16. There shall be free and equal access to all sources of information both within and beyond the borders of the State.

ART. 17. Subject only to the laws governing slander and libel, there shall be freedom of speech and of expression by any means whatsoever, and there shall be reasonable access to all channels of communication. Censorship shall not be permitted.

ART. 18. There exists a duty towards society to present information and news in a fair and impartial manner.

ART. 19. There shall be freedom of peaceful assembly.

ART. 20. There shall be freedom to form associations for purposes not inconsistent with this Bill of Rights.

ART. 21. Every one has the right to establish institutions in conformity with conditions laid down by the law.

ART. 22. Every one has a right to own personal property.

His right to share in the ownership of industrial, commercial and other profit-making enterprises is governed by the law of the State within which such enterprises are situated.

The State may regulate the acquisition and use of private property and determine those things that are susceptible of private appropriation.

No one shall be deprived of his property without just compensation.

ART. 23. No one shall be required to pay any tax or be subjected to any public charge that has not been imposed by the law.

ART. 24. There shall be equal opportunity of access to all vocations and professions not having a public character.

ART. 25. Everything that is not prohibited by law is permitted.

ART. 26. No one shall be convicted of crime except by judgement of a court of law, in conformity with the law, and after a fair trial at which he has had an opportunity for a full public hearing.

Nor shall anyone be convicted of crime unless he has violated some law in effect at the time of the act charged as an offense, nor be subjected to a penalty greater than that applicable at the time of the commission of the offense.

ART. 27. There shall be access to independent and impartial tribunals for the determination of rights and duties under the law.

Every one has the right to consult with and to be represented by counsel.

ART. 28. Every one has the right, either individually or in association with others, to petition the government of his State or the United Nations for redress of grievance.

ART. 29. Every one has the right, either individually or with others, to resist oppression and tyranny.

ART. 30. Every one has the right to take an effective part in the government of the State of which he is a citizen. The State has a duty to conform to the wishes of the people as manifested by democratic elections. Elections shall be periodic, free and fair.

ART. 31. Every one shall have equal opportunity of access to all public functions in the State of which he is a citizen.

Appointments to the civil service shall be by competitive examination.

ART. 32. Every one has the right to a nationality.

Every one is entitled to the nationality of the State where he is born unless and until on attaining majority he declares for the nationality open to him by virtue of descent.

No one shall be deprived of his nationality by way of punishment or be deemed to have lost his nationality in any other way unless he concurrently acquires a new nationality.

ART. 33. No alien who has been legally admitted to the territory of a State may be expelled therefrom except in pursuance of a judicial decision or recommendation as a punishment for offenses laid down by law as warranting expulsion.

ART. 34. Every State shall have the right to grant asylum to political refugees.

ART. 35. Every one has the right to medical care. The State shall promote public health and safety.

ART. 36. Every one has the right to education.

Each State has the duty to require that every child within its territory receive a primary education. The State shall maintain adequate and free facilities for such education. It shall also promote facilities for higher education without distinction as to the race, sex, language, religion, class or wealth of the persons entitled to benefit therefrom.

ART. 37. Every one has the right and the duty to perform socially useful work.

ART. 38. Every one has the right to good working conditions.

ART. 39. Every one has the right to such equitable share of the national income as the need for his work and the increment it makes to the common welfare may justify.

ART. 40. Every one has the right to such public help as may be necessary to make it possible for him to support his family.

ART. 41. Every one has the right to social security. The State shall maintain effective arrangements for the prevention of unemployment and for insurance against the risks of unemployment, accident, disability, sickness, old age and other involuntary or undeserved loss of livelihood.

ART. 42. Every one has the right to good food and housing and to live in surroundings that are pleasant and healthy.

ART. 43. Every one has the right to a fair share of rest and leisure.

ART. 44. Every one has the right to participate in the cultural life of the community, to enjoy the arts and to share in the benefits of science.

ART. 45. No one shall suffer any discrimination whatsoever because of race, sex, language, religion, or political creed. There shall be full equality before the law in the enjoyment of the rights enumerated in this Bill of Rights.

ART. 46. In States inhabited by a substantial number of persons of a race, language or religion other than those of the majority of the population, persons belonging to such ethnic, linguistic or religious minorities shall have the right to establish and maintain, out of an equitable proportion of any public funds available for the purpose, their schools and cultural and religious institutions, and to use their own language before the courts and other authorities and organs of the State and in the Press and in public assembly.

ART. 47. It is the duty of each Member State to respect and protect the rights enunciated in this Bill of Rights. The State shall, when necessary, co-operate with other States to that end.

ART. 48. The provisions of this International Bill of Rights shall be deemed fundamental principles of international law and of the national law of each of the Member States of the United Nations. Their observance is therefore a matter of international concern and it shall be within the jurisdiction of the United Nations to discuss any violation thereof.

THE "CASSIN DRAFT"

Suggestions Submitted by the Representative
of France for Articles of the International
Declaration of Human Rights

PREAMBLE

1. Ignorance and contempt of human rights have been among the principal causes of the sufferings of humanity and particularly of the massacres which have polluted the earth in two world wars;

2. There can be no peace unless human rights and freedoms are respected and, conversely, human freedom and dignity cannot be respected as long as war and the threat of war are not abolished;

3. It was proclaimed as the supreme aim of the recent conflict that human beings should enjoy freedom of speech and worship and be free from fear and want;

4. In the Charter of 26 June 1945 we reaffirmed our faith in fundamental human rights, in the dignity and worth of the human person and in the equal rights of men and women;

5. It is one of the purposes of the United Nations to achieve international co-operation in promoting and encouraging respect for human rights and fundamental freedoms for all without distinction as to race, sex, language, or religion;

6. The enjoyment of such rights and freedoms by all persons must be protected by the community of nations and guaranteed by international as well as municipal law,

Now, therefore, we the Peoples of the United Nations have resolved to define in a solemn Declaration the essential rights and fundamental freedoms of man, so that this Bill, being constantly present in the minds of all men, may unceasingly remind them of their rights and duties and so that the United Nations and its Members may constantly apply the principles hereby formulated,

And we have therefore adopted the following Bill:

CHAPTER I, GENERAL PRINCIPLES

ART. 1. All men, being members of one family are free, possess equal dignity and rights, and shall regard each other as brothers.

ART. 2. The object of society is to enable all men to develop, fully and in security, their physical, mental and moral personality, without some being sacrificed for the sake of others.

ART. 3. As human beings cannot live and achieve their objects without the help and support of society, each man owes to society fundamental duties which are: obedience to law, exercise of a useful activity, acceptance of the burdens and sacrifices demanded for the common good.

ART. 4. The rights of all persons are limited by the rights of others.

ART. 5. The law is the same for all. It applies to public authorities and judges in the same way as to private persons. Anything not prohibited by law is permissible.

ART. 6. The rights and freedoms hereinafter declared shall apply to all persons. No person shall suffer discrimination by reasons of his race, sex, language, religion, or opinions.

CHAPTER 2, RIGHT TO LIFE AND PHYSICAL INVIOLABILITY

ART. 7. Every human being has the right to life and to the respect of his physical inviolability.

No person, even if found guilty, may be subjected to torture, cruelty, or degrading treatment.

CHAPTER 3, PERSONAL FREEDOM

ART. 8. Everyone has the right to personal liberty and security.

ART. 9. Private life, the home, correspondence and reputation are inviolable and protected by law.

ART. 10. No person may be arrested or detained save in cases provided for and in accordance with the procedure prescribed by law. Any person arrested or detained shall have the right to immediate judicial determination of the legality of the proceedings taken against him.

ART. 11. Every accused shall be presumed innocent until found guilty.

No person may be punished except in pursuance of a judgement of an independent and impartial court of law, delivered after a fair and public trial, at which he has had a full hearing or has been legally summoned, and has been given all the guarantees necessary for his defence.

ART. 12. No person may be convicted of a crime unless he has violated a law in force at the time of the act charged as an offence, nor suffer a penalty greater than that legally applicable at the time of the commission of the offence.

ART. 13. Slavery, being inconsistent with human dignity, is prohibited.

No public authority may exact personal service or work except by virtue of the law and for the common interest.

ART. 14. Subject to any general legislative measures adopted in the interest of security and the common good, there shall be liberty of movement and free choice of residence within the State; individuals may also freely emigrate or expatriate themselves.

CHAPTER 4, LEGAL STATUS

ART. 15. Every individual has a legal personality everywhere.

ART. 16. No person may be deprived of the personal exercise of his civil rights except in virtue of a general law based on consideration of age, or of a mental or other condition requiring protection, or as a punishment for a criminal offence.

ART. 17. Every person has the right to contract marriage in accordance with the laws.

ART. 18. All private occupations or professions shall be open to all on equal terms.

ART. 19. Every person has a right to own property.

No person shall be deprived of his property except in the public interest and in return for just compensation.

The State may determine the property capable of private appropriation and regulate the acquisition and use of such property.

The right to full or part ownership of any industrial, commercial or other profit-making private or collective enterprise, is governed by the law of the country within which such enterprise is situated.

ART. 20. Every person shall have access whether as plaintiff or defendant, to independent and impartial tribunals for the determination of his rights, liabilities and obligations under the law. He shall have the right to obtain legal advice and, if necessary, to be represented by counsel.

CHAPTER 5, PUBLIC FREEDOMS

ART. 21. The personal freedom of conscience, belief and opinion is an absolute and sacred right.

The practice of a private or public creed and the expression of conflicting convictions may not be subjected to any restraints except those necessary to protect public order, morality and the rights and freedoms of others.

ART. 22. No person may be molested for his opinions, even if they derive from other than national sources.

Every person is equally free to change, affirm, or impart his opinion, or to hear and discuss the opinions of others.

ART. 23. There shall be freedom of expression by word of mouth, in writing, in the Press, in books or by visual, audible or other means; provided, however, that the author, and the publishers, printers and others concerned shall be answerable for any abuse of this right by defamation of character or failure to present information and news in a true and impartial manner.

ART. 24. The freedom of assembly and of association for political, cultural, scientific, sporting, economic and social purposes compatible with this Bill is recognized and guaranteed, subject only to the protection of public order.

ART. 25. No State may deny any individual the right, either for himself or in association with others, to petition the authorities or Government of his country or of his residence, or the United Nations, for the redress of grievances.

ART. 26. Whenever a Government seriously or systematically violates the fundamental human rights and freedoms, individuals and peoples have the right to resist oppression and tyranny, without prejudice to their right of appeal to the United Nations.

CHAPTER 6, POLITICAL RIGHTS

ART. 27. Every person has an equal right to take part, directly or through his representatives, in the formation of the law, the institution of the taxes necessary for public expenditures and generally the government of the State of which he is a citizen. Each citizen shall bear his share of public expenses according to his means.

ART. 28. The Government shall conform to the wishes of the people, as expressed in democratic elections. Elections shall be periodic, free and fair.

ART. 29. The protection of human rights requires a public force. Such force shall be instituted for the service of all and not for the private use of those to whom it is entrusted. Each citizen should regard it as an honour to perform military service in States where such service exists.

ART. 30. All public offices shall be open to all citizens equally; such offices may not be considered as privileges or favours, but should be granted to the ablest on the basis of competitive examinations or on the grounds of their qualifications.

ART. 31. There can be no guarantees of human rights where the authors of or accessories to arbitrary acts go unpunished and where there is no provision establishing the liability of public authorities or their agents.

CHAPTER 7, NATIONALITY AND PROTECTION OF ALIENS

ART. 32. Every person has the right to a nationality.

It is the duty of the United Nations and Member States to prevent statelessness as being inconsistent with human rights and the interests of the human community.

ART. 33. Every State has the right to grant asylum to political refugees.

ART. 34. No alien legally admitted to the territory of a State may be expelled therefrom without being given a hearing. If his residence is of at least one year's standing, his expulsion may not take place except in pursuance of a judicial decision or recommendation for reasons recognized by law.

CHAPTER 8, SOCIAL, ECONOMIC, AND CULTURAL RIGHTS

ART. 35. All persons have the right and the duty to do work useful to society and to develop their personalities fully.

ART. 36. Services may be hired for a term, but no person may alienate his person or place himself in a state of servitude to another.

ART. 37. Human labour is not a chattel. It must be performed in suitable conditions. It must be justly remunerated according to its quality, duration and purpose, and must yield a decent standard of living to the worker and his family.

ART. 38. Every worker has the right to protect his professional interests. In particular, he may, either in person or through his representatives or his trade union organization, take part in the collective determination of conditions of work, the preparation of general plans of production or distribution, and in the supervision and management of the undertaking in which he works.

ART. 39. Every human being has the right to assistance from the community to protect his health. General measures should, in addition, be taken to promote public hygiene and the betterment of housing conditions and nutrition.

ART. 40. Every person has the right to social security. The community should take steps to prevent unemployment and to organize with contributions from those concerned insurance against disability, illness, old age and all other involuntary and undeserved loss of work and of livelihood.

Mothers and children have the right to special attention, care and resources.

ART. 41. All persons have an interest in learning and a right to education. Primary education is obligatory for children and the community shall provide appropriate and free facilities for such education.

Access to higher education should be facilitated by the grant of equal opportunities to all young persons and adults without distinction as to race, sex, language, religion, social standing or financial means.

Vocational and technical training should be generalized.

ART. 42. Every person has the right to a fair share of rest and leisure and to a knowledge of the outside world.

Every person has the right to participate in the cultural life of the community, to enjoy the arts and to share in the benefits of science.

ART. 43. The authors of all artistic, literary and scientific works and inventors shall retain, in addition to the just remuneration of their labour, a moral right to their work or discovery which shall not disappear even after such work or discovery has become the common property of mankind.

ART. 44. In all countries where there are substantial communities of a race, language or religion other than that of the majority of the inhabitants, persons belonging to such ethnical, linguistic or religious minorities shall have the right, within the limits required by public order, to open and maintain schools and religious or cultural institutions. Subject to the same limitations, they may use their language in the Press, at public meetings and when appearing before the courts or other authorities of the State.

ART. 45. The provisions of the present International Bill of Human Rights are part of the fundamental principles of international law and shall become an integral part of the municipal law of the States Members of the United Nations; their application is a matter of concern to public international order, and the United Nations is competent to take cognizance of violations of the said provisions.

ART. 46. Each State Member of the United Nations has the duty to take such legal measures and make such legal arrangements as may be necessary within the scope of its jurisdiction to apply and ensure respect for the rights and freedoms proclaimed in the present Bill. If necessary, members shall co-operate to this end.

The United Nations and its specialized agencies shall recommend all such international conventions, and shall each take such measures as may be necessary to give full effect to the provisions of the Charter and of the present Bill to safeguard these rights and freedoms throughout the world.

THE JUNE 1947 HUMAN RIGHTS COMMISSION DRAFT

Suggestions of the Drafting

Committee for Articles of an International

Declaration on Human Rights

ARTICLE I

All men are brothers. Being endowed with reason and conscience, they are members of one family. They are free, and possess equal dignity and rights.

ARTICLES 2, 3 AND 4

First alternative (three articles)

ART. 2. The object of society is to afford each of its members equal opportunity for the full development of his spirit, mind and body.

ART. 3. As human beings cannot live and develop themselves without the help and support of society, each one owes to society fundamental duties which are: obedience to law, exercise of a useful activity, willing acceptance of obligations and sacrifices demanded for the common good.

ART. 4. In the exercise of his rights, everyone is limited by the rights of others.

Second alternative (one article only)

ART. 2. These rights are limited only by the equal rights of others. Man also owes duties to society through which he is enabled to develop his spirit, mind and body in wider freedom.

ARTICLE 5

All are equal before the law and entitled to equal protection of the law. Public authorities and judges, as well as individuals are subject to the rule of law.

282 · *A World Made New*

ARTICLE 6

Every one is entitled to the rights and freedoms set forth in this Declaration, without distinction as to race, sex, language, or religion.

[1. The drafting committee suggested that this matter be referred to the Sub-Commission on the Prevention of Discrimination and the Protection of Minorities, for thorough consideration. 2. The view was expressed that the substance of this article might be included in the Preamble to the Declaration, in which case it could be omitted here.]

ARTICLE 7

Every one has the right to life, to personal liberty and to personal security.

Additional text (Chilean proposal)

Unborn children and incurables, mentally defectives and lunatics, shall have the right to life.

All persons shall have the right to the enjoyment of conditions of life enabling them to live in dignity and to develop their personality adequately.

Persons unable to maintain themselves by their own efforts shall be entitled to maintenance and assistance.

Alternative text (Lebanon)

Every one has the right to life and bodily integrity from the moment of conception, regardless of physical or mental condition, to liberty and security of person.

ARTICLE 8

No one shall be deprived of his personal liberty or kept in custody except in cases prescribed by law and after due process. Every one placed under arrest or detention shall have the right to immediate judicial determination of the legality of any detention to which he may be subject.

[1. There was a feeling in the drafting committee that articles 8, 9, and 10 would need to be reconsidered in the light of any convention that might be recommended for adoption. 2. The representative of the United States felt that the following alternative wording for the second sentence might be considered:

"Every one placed under arrest or detention shall have the right to release on bail and if there is a question as to the correctness of the arrest shall have the right to have the legality of any detention to which he may be subject determined in a reasonable time."]

ARTICLE 9

No one shall be held guilty of any offence until legally convicted.

No one shall be convicted or punished for any offence except by judgement of an independent and impartial court of law, rendered in conformity with law after a fair and public trial at which he has had an opportunity for a full hearing and has been given all guarantees necessary for his defence.

ARTICLE 10

No one can be convicted of crime unless he has violated some law in effect at the time of the act charged as an offence nor be subjected to a penalty greater than that applicable at the time of the commission of the offence.

No one, even if convicted for a crime, can be subjected to torture.

ARTICLE 11

Slavery, which is inconsistent with the dignity of man, is prohibited in all its forms.

[1. The consensus of opinion of the drafting committee was that the substance of the following sentence, which formed a part of this article, might be included and elaborated in a Convention: "Public authority may impose a personal service or work only by application of a law and for the common interest."]

ARTICLE 12

The privacy of the home and of correspondence and respect for reputation shall be protected by law.

Alternative text (Chile and France)

The inviolability of privacy, home, correspondence and of reputation shall be protected by law.

ARTICLE 13

There shall be liberty of movement and free choice of residence within the borders of each State. This freedom may be regulated by any general law adopted in the interest of national welfare and security.

Individuals may freely emigrate or renounce their nationality.

[The committee expressed the opinion that this text should be passed on to the Sub-Commission on the Prevention of Discrimination and the Protection of Minorities for further consideration.]

ARTICLE 14

Every one has the right to escape persecution on grounds of political or other beliefs or on grounds of racial prejudice by taking refuge on the territory of any State willing to grant him asylum.

ARTICLE 15

Every one has the right to a status in law and to the enjoyment of fundamental civil rights.

Every one shall have access to independent and impartial tribunals for the determination of his rights, liabilities and obligations under the law. He shall have the right to consult with and to be represented by counsel.

[1. In considering this article, the drafting committee discussed the right to contract marriage, but decided to wait until the Sub-Commission on the Prevention of Discrimination and the Protection of Minorities had reviewed recommendations made on this subject by the Commission on the Status of Women and had reported back to the Commission on Human Rights on its findings. 2. The representative of France suggested the following text in French to replace the second sentence of the second paragraph of this article: "*Il aura le droit d'être assisté et, toutes les fois que sa comparution personnelle ne sera pas exigée par la loi, representé par un conseil.*"]

ARTICLE 16

There shall be equal opportunity for all to engage in all vocations and professions not constituting public employment.

[The drafting committee expressed the opinion that the rights of foreigners in relation to this article should be the subject of a Convention.]

ARTICLE 17

Every one has a right to own personal property.

No one shall be deprived of his property except for public welfare and with just compensation.

The State may determine those things, rights and enterprises that are susceptible of private appropriation and regulate the acquisition and use of such property.

[1. The representative of the United States stated the opinion that it was sufficient to say, "Every one has a right to own property," and objected to the use of the word *personal* as qualifying "property" because of its technical meaning (chattels as distinguished from real property) in English-American law. 2. The representatives of Australia and of the United Kingdom stated the opinion that the article should be deleted altogether. 3. The representative of Chile felt that the concept of the right to property, as stated in the draft submitted by his government, should be included.]

ARTICLE 18

Every one has the right to a nationality.

[The drafting committee expressed the opinion that this article should be considered at greater length as the subject of a Convention.]

ARTICLE 19

No alien legally admitted to the territory of a State may be expelled therefrom without having a fair hearing.

[Members of the drafting committee appreciated that the subject of the article constitutes a difficult problem and stated the opinion that it needed further consideration.]

ARTICLE 20

Individual freedom of thought and conscience, to hold or change beliefs, is an absolute and sacred right.

The practice of a private or public worship, religious observances, and manifestations of differing convictions can be subject only to such limitations as are necessary to protect public order, morals and the rights and freedoms of others.

Alternative text (United Kingdom)

1. Every person shall be free to hold any religious or other belief dictated by his conscience and to change his belief.

2. Every person shall be free to practice, either alone or in community with other persons of like mind, any form of religious worship and observance, subject only to such restrictions, penalties or liabilities as are strictly necessary to prevent the commission of acts which offend laws passed in the interests of humanity and morals, to preserve public order and to ensure the rights and freedoms of other persons.

3. Subject only to the same restrictions, every person of full age and sound mind shall be free to give and receive any form of religious teaching and to endeavour to persuade other persons of full age and sound mind of the truth of his beliefs, and in the case of a minor the parent or guardian shall be free to determine what religious teaching he shall receive.

ARTICLE 21

Every one is free to hold or impart his opinion, or to receive and seek information and the opinion of others from sources wherever situated.

Alternative text (France)

The representative of France suggested that this article read in French as follows:

"Personne ne peut être inquiété en raison de ses opinions.

"Chacun est libre de soutenir ou d'exprimer son opinion, de connaître celle des autres, de recevoir ou de rechercher des informations à toutes les sources possibles."

ARTICLE 22

There shall be freedom of expression either by word, in writing, in the Press, in books or by visual, auditive or other means. There shall be equal access to all channels of communication.

[This would need to be considered by the Sub-Commission on Freedom of Information and of the Press for possible inclusion in the Convention or the Declaration and would have to be elaborated further.]

ARTICLE 23

There shall be freedom of peaceful assembly and of association for political, religious, cultural, scientific, professional and other purposes.

[This would need to be considered for possible inclusion in the Convention or the Declaration and would have to be elaborated further.]

ARTICLE 24

No State shall deny to any individual the right, either individually or in association with others, to petition or to communicate with the Government of his State or of his residence or the United Nations.

ARTICLE 25

When a Government, group or individual seriously or systematically tramples the fundamental human rights and freedoms, individuals and peoples have the right to resist oppression and tyranny.

[There was a substantial expression of opinion in favor of including this article in the Preamble instead of as an article.]

ARTICLE 26

Every one has the right to take an effective part in his Government directly or through his representatives.

Alternative text (Chile, France and Lebanon)

Every one has the right to take an effective part directly or through his representatives in the formulation of law, the framing of a tax policy for public expenses, and his government whether State or territorial.

ARTICLE 27

The State can derive its authority only from the will of the people and has a duty to conform to the wishes of the people. These wishes shall be manifested particularly by democratic elections, which shall be periodic, free, and by secret ballot.

ARTICLE 28

Every one shall have equal opportunity to engage in public employment and to hold public office in the State of which he is a citizen. Access to examinations for public employment shall not be a matter of privilege or favour.

[It was felt that the article might be referred to the Sub-Commission on the Prevention of Discrimination and the Protection of Minorities, after which it might be elaborated further.]

ARTICLE 29

Every one has the right to perform socially useful work.

ARTICLE 30

Human labour is not a merchandise. It shall be performed in good conditions and shall secure a decent standard of living to the worker and his family.

ARTICLE 31

Every one has the right to education. Primary education shall be free and compulsory. There shall be equal access for all to such facilities for technical, cultural and higher education as can be provided by the State or community on the basis of merit and without distinction as to race, sex, language, religion, social standing, political affiliation or financial means.

ARTICLE 32

Every one has the right to a fair share of rest and leisure.

ARTICLE 33

Every one, without distinction as to economic or social conditions, has a right to the highest attainable standard of health.

The responsibility of the State and community for the health and safety of its people can be fulfilled only by provision of adequate health and social measures.

[The drafting committee suggested that each article referring to economic and social rights should be referred to the appropriate specialized agencies for their consideration and comment.]

ARTICLE 34

Every one has the right to social security. To the utmost of its possibilities, the State shall undertake measures for the promotion of full employment and for the security of the individual against unemployment, disability, old age and all other loss of livelihood for reasons beyond his control.

Mothers and children have the right to special regard, care and resources.

ARTICLE 35

Every one has the right to participate in the cultural life of the community, to enjoy the arts, and to share in the benefits that result from scientific discoveries.

[It was the opinion of some of the members that the thought behind this article should be included in the Preamble.]

ARTICLE 36

In States inhabited by a substantial number of persons of a race, language or religion other than those of the majority of the population, persons belonging to such ethnic, linguistic or religious minorities shall have the right as far as compatible with public order to establish and maintain their schools and cultural or religious institutions, and to use their own language in the Press, in public assembly and before the courts and other authorities of the State.

[In view of the supreme importance of this article to many countries, the drafting committee felt that it could not prepare a draft article without thorough pre-examination by the Commission on Human Rights and suggested that it might if necessary be referred to the Sub-Commission on the Prevention of Discrimination and the Protection of Minorities for examination of the minority aspects.

The consensus of opinion of the drafting committee was that the substance of the following draft article might receive consideration for inclusion in an International Convention:

"Authors of all artistic, literary and scientific works and inventors shall retain, in addition to the just remuneration of their labour, a moral right on their work and/or discovery which shall not disappear even after such work and/or discovery shall have become the common property of mankind."]

THE GENEVA DRAFT

Draft International Declaration on Human Rights

ART. 1. All men are born free and equal in dignity and rights. They are endowed by nature with reason and conscience, and should act towards one another like brothers.

ART. 2. In the exercise of his rights every one is limited by the rights of others and by the just requirements of the democratic State. The individual owes duties to society through which he is enabled to develop his spirit, mind and body in wider freedom.

ART. 3. 1. Every one is entitled to all the rights and freedoms set forth in this Declaration, without distinction of any kind, such as race (which includes colour), sex, language, religion, political or other opinion, property status, or national or social origin.

2. All are equal before the law regardless of office or status and entitled to equal protection of the law against any arbitrary discrimination, or against any incitement to such discrimination, in violation of this Declaration.

ART. 4. Every one has the right to life, to liberty and security of person.

ART. 5. No one shall be deprived of his personal liberty or kept in custody except in cases prescribed by law and after due process. Every one placed under arrest or detention shall have the right to immediate judicial determination of the legality of any detention to which he may be subject and to trial within a reasonable time or to release.

ART. 6. Every one shall have access to independent and impartial tribunals in the determination of any criminal charge against him, and of his rights and obligations. He shall be entitled to a fair hearing of his case and to have the aid of a qualified representative of his own choice, and if he appears in person to have the procedure explained to him in a manner in which he can understand it and to use a language which he can speak.

ART. 7. 1. Any person is presumed to be innocent until proved guilty. No one shall be convicted or punished for crime or other offence except after fair public trial at which he has been given all guarantees necessary for his defence. No person shall be held guilty of any offence on account of any act or omission which did not constitute such an offence at the time when it was committed, nor shall he be liable to any greater punishment than that prescribed for such offence by the law in force at the time when the offence was committed.

2. Nothing in this article shall prejudice the trial and punishment of any person for the commission of any act which, at the time it was committed, was criminal according to the general principles of law recognized by civilized nations.

3. No one shall be subjected to torture, or to cruel or inhuman punishment or indignity.

ART. 8. Slavery, in all its forms, being inconsistent with the dignity of man, shall be prohibited by law.

ART. 9. Every one shall be entitled to protection under law from unreasonable interference with his reputation, his privacy and his family. His home and correspondence shall be inviolable.

ART. 10. 1. Subject to any general law not contrary to the purposes and principles of the United Nations Charter and adopted for specific reasons of security or in general interest, there shall be liberty of movement and free choice of residence within the border of each State.

2. Individuals shall have the right to leave their own country and, if they so desire, to acquire the nationality of any country willing to grant it.

ART. 11. Every one shall have the right to seek and be granted asylum from persecution. This right will not be accorded to criminals nor to those whose acts are contrary to the principles and aims of the United Nations.

ART. 12. Every one has the right, everywhere in the world, to recognition as a person before the law and to the enjoyment of fundamental civil rights.

ART. 13. 1. The family deriving from marriage is the natural and fundamental unit of society. Men and women shall have the same freedom to contract marriage in accordance with the law.

2. Marriage and the family shall be protected by the State and society.

ART. 14. 1. Every one has the right to own property in conformity with the laws of the State in which such property is located.

2. No one shall be arbitrarily deprived of his property.

ART. 15. Every one has the right to a nationality.

All persons who do not enjoy the protection of any Government shall be placed under the protection of the United Nations. This protection shall not be accorded to criminals nor to those whose acts are contrary to the principles and aims of the United Nations.

ART. 16. 1. Individual freedom of thought and conscience, to hold and change beliefs, is an absolute and sacred right.

2. Every person has the right, either alone or in community with other persons of like mind and in public or private, to manifest his beliefs in worship, observance, teaching and practice.

(With regard to the following two articles, 17 and 18, the Commission decided not to elaborate a final text until it had before it the views of the Sub-Commission on Freedom of Information and of the Press and of the United Nations Conference on Freedom of Information.)

[ART. 17.] (1. Every one is free to express and impart opinions, or to receive and seek information and the opinion of others from sources wherever situated.

2. No person may be interfered with on account of his opinions.)

[ART. 18.] (There shall be freedom of expression either by word, in writing, in the Press, in books or by visual, auditive or other means. There shall be equal access to all channels of communication.)

ART. 19. Every one has the right to freedom of peaceful assembly and to participate in local, national and international associations for purposes of a political, economic, religious, social, cultural, trade union or any other character, not inconsistent with this Declaration.

ART. 20. Every one has the right, either individually, or in association with others, to petition or to communicate with the public authorities of the State of which he is a national or in which he resides, or with the United Nations.

ART. 21. Every one without discrimination has the right to take an effective part in the government of his country. The State shall conform to the will of the people as manifested by elections which shall be periodic, free, fair and by secret ballot.

ART. 22. 1. Every one shall have equal opportunity to engage in public employment and to hold public office in the State of which he is a citizen or a national.

2. Access to public employment shall not be a matter of privilege or favour.

ART. 23. 1. Every one has the right to work.

2. The State has a duty to take such measures as may be within its power to ensure that all persons ordinarily resident in its territory have an opportunity for useful work.

3. The State is bound to take all necessary steps to prevent unemployment.

ART. 24. 1. Every one has the right to receive pay commensurate with his ability and skill, to work under just and favourable conditions and to join trade unions for the protection of his interests in securing a decent standard of living for himself and his family.

2. Women shall work with the same advantages as men and receive equal pay for equal work.

ART. 25. Every one without distinction as to economic and social conditions has the right to the preservation of his health through the highest standard of food, clothing, housing and medical care which the resources of the State or community can provide. The responsibility of the State and community for the health and safety of its people can be fulfilled only by provision of adequate health and social measures.

ART. 26. 1. Every one has the right to social security. The State has a duty to maintain or ensure the maintenance of comprehensive measures for the security of the individual against the consequence of unemployment, disability, old age and all other loss of livelihood for reasons beyond his control.

2. Motherhood shall be granted special care and assistance. Children are similarly entitled to special care and assistance.

ART. 27. Every one has the right to education. Fundamental education shall be free and compulsory. There shall be equal access for higher education as can be provided by the State or community on the basis of merit and without distinction as to race, sex, language, religion, social standing, financial means, or political affiliation.

ART. 28. Education will be directed to the full physical, intellectual, moral and spiritual development of the human personality, to the strengthening of respect for human rights and fundamental freedoms and to the combating of the spirit of intolerance and hatred against other nations or racial or religious groups everywhere.

ART. 29. 1. Every one has the right to rest and leisure.

2. Rest and leisure should be ensured to every one by laws or contracts providing in particular for reasonable limitations on working hours and for periodic vacations with pay.

ART. 30. Every one has the right to participate in the cultural life of the community, to enjoy the arts and to share in the benefits that result from scientific discoveries.

ART. 31. (The Commission did not take a decision on the two texts that follow. They are reproduced here for further consideration.)

(Text proposed by the drafting committee:

In States inhabited by a substantial number of persons of a race, language or religion other than those of the majority of the population, persons belonging to such ethnic, linguistic or religious minorities shall have the right, as far as compatible with public order, to establish and maintain schools and cultural or religious institutions, and to use their own language in the Press, in public assembly and before the courts and other authorities of the State.)

(Text proposed by the Sub-Commission on the Prevention of Discrimination and the Protection of Minorities:

In States inhabited by well-defined ethnic, linguistic or religious groups which are clearly distinguished from the rest of the population, and which want to be accorded differential treatment, persons belonging to such groups shall have the right, as far as is compatible with public order and security, to establish and maintain their schools and cultural or religious institutions and to use their own language and script in the Press, in public assembly and before the courts and other authorities of the State, if they so choose.)

ART. 32. All laws in any State shall be in conformity with the purposes and principles of the United Nations as embodied in the Charter, in so far as they deal with human rights.

ART. 33. Nothing in this Declaration shall be considered to recognize the right of any State or person to engage in any activity aimed at the destruction of any of the rights and freedoms prescribed herein.

THE LAKE SUCCESS DRAFT

Draft International Declaration of Human Rights

PREAMBLE

WHEREAS recognition of the inherent dignity and of the equal and inalienable rights of all members of the human family is the foundation of freedom, justice, and peace in the world, and

WHEREAS disregard and contempt for human rights resulted, before and during the Second World War, in barbarous acts which outraged the conscience of mankind and made it apparent that the fundamental freedoms were one of the supreme issues of the conflict, and

WHEREAS it is essential, if mankind is not to be compelled as a last resort to rebel against tyranny and oppression, that human rights should be protected by a regime of law, and

WHEREAS the peoples of the United Nations have in the Charter determined to reaffirm faith in fundamental human rights, and in the dignity and worth of the human person and to promote social progress and better standards of life in larger freedom; and

WHEREAS Member states have pledged themselves to achieve, in co-operation with the organization, the promotion of universal respect for and observance of human rights and fundamental freedoms; and

WHEREAS a common understanding of these rights and freedoms is of the greatest importance for the full realization of this pledge,

Now therefore the General Assembly

PROCLAIMS this Declaration of Human Rights as a common standard of achievement for all peoples and all nations, to the end that every individual and every organ of society keeping this Declaration constantly in mind shall strive by teaching and education to promote respect for these rights and freedoms and by progressive measures, national and international, to secure their universal and effective recognition and observance, both among the peoples of Member states themselves and among the peoples of territories under their jurisdiction.

ARTICLE 1

All human beings are born free and equal in dignity and rights. They are endowed by nature with reason and conscience, and should act towards one another in a spirit of brotherhood.

ARTICLE 2

Everyone is entitled to all the rights and freedoms set forth in this Declaration, without distinction of any kind, such as race, color, sex, language, religion, political or other opinion, property or other status, or national or social origin.

ARTICLE 3

Everyone has the right to life, liberty, and security of person.

ARTICLE 4

1. No one shall be held in slavery or involuntary servitude.
2. No one shall be subjected to torture or to cruel, inhuman, or degrading treatment or punishment.

ARTICLE 5

Everyone has the right to recognition, everywhere, as a person before the law.

ARTICLE 6

All are equal before the law and are entitled without any discrimination to equal protection of the law against any discrimination in violation of this Declaration and against any incitement to such discrimination.

ARTICLE 7

No one shall be subjected to arbitrary arrest or detention.

ARTICLE 8

In the determination of his rights and obligations and of any criminal charge against him everyone is entitled in full equality to a fair hearing by an independent and impartial tribunal.

ARTICLE 9

1. Everyone charged with a penal offence has the right to be presumed innocent until proved guilty according to law in a public trial at which he has had all the guarantees necessary for his defence.

2. No one shall be held guilty of any offence on account of any act or omission which did not constitute an offence, under national or international law, at the time when it was committed.

ARTICLE 10

No one shall be subjected to unreasonable interference with his privacy, family, home, correspondence, or reputation.

ARTICLE 11

1. Everyone has the right to freedom of movement and residence within the borders of each state.

2. Everyone has the right to leave any country, including his own.

ARTICLE 12

1. Everyone has the right to seek and be granted, in other countries, asylum from persecution.

2. Prosecutions genuinely arising from nonpolitical crimes or from acts contrary to the purposes and principles of the United Nations do not constitute persecution.

ARTICLE 13

No one shall be arbitrarily deprived of his nationality or denied the right to change his nationality.

ARTICLE 14

1. Men and women of full age have the right to marry and to found a family and are entitled to equal rights as to marriage.

2. Marriage shall be entered into only with the full consent of both intending spouses.

3. The family is the natural and fundamental group unit of society and is entitled to protection.

ARTICLE 15

1. Everyone has the right to own property alone as well as in association with others.

2. No one shall be arbitrarily deprived of his property.

ARTICLE 16

Everyone has the right to freedom of thought, conscience, and religion; this right includes freedom to change his religion or belief, and freedom, either alone or in community with others and in public or private, to manifest his religion or belief in teaching, practice, worship, and observance.

ARTICLE 17

Everyone has the right to freedom of opinion and expression; this right includes freedom to hold opinions without interference and to seek, receive and impart information and ideas through any media and regardless of frontiers.

ARTICLE 18

Everyone has the right to freedom of assembly and association.

ARTICLE 19

1. Everyone has the right to take part in the government of his country, directly or through his freely chosen representatives.

2. Everyone has the right of access to public employment in his country.

3. Everyone has the right to a government which conforms to the will of the people.

ARTICLE 20

Everyone, as a member of society, has the right to social security and is entitled to the realization, through national effort and international co-operation, and in accordance with the organization and resources of each state, of the economic, social, and cultural rights set out below.

ARTICLE 21

1. Everyone has the right to work, to just and favorable conditions of work and pay and to protection against unemployment.

2. Everyone has the right to equal pay for equal work.

3. Everyone is free to form and to join trade unions for the protection of his interests.

ARTICLE 22

1. Everyone has the right to a standard of living, including food, clothing, housing, and medical care, and to social services, adequate for the health and well-

being of himself and his family and to security in the event of unemployment, sickness, disability, old age, or other lack of livelihood in circumstances beyond his control.

2. Mother and child have the right to special care and assistance.

ARTICLE 23

1. Everyone has the right to education. Elementary and fundamental education shall be free and compulsory and there shall be equal access on the basis of merit to higher education.

2. Education shall be directed to the full development of the human personality, to strengthening respect for human rights and fundamental freedoms, and to combating the spirit of intolerance and hatred against other nations and against racial and religious groups everywhere.

ARTICLE 24

Everyone has the right to rest and leisure.

ARTICLE 25

Everyone has the right to participate in the cultural life of the community, to enjoy the arts, and to share in scientific advancement.

ARTICLE 26

Everyone is entitled to a good social and international order in which the rights and freedoms set out in this Declaration can be fully realized.

ARTICLE 27

1. Everyone has duties to the community which enables him freely to develop his personality.

2. In the exercise of his rights, everyone shall be subject only to such limitations as are necessary to secure due recognition and respect for the rights of others and the requirements of morality, public order and general welfare in a democratic society.

ARTICLE 28

Nothing in this Declaration shall imply the recognition of the right of any state or person to engage in any activity aimed at the destruction of any of the rights and freedoms prescribed herein.

NOTE: *The Commission has not considered the following article since measures of implementation were not considered in its third session:*

Everyone has the right, either individually or in association with others, to petition or to communicate with the public authorities of the state of which he is a national or in which he resides, or with the United Nations.

THE THIRD COMMITTEE DRAFT

Draft Universal Declaration of Human Rights

TEXT OF THE THIRD COMMITTEE

TEXT OF THE SUBCOMMITTEE

PREAMBLE

Whereas recognition of the inherent dignity and of the equal and inalienable rights of all members of the human family is the foundation of freedom, justice and peace in the world; and

Whereas disregard and contempt for human rights have resulted in barbarous acts which have outraged the conscience of mankind, and the advent of a world in which human beings shall enjoy freedom of speech and belief and freedom from fear and want has been proclaimed as the highest aspiration of the common people; and

Whereas it is essential, if man is not to be compelled to have recourse, as a last resort, to rebellion against tyranny and oppression, that human rights should be protected by the rule of law; and

PREAMBLE

Whereas recognition of the inherent dignity and of the equal and inalienable rights of all members of the human family is the foundation of freedom, justice and peace in the world; and

Whereas disregard and contempt for human rights have resulted in barbarous acts which have outraged the conscience of mankind, and the advent of a world in which human beings shall enjoy freedom of speech and belief and freedom from fear and want has been proclaimed as the highest aspiration of the common people; and

Whereas it is essential, if man is not to be compelled to have recourse, as a last resort, to rebellion against tyranny and oppression, that human rights should be protected by the rule of law;
and

Whereas it is essential to promote the development of friendly relations between nations; and

Whereas the peoples of the United Nations have in the Charter determined to reaffirm faith in fundamental human rights, in the dignity and worth of the human person and in the equal rights of men and women and to promote social progress and better standards of life in larger freedom; and

Whereas Member States have pledged themselves to achieve, in co-operation with the Organization, the promotion of universal respect for and observance of human rights and fundamental freedoms; and

Whereas a common understanding of these rights and freedoms is of the greatest importance for the full realization of this pledge;

Now therefore, *The General Assembly*

Proclaims this Declaration of Human Rights as a common standard of achievement for all peoples and all nations, to the end that every individual and every organ of society, keeping this Declaration constantly in mind, shall strive by teaching and education to promote respect for these rights and freedoms and by progressive measures, national and international, to secure their universal and effective recognition and observance, both among the peoples of Member States themselves and among the peoples of territories under their jurisdiction.

Whereas it is essential to promote the development of friendly relations between nations; and

Whereas the peoples of the United Nations have in the Charter reaffirmed their faith in fundamental human rights, in the dignity and worth of the human person and in the equal rights of men and women and determined to promote social progress and better standards of life in larger freedom; and

Whereas Member States have pledged themselves to achieve, in co-operation with the United Nations, the promotion of universal respect for and observance of human rights and fundamental freedoms; and

Whereas a common understanding of these rights and freedoms is of the greatest importance for the full realization of this pledge;

Now therefore, *The General Assembly*

Proclaims this Universal Declaration of Human Rights as a common standard of achievement for all peoples and all nations, to the end that every individual and every organ of society, keeping this Declaration constantly in mind, shall strive by teaching and education to promote respect for these rights and freedoms and by progressive measures, national and international, to secure their universal and effective recognition and observance, both among the peoples of Member States themselves and among the peoples of territories under their jurisdiction.

ARTICLE I

All human beings are born free and equal in dignity and rights. They are endowed with reason and conscience and

ARTICLE I

All human beings are born free and equal in dignity and rights. They are en-

should act towards one another in a spirit of brotherhood.

dowed with reason and conscience and should act towards one another in a spirit of brotherhood.

ARTICLE 2

1. Everyone is entitled to all the rights and freedoms set forth in this Declaration, without distinction of any kind, such as race, colour, sex, language, religion, political or other opinion, property or other status, birth, or national or social origin.

2. The rights proclaimed in this Declaration also apply to any person belonging to the population of Trust and Non-Self-Governing Territories (*additional article*).

ARTICLE 2

1. Everyone is entitled to all the rights and freedoms set forth in this Declaration, without distinction of any kind, such as race, colour, sex, language, religion, birth, national or social origin, political or other opinion, or property or other status.

2. Furthermore, no distinction shall be made on the basis of the political status of the country to which a person belongs.

ARTICLE 3

Everyone has the right to life, liberty and security of person.

ARTICLE 3

Everyone has the right to life, liberty and security of person.

ARTICLE 4

Slavery and the slave trade are prohibited in all their aspects.

No one shall be held in slavery or servitude.

No one shall be subjected to torture or to cruel, inhuman or degrading treatment or punishment.

ARTICLE 4

No one shall be held in slavery or servitude; slavery and the slave trade shall be prohibited in all their forms.

ARTICLE 4(A)

No one shall be subjected to torture or to cruel, inhuman or degrading treatment or punishment.

ARTICLE 5

Every human being has the right to recognition everywhere as a person before the law.

ARTICLE 5

Everyone has the right to recognition everywhere as a person before the law.

ARTICLE 6

All are equal before the law and are entitled without any discrimination to equal protection of the law and equal

ARTICLE 6

All are equal before the law and are entitled without any discrimination to

protection against any discrimination in violation of this Declaration and against any incitement to such discrimination.

Everyone has the right to an effective remedy by the competent national tribunals for acts violating the fundamental rights granted him by the constitution or by law.

ARTICLE 7

No one shall be subjected to arbitrary arrest, detention or exile.

ARTICLE 8

In the determination of his rights and obligations and of any criminal charge against him, everyone is entitled in full equality to a fair and public hearing by an independent and impartial tribunal.

ARTICLE 9

1. Everyone charged with a penal offence has the right to be presumed innocent until proved guilty according to law in a public trial at which he has had all the guarantees necessary for his defence.

2. No one shall be held guilty of any penal offence on account of any act or omission which did not constitute a penal offence, under national or international law, at the time when it was committed. Nor shall a heavier penalty be imposed than the one that was applicable at the time the penal offence was committed.

ARTICLE 10

No one shall be subjected to arbitrary interference with his privacy, family, home or correspondence, nor to attacks upon his honour and reputation.

equal protection of the law. All are entitled to equal protection against any discrimination in violation of this Declaration and against any incitement to such discrimination.

ARTICLE 6(A)

Everyone has the right to an effective remedy by the competent national tribunals for acts violating the fundamental rights granted him by the constitution or by law.

ARTICLE 7

No one shall be subjected to arbitrary arrest, detention or exile.

ARTICLE 8

Everyone is entitled in full equality to a fair and public hearing by an independent and impartial tribunal, in the determination of his rights and obligations and of any criminal charge against him.

ARTICLE 9

1. Everyone charged with a penal offence has the right to be presumed innocent until proved guilty according to law in a public trial at which he has had all the guarantees necessary for his defence.

2. No one shall be held guilty of any penal offence on account of any act or omission which did not constitute a penal offence, under national or international law, at the time when it was committed. Nor shall a heavier penalty be imposed than the one that was applicable at the time the penal offence was committed.

Everyone has the right to the protection of the law against such interference or attacks.

ARTICLE 11

1. Everyone has the right to freedom of movement and residence within the borders of each State.

2. Everyone has the right to leave any country, including his own, and to return to his country.

ARTICLE 12

1. Everyone has the right to seek and to enjoy in other countries asylum from persecution.

2. Prosecutions genuinely arising from nonpolitical crimes or from acts contrary to the purposes and principles of the United Nations do not constitute persecution.

ARTICLE 13

1. Everyone has the right to a nationality.

2. No one shall be arbitrarily deprived of his nationality or denied the right to change his nationality.

ARTICLE 14

1. Without any limitation due to race, nationality or religion, men and women of full age have the right to marry and to found a family and are entitled to equal rights as to marriage.

2. Marriage shall be entered into only with the free and full consent of the intending spouses. Men and women shall enjoy equal rights both during marriage and at its dissolution.

ARTICLE 10

No one shall be subjected to arbitrary interference with his privacy, family, home or correspondence, nor to attacks upon his honour and reputation. Everyone has the right to the protection of the law against such interference or attacks.

ARTICLE 11

1. Everyone has the right to freedom of movement and residence within the borders of each State.

2. Everyone has the right to leave any country, including his own, and to return to his country.

ARTICLE 12

1. Everyone has the right to seek and to enjoy in other countries asylum from persecution.

2. This right may not be invoked in the case of prosecutions genuinely arising from non-political crimes or from acts contrary to the purposes and principles of the United Nations.

ARTICLE 13

1. Everyone has the right to a nationality.

2. No one shall be arbitrarily deprived of his nationality nor denied the right to change his nationality.

ARTICLE 14

1. Men and women of full age, without any limitation due to race, nationality or religion, have the right to marry and to found a family. They are entitled to equal rights as to marriage, during marriage and at its dissolution.

3. The family is the natural and fundamental group unit of society and is entitled to protection by society and the State.

ARTICLE 15

1. Everyone has the right to own property alone as well as in association with others.

2. No one shall be arbitrarily deprived of his property.

ARTICLE 16

Everyone has the right to freedom of thought, conscience and religion; this right includes freedom to change his religion or belief, and freedom either alone or in community with others and in public or private, to manifest his religion or belief in teaching, practice, worship and observance.

ARTICLE 17

Everyone has the right to freedom of opinion and expression; this right includes freedom to hold opinions without interference and to seek, receive and impart information and ideas through any media and regardless of frontiers.

ARTICLE 18

Everyone has the right to freedom of peaceful assembly and association.

No one may be compelled to belong to an association.

ARTICLE 19

1. Everyone has the right to take part in the government of his country, di-

2. Marriage shall be entered into only with the free and full consent of the intending spouses.

3. The family is the natural and fundamental group unit of society and is entitled to protection by society and the State.

ARTICLE 15

1. Everyone has the right to own property alone as well as in association with others.

2. No one shall be arbitrarily deprived of his property.

ARTICLE 16

Everyone has the right to freedom of thought, conscience and religion; this right includes freedom to change his religion or belief, and freedom either alone or in community with others and in public or private, to manifest his religion or belief, in teaching, practice, worship and observance.

ARTICLE 17

Everyone has the right to freedom of opinion and expression; this right includes freedom to hold opinions without interference and to seek, receive and impart information and ideas through any media and regardless of frontiers.

ARTICLE 18

1. Everyone has the right to freedom of peaceful assembly and association.

2. No one may be compelled to belong to an association.

rectly or through freely chosen representatives.

2. Everyone has the right of equal
access to public service in his country.

3. The will of the people shall be the
basis of the authority of government;
this will shall be expressed in periodic
and genuine elections which shall be
universal and equal and shall be held by
secret vote or by equivalent free voting
procedures.

ARTICLE 20

Everyone, as a member of society,
has the right to social security and is
entitled to the realization through national effort and international cooperation, and in accordance with the
organization and resources of each
State, of the economic, social and cultural rights indispensable for his dignity and the free development of his
personality.

ARTICLE 21

1. Everyone has the right to work, to
free choice of employment, to just and
favourable conditions of work and to
protection against unemployment.

2. Everyone, without any discrimination, has the right to equal pay for
equal work.

Everyone who works has the right to
just and favourable remuneration insur-
ing for his family and himself an existence worthy of human dignity and
supplemented, if necessary, by other
means of social protection.

3. Everyone has the right to form
and to join trade unions for the protection of his interests.

ARTICLE 19

1. Everyone has the right to take part
in the government of his country, directly or through freely chosen representatives.

2. Everyone has the right of equal
access to public service in his country.

3. The will of the people shall be the
basis of the authority of government;
this will shall be expressed in periodic
and genuine elections which shall be by
universal and equal suffrage and shall
be held by secret vote or by equivalent
free voting procedures.

ARTICLE 20

Everyone, as a member of society,
has the right to social security and is entitled to the realization through national
effort and international co-operation
and in accordance with the organization
and resources of each State, of the economic, social and cultural rights indispensable for his dignity and the free
development of his personality.

ARTICLE 21

1. Everyone has the right to work, to
free choice of employment, to just and
favourable conditions of work and to
protection against unemployment.

2. Everyone, without any discrimination, has the right to equal pay for
equal work.

3. Everyone who works has the right
to just and favourable remuneration in-
suring for himself and his family an existence worthy of human dignity, and
supplemented, if necessary, by other
means of social protection.

ARTICLE 22

1. Everyone has the right to a standard of living adequate for the health and well-being of his family and himself, including food, clothing, housing and medical care and necessary social services and to security in the event of unemployment, sickness, disability, widowhood, old age or other lack of livelihood in circumstances beyond his control.

2. Motherhood and childhood have the right to special care and assistance.

3. Children born out of wedlock shall enjoy the same social protection as those born in marriage.

ARTICLE 23

1. Everyone has the right to education, which shall be free, at least in so far as elementary and fundamental education are concerned. Elementary education shall be compulsory. Technical and professional education shall be made generally available. There shall be equal access to higher education on the basis of merit.

2. Education shall be directed to the full development of the human personality, to the strengthening of respect for human rights and fundamental freedoms and to the promotion of understanding, tolerance, and friendship among all nations, racial or religious groups, as well as of the activities of the United Nations for the maintenance of peace.

3. Parents have a prior right to choose the kind of education that shall be given to their children.

ARTICLE 24

Everyone has the right to rest and leisure, to reasonable limitation of

4. Everyone has the right to form and to join trade unions for the protection of his interests.

ARTICLE 22

1. Everyone has the right to a standard of living adequate for the health and well-being of himself and of his family, including food, clothing, housing and medical care and necessary social services, and the right to security in the event of unemployment, sickness, disability, widowhood, old age or other lack of livelihood in circumstances beyond his control.

2. Motherhood and childhood are entitled to special care and assistance. All children, whether born in or out of wedlock, shall enjoy the same social protection.

ARTICLE 23

1. Everyone has the right to education. Education shall be free, at least in the elementary and fundamental stages. Elementary education shall be compulsory. Technical and professional education shall be made generally available. There shall be equal access to higher education on the basis of merit.

2. Education shall be directed to the full development of the human personality and to the strengthening of respect for human rights and fundamental freedoms. It shall promote understanding, tolerance, and friendship among all nations, racial or religious groups, and shall further the activities of the United Nations for the maintenance of peace.

3. Parents have a prior right to choose the kind of education that shall be given to their children.

working hours and to periodic holidays with pay.

ARTICLE 25

Everyone has the right freely to participate in the cultural life of the community, to enjoy the arts and to share in scientific advancement and its benefits.

Everyone has the right to the protection of the moral and material interests resulting from any scientific, literary or artistic production of which he is the author.

ARTICLE 26

Everyone is entitled to a social and international order in which the rights and freedoms set out in this Declaration can be fully realized.

ARTICLE 27

1. Everyone has duties to the community in which alone the free and full development of his personality is possible.

2. In the exercise of his rights and freedoms, everyone shall be subject only to such limitations as are prescribed by law solely for the purpose of securing due recognition and respect for the rights and freedoms of others and of meeting the just requirements of morality, public order and the general welfare in a democratic society.

3. These rights and freedoms can in no case be exercised contrary to the purposes and principles of the United Nations.

ARTICLE 28

Nothing in this Declaration shall imply the recognition of the right of any

ARTICLE 24

Everyone has the right to rest and leisure, to reasonable limitation of working hours and to periodic holidays with pay.

ARTICLE 25

1. Everyone has the right freely to participate in the cultural life of the community, to enjoy the arts and to share in scientific advancement and its benefits.

2. Everyone has the right to the protection of the moral and material interests resulting from any scientific, literary or artistic production of which he is the author.

ARTICLE 26

Everyone is entitled to a social and international order in which the rights and freedoms set out in this Declaration can be fully realized.

ARTICLE 27

1. Everyone has duties to the community in which alone the free and full development of his personality is possible.

2. In the exercise of his rights and freedoms everyone shall be subject only to such limitations as are prescribed by law solely for the purpose of securing due recognition and respect for the rights and freedoms of others and the just requirements of morality, public order and the general welfare in a democratic society.

3. These rights and freedoms may in no case be exercised contrary to the purposes and principles of the United Nations.

State, group or person to engage in any activity or to perform any act aimed at the destruction of any of the rights and freedoms prescribed herein.

ADDITIONAL ARTICLE

The rights proclaimed in this Declaration also apply to any person belonging to the population of Trust and Non-Self-Governing Territories.

ARTICLE 28

Nothing in this Declaration shall imply the recognition of the right of any State, group or person to engage in any activity or to perform any act aimed at the destruction of any of the rights and freedoms prescribed herein.

(See paragraph 2 of article 2)

UNIVERSAL DECLARATION
OF HUMAN RIGHTS

PREAMBLE

WHEREAS recognition of the inherent dignity and of the equal and inalienable rights of all members of the human family is the foundation of freedom, justice and peace in the world.

WHEREAS disregard and contempt for human rights have resulted in barbarous acts which have outraged the conscience of mankind, and the advent of a world in which human beings shall enjoy freedom of speech and belief and freedom from fear and want has been proclaimed as the highest aspiration of the common people.

WHEREAS it is essential, if man is not to be compelled to have recourse, as a last resort, to rebellion against tyranny and oppression, that human rights should be protected by the rule of law.

WHEREAS it is essential to promote the development of friendly relations between nations.

WHEREAS the peoples of the United Nations have in the Charter reaffirmed their faith in fundamental human rights, in the dignity and worth of the human person and in the equal rights of men and women and have determined to promote social progress and better standards of life in larger freedom.

WHEREAS Member States have pledged themselves to achieve, in cooperation with the United Nations, the promotion of universal respect for and observance of human rights and fundamental freedoms.

WHEREAS a common understanding of these rights and freedoms is of the greatest importance for the full realization of this pledge.

Now, Therefore,
The General Assembly
Proclaims

This universal declaration of human rights as a common standard of achievement for all peoples and all nations, to the end that every individual and every organ of society, keeping this Declaration constantly in mind, shall strive by teaching and education to promote respect for these rights and freedoms and by progressive measures, national and international, to secure their universal and effective recognition and observance, both among the peoples of Member States themselves and among the peoples of territories under their jurisdiction.

ARTICLE 1. All human beings are born free and equal in dignity and rights. They are endowed with reason and conscience and should act towards one another in a spirit of brotherhood.

ARTICLE 2. Everyone is entitled to all the rights and freedoms set forth in this Declaration, without distinction of any kind, such as race, colour, sex, language, religion, political or other opinion, national or social origin, property, birth or other status.

Furthermore, no distinction shall be made on the basis of the political, jurisdictional or international status of the country or territory to which a person belongs, whether it be independent, trust, non-self-governing or under any other limitation of sovereignty.

ARTICLE 3. Everyone has the right to life, liberty and security of person.

ARTICLE 4. No one shall be held in slavery or servitude; slavery and the slave trade shall be prohibited in all their forms.

ARTICLE 5. No one shall be subjected to torture or to cruel, inhuman or degrading treatment or punishment.

ARTICLE 6. Everyone has the right to recognition everywhere as a person before the law.

ARTICLE 7. All are equal before the law and are entitled without any discrimination to equal protection of the law. All are entitled to equal protection against any discrimination in violation of this Declaration and against any incitement to such discrimination.

ARTICLE 8. Everyone has the right to an effective remedy by the competent national tribunals for acts violating the fundamental rights granted him by the constitution or by law.

ARTICLE 9. No one shall be subjected to arbitrary arrest, detention or exile.

ARTICLE 10. Everyone is entitled in full equality to a fair and public hearing by an independent and impartial tribunal, in the determination of his rights and obligations and of any criminal charge against him.

ARTICLE 11. (1) Everyone charged with a penal offense has the right to be presumed innocent until proved guilty according to law in a public trial at which he has had all the guarantees necessary for his defense.

(2) No one shall be held guilty of any penal offense or of any act or omission which did not constitute a penal offense, under national or international law, at the time when it was committed. Nor shall a heavier penalty be imposed than the one that was applicable at the time the penal offense was committed.

ARTICLE 12. No one shall be subject to arbitrary interference with his privacy, family, home or correspondence, nor to attacks upon his honour and reputation. Everyone has the right to the protection of the law against such interference or attacks.

ARTICLE 13. (1) Everyone has the right to freedom of movement and residence within the borders of each state.

(2) Everyone has the right to leave any country, including his own, and to return to his country.

ARTICLE 14. (1) Everyone has the right to seek and to enjoy in other countries asylum from persecution.

(2) This right may not be invoked in the case of prosecutions genuinely arising from non-political crimes or from acts contrary to the purposes and principles of the United Nations.

ARTICLE 15. (1) Everyone has the right to a nationality.

(2) No one shall be arbitrarily deprived of his nationality nor denied the right to change his nationality.

ARTICLE 16. (1) Men and women of full age, without any limitation due to race, nationality or religion, have the right to marry and to found a family. They are entitled to equal rights as to marriage, during marriage, and at its dissolution.

(2) Marriage shall be entered into only with the free and full consent of the intending spouses.

(3) The family is the natural and fundamental group unit of society and is entitled to protection by society and the State.

ARTICLE 17. (1) Everyone has the right to own property alone as well as in association with others.

(2) No one shall be arbitrarily deprived of his property.

ARTICLE 18. Everyone has the right to freedom of thought, conscience and religion; this right includes freedom to change his religion or belief, and freedom, either alone or in community with others and in public or private, to manifest his religion or belief in teaching, practice, worship and observance.

ARTICLE 19. Everyone has the right to freedom of opinion and expression; this right includes freedom to hold opinions without interference and to seek, receive and impart information and ideas through any media and regardless of frontiers.

ARTICLE 20. (1) Everyone has the right to freedom of peaceful assembly and association.

(2) No one may be compelled to belong to an association.

ARTICLE 21. (1) Everyone has the right to take part in the government of his country, directly or through freely chosen representatives.

(2) Everyone has the right of equal access to public service in his country.

(3) The will of the people shall be the basis of the authority of government; this

will shall be expressed in periodic and genuine elections which shall be by universal and equal suffrage and shall be held by secret vote or by equivalent free voting procedures.

ARTICLE 22. Everyone, as a member of society, has the right to social security and is entitled to realization, through national effort and international co-operation and in accordance with the organization and resources of each State, of the economic, social and cultural rights indispensable for his dignity and the free development of his personality.

ARTICLE 23. (1) Everyone has the right to work, to free choice of employment, to just and favourable conditions of work and to protection against unemployment.

(2) Everyone, without any discrimination, has the right to equal pay for equal work.

(3) Everyone who works has the right to just and favourable remuneration ensuring for himself and his family an existence worthy of human dignity, and supplemented, if necessary, by other means of social protection.

(4) Everyone has the right to form and to join trade unions for protection of his interests.

ARTICLE 24. Everyone has the right to rest and leisure, including reasonable limitation of working hours and periodic holidays with pay.

ARTICLE 25. (1) Everyone has the right to a standard of living adequate for the health and well-being of himself and his family, including food, clothing, housing and medical care and necessary social services, and the right to security in the event of unemployment, sickness, disability, widowhood, old age or other lack of livelihood in circumstances beyond his control.

(2) Motherhood and childhood are entitled to special care and assistance. All children, whether born in or out of wedlock, shall enjoy the same social protection.

ARTICLE 26. (1) Everyone has the right to education. Education shall be free, at least in the elementary and fundamental states. Elementary education shall be compulsory. Technical and professional education shall be made generally available and higher education shall be equally accessible to all on the basis of merit.

(2) Education shall be directed to the full development of the human personality and to the strengthening of respect for human rights and fundamental freedoms. It shall promote understanding, tolerance and friendship among all nations, racial or religious groups, and shall further the activities of the United Nations for the maintenance of peace.

(3) Parents shall have a prior right to choose the kind of education that shall be given to their children.

ARTICLE 27. (1) Everyone has the right freely to participate in the cultural life of the community, to enjoy the arts and to share in scientific advancement and its benefits.

(2) Everyone has the right to the protection of the moral and material interests resulting from any scientific, literary or artistic production of which he is the author.

ARTICLE 28. Everyone is entitled to a social and international order in which the rights and freedoms set forth in this Declaration can be fully realized.

ARTICLE 29. (1) Everyone has duties to the community in which alone the free and full development of his personality is possible.

(2) In the exercise of his rights and freedoms, everyone shall be subject only to such limitations as are determined by law solely for the purpose of securing due recognition and respect for the rights and freedoms of others and of meeting the just requirements of morality, public order and the general welfare in a democratic society.

(3) These rights and freedoms may in no case be exercised contrary to the purposes and principles of the United Nations.

ARTICLE 30. Nothing in this Declaration may be interpreted as implying for any State, group or person any right to engage in any activity or to perform any act aimed at the destruction of any of the rights and freedoms set forth herein.

INDEX

Page numbers in italics refer to illustrations.

Churchill, Roosevelt, and Stalin (p. 2): Bettmann/Corbis; Eleanor Roosevelt and Harry Truman in the Oval Office (p. 23): New York Public Library; Eleanor Roosevelt cartoon (p. 37): Alois Derso and Emery Kelen, *United Nations Sketchbook: A Cartoon History of the United Nations* (New York: Funk & Wagnalls, 1950)/reprinted with permission of Betty Kelen; Eleanor Roosevelt at the first meeting of the drafting committee, June 9, 1947 (p. 52): United Nations Photo Library; Eleanor Roosevelt and John P. Humphrey (p. 81): Bettmann/Corbis; Eleanor Roosevelt conferring with René Cassin and Charles Malik (p. 101): United Nations Photo Library; Alexei Pavlov and Charles Malik (p. 122): Library of Congress; P. C. Chang and Charles Malik (p. 145); Library of Congress; "Cassin's Portico" (p. 172): Katherine G. Lev; Charles Malik and Eleanor Roosevelt at the 1951 Geneva meeting of the Human Rights Commission (p. 192): United Nations Photo Service; Eleanor Roosevelt and "a job well done" (p. 220): United Nations Photo Service.

ABOUT THE AUTHOR

MARY ANN GLENDON is the Learned Hand Professor of Law at Harvard University. She led the Holy See's delegation to the Beijing Women's Conference in 1995, the first woman ever to lead a Vatican delegation, and has been featured on Bill Moyers's *World of Ideas.* She is the author of *Rights Talk; A Nation Under Lawyers; Comparative Legal Traditions* (a classic textbook on comparative law); *Abortion and Divorce in Western Law,* winner of the Scribes Book Award; and *The Transformation of Family Law,* winner of the Order of the Coif Prize, the legal academy's highest award for scholarship. She is a member of the American Academy of Arts and Sciences and the International Academy of Comparative Law, and former president of the UNESCO-sponsored International Association of Legal Science.

ABOUT THE TYPE

This book was set in Times Roman, designed by Stanley Morrison specifically for *The Times* of London. The typeface was introduced in the newspaper in 1932. Times Roman had its greatest success in the United States as a book and commercial typeface, rather than one used in newspapers.